Austro-Hungarian army supply train passes Jezierna, 1914. Public domain via Picryl. Source: Austrian National Library

Memorial Book of Jezierna (Ozerna, Ukraine)

Translation of
Sefer Jezierna

Original Book Edited by: Y. Sigelman

Originally published in Haifa 1971

A Publication of JewishGen, Inc
Edmond J. Safra Plaza, 36 Battery Place, New York, NY 10280
646.494.5972 | info@JewishGen.org | www.jewishgen.org

Memorial Book of Jezierna (Ozerna, Ukraine)
Translation of *Sefer Jezierna*

Copyright © 2022 by JewishGen, Inc. All rights reserved.
First Printing: December 2022, Kislev 5783

Editor of Original Yizkor Book: Y. Sigelman
Project Coordinators: Suri Edell-Greenberg and Talila Charap-Friedman
Reproduction of Photographs: Maury Greenberg
Cover Design: Nina Schwartz, Impulse Graphics
Layout: Jonathan Wind
Name indexing: Stefanie Holzman

Printed in the United States of America by Lightning Source, Inc.

Library of Congress Control Number (LCCN): 2021941968

ISBN: 978-1-954176-18-8 (hard cover: 230 pages, alk. paper)

About JewishGen.org

JewishGen, an affiliate of the Museum of Jewish Heritage - A Living Memorial to the Holocaust, serves as the global home for Jewish genealogy.

Featuring unparalleled access to 30+ million records, it offers unique search tools, along with opportunities for researchers to connect with others who share similar interests. Award winning resources such as the Family Finder, Discussion Groups, and ViewMate, are relied upon by thousands each day.

In addition, JewishGen's extensive informational, educational and historical offerings, such as the Jewish Communities Database, Yizkor Book translations, InfoFiles, Family Tree of the Jewish People, and KehilaLinks, provide critical insights, first-hand accounts, and context about Jewish communal and familial life throughout the world.

Offered as a free resource, JewishGen.org has facilitated thousands of family connections and success stories, and is currently engaged in an intensive expansion effort that will bring many more records, tools, and resources to its collections.

Please visit https://www.jewishgen.org/ to learn more.

Executive Director: Avraham Groll

About the JewishGen Yizkor Book Project

Yizkor Books (Memorial Books) were traditionally written to memorialize the names of departed family and martyrs during holiday services in the synagogue (a practice that still exists in many synagogues today).

Over the centuries, as a result of countless persecutions and horrific atrocities committed against the Jews, Yizkor Books (Sefer Zikaron in Hebrew) were expanded to include more historical information, such as biographical sketches of famous personalities and descriptions of daily town life.

Following the Holocaust, the idea of remembrance and learning took on an urgent and crucial importance. Survivors of the Holocaust sought out other surviving residents of their former towns to memorialize and document the names and way of life of those who were ruthlessly murdered by the Nazis. These remembrances were documented in Yizkor Books, hundreds of which were published in the first decades after the Holocaust.

Most of these books were published privately, or through landsmanshaftn (social organizations comprised of members originating from the same European town or region) that still existed, and were often distributed free of charge. Sadly, the languages used to document these crucial histories and links to our past, Yiddish and Hebrew, are no longer commonly understood by a significant percentage of Jews today. As a result, JewishGen has undertaken the sacred responsibility of translating these books into English so that the culture and way of life of these communities will be preserved and transmitted to future generations.

In 1986, a group of farsighted JewishGenners started a project to pool their efforts together in groups based upon their ancestors from each town and donate money to get the Yizkor books of their ancestral towns translated into English. As the translated material became available, it was made accessible for free at www.JewishGen.org/Yizkor. Hardcover copies can be purchased by visiting https://www.jewishgen.org/Yizkor/ybip.html (see below).

It is our hope that the translation of these books into English (and other languages) will assist the countless Jewish family researchers who are so desperately seeking to forge a connection with their heritage.

Director of JewishGen Yizkor Book Project: Lance Ackerfeld

About JewishGen Press

JewishGen Press (formerly the Yizkor Books-in-Print Project) is the publishing division of JewishGen.org, and provides a venue for the publication of non-fiction books pertaining to Jewish genealogy, history, culture, and heritage.

In addition to the Yizkor Book category, publications in the Other Non-Fiction category include Shoah memoirs and research, genealogical research, collections of genealogical and historical materials, biographies, diaries and letters, studies of Jewish experience and cultural life in the past, academic theses, and other books of interest to the Jewish community.

Please visit https://www.jewishgen.org/Yizkor/ybip.html to learn more.

Director of JewishGen Press: Joel Alpert
Managing Editor - Jessica Feinstein
Publications Manager - Susan Rosin

Notes to the Reader

The images in the original book were reproduced from photographs from the time of the first edition. These reproductions were already of poor quality, being pre-war and at least 30 or more years old. As a result the images in the book are not very good and the best achievable.

A reader can view the original scans of the book on the websites listed below.

The original book can be seen online at the Yiddish Book Center website:

https://www.yiddishbookcenter.org/collections/yizkor-books/yzk-nybc313799/siegelman-yitshak-dol-sefer-yezernah

or

at the New York Public Library Digital Collections website:

https://digitalcollections.nypl.org/items/8747f7b0-79b9-0133-a571-00505686a51c

To obtain a list of Shoah victims from Jezierna (Ozerna, Ukraine) the reader should access the Yad Vashem web site listed below; one can also search for specific family names using family name option. These lists are continually updated by Yad Vashem, so it is worthwhile to periodically search these lists.

There is more valuable information (including the Pages of Testimony, etc.) available on this website: https://yvng.yadvashem.org/

A list of all books available from JewishGen Press along with prices is available at: https://www.jewishgen.org/Yizkor/ybip.html

English Translation Editor's Comments

My father Yizchak (Israel) Edell z'l was born in Jezierna in 1909, into the Eidel, Packet, Fuchs and Engel families. His immediate family emigrated to Toronto Canada in 1914, and many of their extended family were fortunate to join them before the outbreak of WW2. The spelling of the Austrian surname Eidel was changed to Edell.

My interest in genealogy was sparked by my cousin Sara Edell-Schafler-Kelman z"l, who traveled to Europe several times, to search through government records for information about families from Jezierna and other shtetls. My interest in Jezierna was stimulated by the stories told by my aunt Anne Edell z"l, about her life as a young girl in Ozerna.

For several years, I volunteered with JewishGen's program of transcribing Birth, Marriage and Death records, which were available for towns in Austria/Poland, present-day Ukraine.

In 2008, I joined the website www.soc-genealogy.jewish/Jezierna organized and managed by Andrew Rosen z"l, of Tucson, Arizona, for the shtetl's descendants. There are several villages and towns with 'Jezior' (Polish for water/lake) as part of their name. Our shtetl was confused with a different town. Thanks to Andy's persistence, both the US Geological Survey Department and JewishGen corrected their information and map location for the town.

The chapters of this Memorial Book were written in anger and with ears, in Yiddish, Hebrew, Polish, German and English. Members of our descendants group suggested that the Yizkor Book should be translated into English so that we and our descendants would be able to read the truth about our ancestors lives and deaths and about the destruction of the Jews of this shtetl.

Among the participants in the descendants' group was Talila Charap-Friedman. She is the granddaughter of Markus Marder, who was the official government chronicler of population records [Metrical Book] of the Jewish community in Jezierna, for successive governments. I was thrilled to discover his signature on the copy of my father's birth record, which was ordered and issued in 1927.

Talila's parents, Sara Marder-Charap and Yitzhak Charap had arrived in Palestine in 1933, and settled in Haifa. Her father was one of the committee members who organized and printed the Jezierna Yizkor Book in Haifa in 1971. Talila rightly insisted that the Yizkor Book should be translated into Hebrew as well. She coordinated volunteers to do this while I managed the fundraising for and the editing of the translation into English. In effect we became co-editors of the translations. Her knowledge of Yiddish and Hebrew contributed to the accuracy of the English version. We helped each other with all problems in all languages.

We began our work in the spring of 2013 and completed the sacred mission in the summer of 2020. Both the English and Hebrew translations of the Jezierna Yizkor Book can be found online at https://www.jewishgen.org/Yizkor/ozerna/Ozerna.html

Acknowledgments:

- Lance Ackerfeld, Yizkor Book Director and Joel Alpert, Director of JewishGen Press.
- JewishGen volunteer experts in computer interface and printing books.
- Donors who provided financial assistance to pay professional translators.
- Volunteer translators, all of whom gave generously of their time and expertise in various languages.
- Zen Eidel z"l, Editor of the chapter - Life of the Jezierna Jews in America.
- Committee of Former Jeziernians in Israel, who wrote, edited and printed the original Sefer Jezierna in 1971.

Suri Edell-Greenberg
English Translation Editor

Hebrew Translation Editor's Comments

To the Reader,

This book was written by our parents for us, their children who were born and raised in Israel. Jezierna was a vague concept for us, 'the Jewish Shtetl" (town) we studied at school, another chapter of the horrible story about the fate of those who stayed there and perished in the Holocaust.

My parents, Sarah of Marder household and Yitchak Charap, like many other parents, did not share their broken hearts with us. They carried their pain, but spared us, their children, from it.

However, it was not just their pain they spared us from, they also withheld the rest of the stories from us. Emerging life stories, rich in endeavor, and the hopes and dreams of their relatives and the town's people. The silencing of the stories and the pain left the characters blurred and faded into a pale background. A net full of holes, of vague knowledge and shredded facts.

I think of how the elders of the town went on their own from Haifa to Jerusalem to unveil the memorial board to the town in the Holocaust Cellar on Mount Zion. They had each other to hug there and to cry. They did not take us, the children, with them.

Drop by drop we became conscious of what had happened there to families and friends who stayed behind. We were busy with our own things, studying, working, raising children, and did not ask questions.

They prepared this book for us, to read when we were ready, when we would want to know. Our parents wrote a large portion of their testimonies in Yiddish, a language we found hard to understand, partly because it, too, was 'silenced'.

Years passed. The Iron Curtain parted. People started traveling to these regions to see, to touch, maybe to try to understand. I also traveled, twice. It was not easy to find Jezierna. We were surprised to discover that the borders had shifted, and the town is now in Ukraine, not in Poland.

Coming there I found that the great Jewish community that used to live there was completely erased. Most people of Polish origin had left, and the majority were Ukrainians, who came after the war. The Jewish cemetery turned into a grazing field, with bits of broken tombstones sticking out of the ground. Near neighboring Zborow, I was led to a monument indicating the site of a mass grave, probably of Jewish victims from the whole area.

With the advent of the internet, I joined a group of Jezierna descendants, many of them were from the USA. I was asked to support them translating the book into English. I said I would be happy to help if we could also make a Hebrew version of the book. Suri Greenberg, born in Toronto to a father from Jezierna, took it upon herself to edit the book in English. We looked for and found Jezierna descendants, both in Israel and abroad, who agreed to donate and support our endeavor. Suri and I worked together in full cooperation. After almost 10 years of hard work, the Hebrew translation of the book was fully online.

I encountered many surprises while working on this text. Many stories found their way to be told. I learned that there was a Jewish cooperative bank in the town, as well as a Hebrew school; and a sage, who was a `miracle maker`, whose grave was honored by Jews and Ukrainians alike. I found a quotation from a Yiddish newspaper that Jezierna excelled in the number of Jews who were agricultural workers! And in another instance came to learn that there were Haaretz newspaper readers in the town… However, alongside these stories the majority of the book is dedicated to the war's horror and its consequences, which includes the story of the fate of the commander of the concentration camp located in the town.

The Yiddish poems in the book, written by Jezierna poets, were added without translation.

 The Jezierna Yizkor book was a joint project of former Jeziernans, initiated by Prof. Menachem Duhl z"l. They assembled many volunteers to write and to raise funds for it. The Hebrew translation was also done mainly by volunteers, almost all of them family members of descendants from Jezierna. The work may not always be professional, but people's willingness to be recruited makes up for it, in my opinion.

Hebrew online translation: http://www.jewishgen.org/yizkor/ozerna/Ozernah.html

Talila (Charap) Friedman

Hebrew Translation Editor

June2022

Translated into English by Sari and Maya Avis

Credits and Captions for Book Cover

Front Cover:

Jezierna on the Wosuczka, c.1915. A wash day during the first World War, with soldiers on patrol. Source: Austrian National Museum. Public domain via Wikimedia Commons.

School chums, c.1935. Courtesy of Dozia Blaustein. Left to right: Unknown, Lusia Fuchs, Dozia Blaustein, Unknown

Back Cover:

Six-year-old Stella (Kochva) Charap brings water from the well, 1937. Courtesy of Ayelet Ophir. Taken by Charap's grandfather, Mordechai Marder.

Unknown farm couple ploughing, c.1935. Courtesy of Talila Charap Friedman. Taken by Mordechai Marder.

Unknown men on a bench, c.1935. Courtesy of Talila Charap Friedman. Taken by Mordechai Marder.

Geopolitical Information

	Town	District	Province	Country
Before WWI (c. 1900):	Jezierna	Złoczów	Galicia	Austrian Empire
Between the wars (c. 1930):	Jezierna	Zborów	Tarnopol	Poland
After WWII (c. 1950):	Ozernyany			Soviet Union
Today (c. 2000):	Ozerna			Ukraine

Alternate names of the Town:

Ozerna [Ukr], Jezierna [Pol], Azierna [Yid], Ozernyany [Rus], Yezirna, Ozernyani, Ozërnaya, Uzirna, Uzyerni, Yezherne, Yezhyerna

Nearby Jewish Communities:

Kozliv 6 miles S

Zboriv 9 miles WNW

Zaliztsi 10 miles N

Yezezhanka 11 miles W

Ternopil 13 miles ESE

Novyy Oleksinets 16 miles NNE

Kozova 16 miles SSW

Pomoryany 18 miles W

Mikulintsy 20 miles SE

Zbarazh 20 miles E

Pidkamin 21 miles N

Stryyivka 22 miles E

Berezhany 22 miles SW

Dunayev 22 miles W

Zolochiv 23 miles WNW

Sasiv 24 miles NW

Zolotnyky 24 miles S

Burkaniv 24 miles S

Strusiv 24 miles SSE

Darakhov 25 miles SSE

Vishnevets 26 miles NE

Narayiv 26 miles WSW

Pidhaytsi 27 miles SSW

Pochayev 27 miles NNE

Vyshnivchyk 28 miles S

Holohory 29 miles WNW

Terebovlya 29 miles SE

Bilyi Kamin 29 miles NW

Jewish Population in 1900: 1,095

Map of Ukraine with **Ozerna** location

Table of Contents

At Home and in the Area

Destruction and Annihilation

Yad Vashem (Memorial)

Appendix

Name Index

Memorial Book of Jezierna
(Ozerna, Ukraine)

49°38' / 25°20'

Translation of *Sefer Jezierna*

Edited by: J. Sigelman

Published in Haifa, 1971

Our sincere appreciation to Yad Vashem
for the submission of the List of Martyrs for placement on the JewishGen web site.

Acknowledgments
Project Coordinators:
Suri Edell-Greenberg and Talila Charap-Friedman

This is a translation from: *Sefer Jezierna* (Memorial book of Jezierna),
Editors: J. Sigelman, Haifa, Committee of Former Residents of Jezierna in Israel 1971 (H,Y, 354 pages)
Note: The original book can be seen online at the NY Public Library site: Jezierna

THERE WAS A TOWN

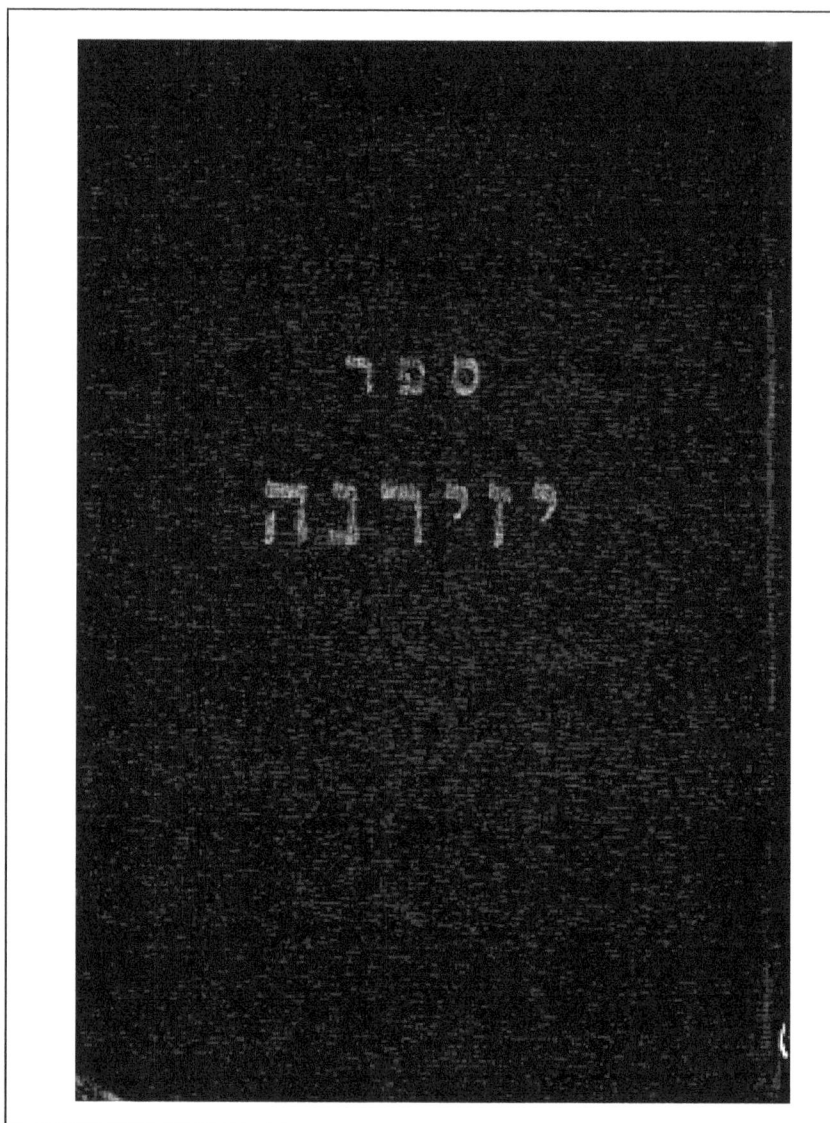

ספר

יזירנה

Committee of Former Jeziernians in Israel

Professor Menachem Duhl, Pesach Altman, Yitzhak Charap, Azriel Zmora, Dora Gottfried, Shlomo Gottfried, Dora Gilad, Chana Yardeni, Shimon Kritz, Lipa Fischer, Yaakov Segal, Aba Katz

Printed in Haifa, Israel- 1971

***

About The Book
Translated from Yiddish by Dorothy Wolfthal, New York
Transcribed & Edited by Zeneth Eidel, New York

With trembling and love we undertake the sacred mission to build a memorial to the holy martyrs of our shtetl, Jezierna, who were annihilated by Nazi hatred in WWII. Since that bitter time, when the axe fell upon the cradle of our childhood, an entire generation has passed, but the blood of our tortured brothers and sisters has not ceased calling to us from the killing fields. We, the survivors, feel the responsibility to create a memorial to our village and its holy martyrs in the form of this book which lies before us. And though we realize that our language is inadequate to express the horror in its full depth – nevertheless we could not consider ourselves free from recording and describing this minimum, which we undertook to do under these circumstances.

Then let these pages recount anew about the destruction and disaster which befell the Jezierna community, as they did upon the whole House of Israel let them tell of the screams of terror of our babies as they were hurled alive into their graves, and of the cries of "SH'MA YISRAEL" [Hear, O Israel] by Jews' open mouths at the abyss into which they were thrown. Let these pages bring to light again the road of sorrow that our dear ones trod in their final walk to the grave.

But this book will tell not only of annihilation but also of the lively life in the not–so–distant past when the Jezierna community stood whole; when there still lived in the *shtetl* – on the Lemberg–Tarnopol line – laboring Jews, ordinary people and intellectuals. And despite the fact that they earned their bread by the sweat of their brows, they still understood how to live a complete and genuine Jewish life. It is noteworthy that, small as our shtetl was, it produced authors and poets, rabbis, school–directors, newspaper editors and great merchants.

And it is our sincere desire that in private solitude, as in communal gatherings, when we page through our book, we will be able to present the long–ago Jezierna, our Yiddish Jezierna, as it developed over the course of generations, with her charming little corners, with her cottages where we lived, with her streets where we ran as youngsters, with her synagogues and worshipers, and above all – with her beloved images (gestalt) which have been torn away from us. Let this book be, for us and for our children after us, a source of pride and inspiration.

The Editors

In the Holocaust Cellar, Mt. Zion

*Left to right: Chaim Gottfried, Chana Yardeni, Dora Gotfried, Elisheva Yafo, Sofia Heliczer
Anderman, Menachem Duhl, Yaakov Kritz, YitzchakCharap, Shlomo Schenhod, Abba Katz, Yehoshua
Glickman, Yaakov Segal, Tova Fuchs, Chaim Zmojre*

***

Acknowledgements

In January 1966, under the initiative of Professor Menachem Duhl and co-operation of Pesach Altman, Yitzhak Charap, Lipa Fischer and Shimon Kritz, a committee of former Jezierna residents, a *landsmenschaft*, was formed, which undertook activities to commemorate the martyrs of the *shtetl*.

The committee dedicated a memorial plaque on Mount Zion [in Jerusalem] and published this memorial Yizkor Book.

The committee's appeal for help was answered by many former Jeziernans in *landsmennschaft* (communal organizations) from Israel and abroad:

The Jezierna group 'Bnei Shlomo' (Sons of Solomon) in the United States, headed by Yosef Zilberberg, secretary; Union of Traditional Jezierna Jews and its secretary Moshe Fuchs.

Among the many individuals are:

from the USA - Yosef Fuchs, Lotta Frankel, Rivka Schwalb, N.Kelman.
from Canada - Ethel Spindel, Chana Katz, David Kurzrok
from Australia - Pepi Scharer and daughters, Helena Fuchs
from Brazil - Yitzchak Wolf Katz
from West Germany - Dr. Norbert Kalafer, Dr. Benzion Rosenfeld
from France - Yaakov Katz, z'l

And in Israel.

Dr. Reuven Avineri, Beno Shteiger, Dvora and Shlomo Gottfried, Dvora Gilad, Yoel Charap, Rosa Herman, Regina Ginzberg, Michael Altman, Magister Sofia Heliczer-Anderman
May they all be blessed.

[Page 11]

Jezierna Jews
by Yehoshua Fuchs (Sam Fox)
Translated from Yiddish by Lily Fox Shine and Cyril Fox

The Shtetl of Jezierna is situated on the road from Zborow to Tarnopol in East Galicia

The Jezierna Rav - Rav Zelig Optavitzer was connected through his family with Zborow and Tarnopol. The Jezierna Rebbe - Rebbe Levi Yitzhak (Monaszohn) was connected to the famous Hasidic Rhiziner dynasty and had a greater Hasidic court and mansion than the Rebbe of Tarnopol and other nearby towns.

About 200 years ago the Empress Maria Theresa of Austria annexed Galicia which became a crown colony in her Empire. There she sent some of her Austrian Jewish population to settle among the gentile Ukrainian and Polish peasants of the area, not a very easy exile for them. The shtetl had a kind and helpful Crown Representative, a Jew by the name of Mendel Yampoler. He led a good and observant Jewish life. He owned a large area of land which included a stream and a mill; land which was rich in arable fields. He organized the construction of a large synagogue which was the pride of the town. There was also the Rebbe's beautiful Court with its great ornamental gates. Another large communal building where young men of the shtetl could learn Talmud and study in the Beth Hamedrash was constructed by a wealthy Jew, Jehoshua Flaum. Examples of typical and prominent Jewish families were the families of Fuchs, Charap and Gottfried.

My father was called Chaim Fuchs and my mother was Feiga Fuchs. My paternal grandfather Avrom Moshe and my maternal grandfather Yitzhak Shlomo were related, both with the name Fuchs. Both great-grandfathers were from the early settlers sent by Maria Theresa. My father traveled through the surrounding neighbourhood and traded with gentile peasants. We are now three brothers, our fourth brother Hersch Volff Fuchs was annihilated with other Jews of the area by the murderous Nazis in 1942.

My older brother Avrom Moshe Fuchs is a well-known Yiddish author who now lives in Israel. Our youngest brother is I.A. Lisky (Itamar Yehuda Fuchs), the editor of the London Jewish Weekly, The Yiddishe Shtimme (The Jewish Voice). He also writes poems, short stories and essays. I left Jezierna in 1914 and have settled in London since then.

The Gottfried family, to whom we are related by marriage, also emigrated to London at the turn of the Century. Their ancestor Reb Avrahom Gottfried also came with the early settlers from Austria. For many years he was the gabbai of the large shul.

The Charap family was also well known in the shtetl. People would stay in their home when visiting the Rebbe. It was always a noisy and lively house because of this. Another Charap family, who lived in a more "enlightened" manner, held court to a group of our society comprising Dr. Hirshhorn, Mordechai Marder the Population Recorder, Ludwig Minz the chemist, and Shmaryahu Imber the Hebrew teacher at the Baron Hirsch school - a brother of Naftali Herz Imber,(who wrote the words of Hatikva), and father of Shmuel Yaakov Imber the Yiddish poet, of the famous Imber family of poets. Also there was Jacob Blaustein, the Director of the school, and Josef Feldman the Polish teacher at the school, and their sons and daughters. These were the more intellectual group of our community. When I left

Jezierna in 1914 there were three hundred Jews. I was told that only one, Yitzhak Pollak, was left after the Shoah 1939-45.

May my memories be bound up with the souls of good innocent Jews of Jezierna who were mercilessly slaughtered by the Nazi murderers in World War II, 1939-45.

Sam Fox, London, 1968-9.

Note by M.D. - *The information in the above article is solely the opinion of Mr. Yehoshua Fuchs z'l.*

Translators of the article are the daughter and son of the author. They added the following information:

Sam Fox (1892-1969) went to London in 1913. He had been apprenticed as a sheet-metal worker in Jezierna, and in the late 1920s opened his own business in London. During World War 2 his factory was largely given over to work for the War Office. He was still working up to a few days before his death at age 77.

An English summary was donated to this book by David Fielker. It was previously published in Shemot (JGS of Great Britain), September 1999.

[Pages 13-14]

The *Tzaddik* of Jezierna
by Gavriel Herman Green, Buenos Aires
Translated from Yiddish by Pamela Russ

What are years? Years are like waves. A person always tries to swim upstream, but the years always run downstream and they disappear farther and deeper into the past.

This is how many, many years have already disappeared. I have already experienced and wandered through many, many lands, and many years have already passed since I have planted my tent here on the shores of La Plata estuary. Nonetheless, I remember my *shtetleh* Jezierna, or as the Jews called it, Ozerna. That's where I was born and where I lived until my tenth year of life.

Of all the hundred and maybe thousands of cities and towns through which I wandered in my youngest years, my place of birth, Jezierna, stands out, and when I remember it, I actually see it in my mind. I see the crooked, wooden houses, the broken wells that often swallowed victims, and I even see the church spires that stretch out in a distance, as if they were calling: Come, go out of this town, look at the world. If you would want to return, you will not get lost, we will show you the way...

I was a child, a poor neglected child, an orphan, so I wandered around the town, rummaging through things, and I saw everything; and most of all I saw the poverty, with which I was very familiar.

There were many Jewish stores in Jezierna, and the Jewish trade was lively in the marketplaces. But no one said that the Jews in Jezierna survived by trading, because according to my childish understanding, I heard only that the Jezierna Jews survived only thanks to the Jezierna *Tzaddik* (righteous man), Reb Schloime Charap.

Reb Shloime'le was not from a rabbinic lineage. He was the son of an innkeeper, but he was a genius and a scholar, and he very quickly became reputed in the region for his knowledge. Once, when there was a fire in Jezierna, and house after house was destroyed and blown away with the smoke, and the wind blew the fire to the Jewish street and to the courtyard, then (this is what I heard tell) Shloime'le stood himself up and began to pray to God - and then a wondrous thing happened, even though the wind blew to the side where Shloime'le was standing, one could clearly see that the fire was struggling with the wind and could not advance; it was even retreating...

There were even people who said that they themselves actually saw how it was as if a supernatural hand was driving the fire back into the wind, and everyone was certain that these powers were a result of the prayers of the young *Tzaddik*, Reb Shloime'le, who struggled with the wind. That's how the entire Jewish population of Jezierna was saved from the terrible fire.

Since then, Reb Shloime'le's name became famous, and Jews from Hungary, Bessarabia, and Romania came to him with notes requesting blessings. Later on, it became known that Reb Shloime'le was not only a brilliant scholar, but he was also brilliant in worldly matters, because Reb Shloime'le was a wise man who gave sage advice to all those who came to see him. That's how everyone knew that the town would long ago have been destroyed by the fire, but thanks to Reb Shloime'le the town survived and the resident Jews earned money from the *Chassidim* who came to Shloime'le for blessings and forgiveness.

How my Jezierna later developed I do not know because it's already been more than half a century since I left there. But one thing I know, that a great-grandchild of the Jezierna Tzaddik Reb Shloime'le today is President of the Galician Society in Argentina - that is the President Shloime Kweller - who is actually named after his famous great-grandfather, Reb Shloime'le.

Note by M.D.- Shloime Kweller originated from Kozlow

[Pages 15-19]

From Jezierna to the Land of Israel
by Chanah Marder-Yardeni, Kiryat Bialik
Translated from Hebrew by Ronit Yardeni-Gura and Ori Yardeni

There once was… well, that's how all legends begin. The Holocaust made the Jewish communities of Europe into legend - a tragic and horrific legend at that. They once were, and are no more.

There once was the city of Jezierna, where we were born and raised… the city of our mothers and fathers, our brothers and sisters. And behold - they are no more!

Chanah Marder (center) and unknown friend go for a ride, c.1932. Courtesy of Talila Charap Friedman.
Taken by Mordechai Marder. [Photo not in original book.]

Jezierna was a lively city, a microcosm of an independent country, complete with its cultural life, its diverse social classes fighting for their survival, its lay leaders, its charity treasurers, its rank-and-file citizens, its political parties with their battles for the hearts and minds of the public, and the task of choosing between them. There were the city's 'shining youth' - young people who were working or studying.

I can still remember the small three-room house that stood on a hilltop. It was the center of intellectual life, where battles raged over different interpretations of the Zionist idea. The largest room was used by *HaZionim Haklali'im* faction, the General Zionists. My father, Mordechai Marder, of blessed memory, was their head spokesperson and their life and soul. *HaNoar Hazioni* youth movement, the natural heirs of the aging *Zionim Haklali'im*, was under their auspices, and was led by personalities like Moshe Altman, Moshe Kelman, Villik Laufer, Mania Hazelnuss and Munio Motzborov. All of them, of blessed memory, were eradicated during the Holocaust. As for myself - may I live to a ripe old age - I was the youngest child of the chairman of the *Zionim Haklali'im*. In the other two rooms, two other groups would convene: the *Hapoel Hazair* youth movement, or the 'Gordonia', and the revisionists, in which my brother-in-law (who was married to my older sister Sarah) was active. So it was that we would be seated around my father's table for a Sabbath or holiday meal, and polemics between the representatives of these three factions from the house on the hill would rage on. When my mother would remind us that it was the

Sabbath day and that it was unseemly of us to argue in deference to the joyous spirit of the Sabbath, we would all respond with "what do you care... this is what we enjoy doing"...

A Zionist Household

This was indeed the epitome of a household in a Jewish town, complete with its conflicts of opinion.

My father, who was born in Zborow, was brought up by his devoutly religious parents, who were determined to raise their only son to be a rabbi and a Torah scholar. He had, however, his own unique perceptions and judgment, as well as a gentle, poetic soul. As a youth he had already rebelled against his parents' principles. Secretly, while studying *Gemara,* he would read the literature of the *Haskalah*, the Enlightenment movement. He reveled in the works of Goethe, Schiller and Zola, and would even quote chapters of their books. Thus my self-taught father would come to acquire a general education, and he was drawn to the Emancipation movement, which had been spreading throughout the enlightened world during his lifetime. He defied stereotypes and he was always following what was going on in the broader world around him. Fueled by his passion for his beliefs, and using his natural gifts of persuasion and eloquence, he even began convincing his friends and other young people to espouse these views.

My mother, of blessed memory, was raised by progressive parents. What was unique about her household was that a private tutor was brought in to teach the four girls in her family. This was very uncommon, especially since the educational program included studying a foreign language in addition to Polish and learning the foundations of social etiquette and cultural norms. My mother's education produced results that were immediately apparent; her peace of mind, her wisdom of life, her nobility. My mother always looked neat and well groomed, though she didn't always lead 'an easy life'.

The extraordinary blend of contrasts in my mother and father found its expression in their children's' upbringing: intellectual awareness, sensitivity and over-achievement attitude from father, on one hand; peace of mind and life wisdom from mother, on the other. Together, these traits produced warmth, culture and vitality - qualities that touched every corner of our home.

Under the influence of his prominent friend Yehoshua Redler-Feldman, otherwise known as the writer Rabbi Binyamin, my father became an ardent and passionate Zionist. For years the two worked together in the town, and later they exchanged letters up until the war and the Holocaust. From then on, my father dedicated his entire being and his passions to the Zionist movement. He would valiantly fight in its defense against the religious right on one hand, and the liberal left on the other.

He was particularly active during preparations for the distribution of *shekalim*, membership certificates, and elections for Zionist congresses. At that time my father would muster all his energy and prepare himself for the struggle ahead. During elections he would invite well-known lecturers to speak to voters in the assembly halls, though his opening remarks at these assemblies were passionate and fiery. His heartfelt words penetrated the hearts of his peers and recruited them to the ranks of his party.

I remember once, during election day for the Zionist congress, my father discovered that two people who had promised him their votes were not in the town; they were: Rachel Shalita, the daughter of Rabbi Shalita, and Frimeleh Feuerstein's grandfather. They had both gone to Zborow. My father promptly rented a wagon that was to be sent to Zborow to bring these two to the ballot station. He would also distribute membership certificates free of charge, and would later replace the money out of his own pocket. It wasn't that he had too much money- he was simply so concerned about the results of the elections, that he was willing to give up on his own needs and those of his family!

The Clandestine Immigration

My father would level criticism at Zionist leaders in the diaspora, saying: "Who is a *Zioni Klali* (General Zionist}? Someone who takes money from another Jew to send a third Jew to Israel. To prove his devotion to the idea of immigration, he planned his family's immigration to the Land of Israel. First, he dispatched his eldest daughter - my sister Sarah, her husband Yitzhak Charap, and his granddaughter, whom he treasured so dearly. Next was his second daughter, my sister Lotta. Still, it stands to reason that what made their sacrifice so great in terms of the pain and suffering they endured, was to take leave of me, the baby of the family, when I emigrated to Israel. After a difficult and emotional struggle, I was given permission to begin pioneer training, which wasn't a common activity in those days. I was our town's first representative to this program. Certificates for legal immigration didn't exist, so I decided to enter the country illegally. My parents didn't bar the way, but the hardships that I endured and the distress that I put my parents through were unbearable.When we arrived in Costanza [Constanta], Romania, I, as well as a thousand others, were loaded onto the 'Katina', a small cargo ship meant to carry potatoes. The ship couldn't even hold 500 people. It didn't have the facilities necessary for passengers, including proper latrines. After trying to approach the Israeli shore for two weeks and then fleeing back towards the sea- having been repelled by the British navy- our ship washed up on a sandbar near a desolate beach on the Isle of Crete. The ship sank just as we managed to get ourselves onto the beach.

Our sirens and SOS signals attracted the attention of another ship of illegal immigrants, called 'Gipo'. Seven hundred people were packed together on board that ship and we joined them- all one thousand of us.

700 women, children and elderly people, who possessed nothing but the shirts on their backs, managed to reach the shores of Israel. Members of the *Hagana*, who had awaited our arrival throughout the rainy and foggy night carried us in on their backs. The rest of the passengers were destined to continue their wandering. We soon found ourselves in a packing house. We were wet and shivering from the cold, but we were given food to eat for the first time in a month of wandering, fresh bread and halva, and even hot drinks. The next day we enjoyed a hot bath and cooked food, provided by representatives of the various movements who came to welcome us and send us to the places designated for our absorption.

***

All throughout that period, my mother and father were anxiously awaiting news from me, and they were worried sick. At that time, they had been hearing rumors of ships of immigrants that were attacked by the British, and that some of the passengers had been killed when the ships sank (and our ship had indeed sunk). They heard about a ship that was burned. When I reached my sister's house in Israel I found a pile of letters from my parents. They had written to me every day, begging for some information on what had happened to me. Here's an excerpt from one of their letters, which exemplifies my parents' dedication to immigration - a process that was also their source of solace during times of trouble:

"According to the legend, the return to Zion during the times of the Messiah will be accompanied by *gilgul mechilot,* rolling in the underworld's tunnels and *chibut hakever,* torments of the grave. It appears that this was decreed - that it would not be easy for the Jews to return to their land. Their pains and torments are great, and we know that illegal immigration has elements of rolling in the underworld's tunnels. Every day we feel horror and astonishment, and we ask ourselves if we have wronged you by letting you set off on such a dangerous path. We don't sleep at all at nighttime and can't bear the burden of these feelings of concern and fear. Still, if we are fated to suffer during our own immigration to Israel we'll accept our fate with love…"

My father devoted his life to the ideal of resurrecting the people of Israel in its own land. My father and mother's dream was to join their children in the land of their forefathers, but they never had the chance to realize that dream…

Six-year-old Stella (Kochva) Charap brings water from the well, 1937. Courtesy of Ayelet Ophir. Taken by Charap's grandfather, Mordechai Marder. Stella and her mother Sarah Marder Charap visited Jezierna from Eretz Israel; it was the last time they ever saw their relatives. Photo not in original book

Jewish students at the Polish government school in Jezierna, with teacher Y. Fuchs

In the Holocaust Cellar
The gentlemen Yaakov Segal and Lipa Fischer before the Unveiling of
the Plaque for the Jezierna Community on the Wall of Remembrance

[Pages 20-24]

The Last Will of our Martyrs
by Menachem Duhl, Haifa
Translated by Ornit Barkai

Our Martyrs left us their last will "Remember! Never Forget!"

Never to forget the slaughterers of our people; to gather all our might to expose their true faces to the world; to expose their crimes and bring them to justice.

We heard this from the victims on their way to the slaughter. Similarly, we heard this even from the Judenrat members just moments before their death, when they finally realized the tragedy of their own people.

The both of us, Tzila Heliczer and myself, gathered all our strength to seek and find Richard Diga, the murderer of the Jews who were imprisoned in what was known as "Jezierna Labor Camp", and bring him to trial. Tzila worked with extraordinary dedication towards this goal.

As soon as the war was over and we were expelled from Brzezany to Silesia, I started to search for Diga. I knew that this murderer was from Bytom in Silesia. So I relied on the security forces of Katowiec, Warsaw, Wroclaw, and the Ministry of Justice in Warsaw.

In 1947, while living in Zabkovice (Lower Silesia), my wife and I were summoned to testify in court about Diga's crimes in Jezierna. In answer to my question, the judge replied "the killer must have been captured already if you were asked to testify."

Months went by and I hadn't heard a thing about Diga's case. I started to ask in the various authorities to find out what happened with the case, but did not get a response. Even the judge did not know anything, but suspected that Diga had escaped to Germany.

* * *

During the Nazi era, Tzila Heliczer was quick to understand that escape was the only way to survive, especially after she witnessed the horrific crimes committed by Diga against Jews in Jezierna. She left town with fake Aryan documents identifying her as Ukrainian, and was lucky to survive while moving from one place to another.

After leaving town she embarked on the wretched life on the road, the constant fear of being discovered, identified and turned in. She changed her address often, even moving to new neighborhoods, but to no avail. In the end she was caught, spent several months in jail withstanding the dreadful Gestapo interrogations and was finally transferred to forced labor in Germany.

Tzila, the daughter of a hand-wringing, caring mother, went through the seven circles of hell. Listening to her hair-raising story, it's hard to believe that a person could survive this. I only bring this up as a fact. It was Tzila who had to tell her story. Her whole life passed in front of her eyes even after the war, and the memory was never erased.

After the war, when Tzila Cymer, maiden name Heliczer, lived in Aachen, West Germany and met with a lawyer to discuss reparations, she told him about what happened to her during the Nazi regime and Diga's name was brought up. Upon hearing his name the lawyer told her that the police were looking for evidence against a war criminal named Richard Diga, and he passed along to the police the information he received from Tzila.

Coincidentally, in 1959, when the Cymer family was looking for an apartment, Tzila stumbled upon the name Richard Diga on an entrance to one of the apartments. Her blood curdled upon noticing that name and her heart pounded hard. Could it be the same Diga, slaughterer of the Jews of Jezierna who lived there? Was he living here peacefully with his family? These thoughts rushed through Tzila's mind. Anxiously, Tzila hurried to the police station. The story had already been reported to the police by her attorney. As it turned out, the man was the cousin of the real Diga, the commander of Jezierna labor camp.

And in a tiny town near the Swiss border, in a beautiful villa, lived Richard Diga with his family. He didn't lack for silver, gold or dollars. In fact, he was swimming in gold and precious items. He was not afraid of anyone. Who would have recognized him there? He lived "like a god in France" as the old saying goes. He had eliminated the Jews, so who would tell on him and turn him in? He knew that eventually the war crimes' statute of limitations would expire and so would his own crimes, and then he would leave the small town and settle in Berlin, or move back to Bytom as a hero.

But finally Tzila was summoned to the prosecutor Dr. Engleberg in Waldshut. He questioned her in great detail and showed her a photo of Diga, which she identified right away. He suggested that she accompany him to the town where Diga lived. And so, accompanied by the prosecutor and the police they left on the fast train. One can only imagine the fear and joy that engulfed her. There, she will finally face that murderer. She would identify him and he will be arrested on the spot.

They arrived in town after a 24-hour ride and went directly to court. They had to wait a while before Diga was brought in. Tzila recognized him immediately and in a state of uncontrolled emotion a scream escaped her lips: "There he is - the murderer of the Jews! " Diga stood there as white as death. He too recognized her. That Jewess, that "dirty Jewess" was standing now in front of him. He knew that there could be no arguments or any nonsense; he was identified and arrested. Later he was transferred to Waldshut, to "a retreat."

We were now faced with the daunting task of collecting testimonies and gathering proofs. Several testimonies were presented by Tzila on the spot. Tzila fulfilled the last will of the Jezierna martyrs.

Her immense courage to undertake a 24-hour long trip surrounded by strangers, and above all Germans, to look the murderer straight in the eye and to recount his crimes, was unfathomable. That is heroism without a doubt, and the driving force behind it was the testament to "Remember! Never Forget!"

This all took place in 1959, 14 years after the war and 16 years after the annihilation of the Jezierna Jews.

Mrs. Henya Helizcer, Tzila's mother, informed us of Diga's arrest. And so, with help from Yad Va'Shem, we began collecting testimonies. This is the list of the witnesses we found:

Australia: Mrs. Peppe Sharer and her daughters Bronia and Frieda.
Cuba: Dora Blaustein - Cyna Blaustein's daughter.
Israel: My wife and I, Mr. Ryski (Engel) - Yiddish actor from Poland who was interred in our camp.
Canada: Chanah Katz-Reichman
USA: New York, Brooklyn: Inzesh, Isidor Steinberg from Borszczów who was in the Jezierna camp.

The major and most significant testimonies were given by Tzila and her mother. At the request of the prosecutor in Waldshut we all gave our evidence about what happened to us, and in all the testimonies Diga was accused of the horrific crimes he committed. However, his case never came to trial. The prosecutor informed Yad VaShem that Diga hanged himself in jail.

That was the end of the man, who for over two years murdered about 20,000 Jews in Jezierna, in a horrible way and in cold blood. He probably did not want to face the few surviving Jews and give them the satisfaction of bringing to trial "The Chief Diga", dressed in a prison uniform, and recounting one by one his horrendous crimes.

May his name and his memory be obliterated!

In the Holocaust Cellar

Left to right: Menachem Duhl, Shlomo Shenhod, Yaakov Segal, Yizchak Charap, Yaakov Kritz, Shmuel Altman

[Page 27]

THE WAY OF LIFE

Shadows Dance

S.Y. Imber

שאָטן־טענץ
עמעץ טייטלט אויף מיין שטערן
מיט אַ פינגער שוואַרץ ווי קויל ;
עמעץ קושט מיין האַנט די דאַרע
מיט אַ קאַלט פאַרפרוירן מויל.
ערגעץ האָט אַ קראָ געשריגן,
דאָרט אין דרויסן -- ווייט, העט-העט.
ס'איז דאָך ווינטער, ס'איז דאָך ווינטער.
ס'איז דאָך אזוי קאַלט אין בעט.
עפעס הוידען זיך געשטאַלטן
אָן אַן אויפהער, אָן אַן ענד
אויף זיין שויבלס קרומע ווענטלעך,
און זיי ברעכן מיט די הענט.
און די עקן שאָטן־פלעקן
מאַלן דאָס און מאַלן יענץ.
און זאַיי סטראַשען און זיי שרעקן
און זיי גייען שטילע טענץ - - -
(1910)

Shmuel Yaakov Imber wrote this poem in Jezierna when he was 21 years old.   The Imber family lived in Jezierna at that time. His father Shmaryahu Imber was a teacher at the Baron Hirsch School. - M. Duhl

[Page 28]

***

Jezierna

by Dr. Nachman Blumenthal, Jerusalem

Translated from Yiddish by Pamela Russ

Introduction:

A person is – someone once said – a world unto himself; a microcosm in which the big world (the macrocosm), a world with so many details, reflects itself. And if this is true for an individual, how much more so is this true for a collective setting, like a Jewish town, a Jewish community. Here we already have what to discuss – as the grandfather of Yiddish literature, Mendele Moicher Sforim, said: "It's a world with small worlds."

And if it's a world, a whole world, so who can undertake to write it's history from beginning to end? It would take years of work, travels across the world, searches and rummages through archives, browsing all the newspapers, interviews with each history writer who originates from these places or who somehow wandered around these parts, and trace every descendant from that place, to wherever and whenever he has roamed, etc.

Who can permit himself to do this?

I believe all this is important to say, since I will attempt to paint the history of the town of Jezierna only with broad strokes. Cut off thousands of kilometers from the city itself, without any chance of accessing any archives or institutions, as much as they could have survived after the destruction that World War Two brought with it, something from our past – since there is no other way, our work must bear the character of distant echoes that once was and is no more. More than this historical outline is likely not necessary for a memorial book … in order to remember.

The *Shtetl* (Jezierna in Polish, Ozerna in Ukrainian)

The old settlement was located near a large lake into which rivulets flowed, and near a small river, Wosuszka, that flows into the Strypa River. From that lake the settlement took its name – Jeziero in Polish, and Ozero in Ukrainian. And these provided a livelihood to the early settlers many years ago. With time, as the settlement grew around both sides of the river, it came to pass that the river split the town into two. Years ago, when the waters rose, the settlement was protected like a natural fortress. One could not get to it easily.

We hear about Jezierna for the first time in a letter from Zygmunt August written in the year 1545, to his father the king of Poland, Zygmunt I (the Elder). The letter was about this specific village that Jan Tarnowski, the great military commander–in–chief of Poland (of "the Crown," that is Poland without Lithuania) had forcefully taken over (justly or unjustly – who can judge this today?) from Duchess Beata Ostrowska.

In about 1615, the settlement was purchased by Yakob Sobieski, the governor of Lublin, father of the future king Jan Sobieski, whose family estates were located in Reussen, part of later East Galicia: such as Olesk, Zlocow, Zhulkiew, etc.). He built a castle, to protect himself on the mountain, located southwest of the settlement at a height of about 400 meters. He also built a Roman Catholic church in the year 1636. Other members of the Sobieski family would also come here to live – the father, and after that the son; then later King Jan III and his son Jakob.

The position of the settlement: a lake, a river with flowing water, and a mountain that had strategic defense capacity were the cause of occasional military campaigns.

Historical Events:

In the year 1649, on the third of August at the time of the Chmielnicki revolt and the wars with him, and the Tatars on one side and the Polish military on the other side, King Jan Kazimierz waited to the rear of Zborow for the bridges to be repaired so that he could pass over to Jezierna, Tarnopol[1] …

On May 29, 1651, during the second assault on Poland, Jezierna was occupied by Chmielnicki. He waited here for the Tatar Khan[2] for several months.

In the year 1655, Jezierna was involved in an agreement between the Poles and the Khan.[3] In that same year, on the ninth of November, there was a confrontation between the Tatars and the Russian military; the Tatars did not want to allow the Russians to pass over the embankments into the city, but this didn't work. At least that's how the Czar's messenger Buturlyn presented this in a letter reporting to the Czar.

Again in 1657, the well–known Polish commander, the great military man and anti–Semite Stefan Schtarnazki [Czarniecki] was there and from there he continued his war with the Swedes…

In the year 1667, the great commander and Grand Marshall Jan Sobiecki, the future king, wrote to his sister Duchess Katarzyna Radziwill that the hordes of Tatars completely destroyed Jezierna, among other towns. "There is no sign of what once was. You cannot find even one peasant for help." – They had all run away.

***

These are more or less the important historical facts of Poland's past that are related to the Jezierna of those times. Jezierna then passes into the hands of the magnate family Radziwill. Moczei Stazhenski buys this village from them; in 1863 half of the settlement belonged to the Ilinski family.[4]

At the first partitioning of Poland in 1772, Jezierna is transferred to Austria as a part of the kingdom of Galicia and then remains in Austria (afterwards Austria–Hungary) until the end, which began in November 1918, when the huge empire fell apart. Jezierna is taken over by the Ukraine which creates its western Ukrainian republic in that part of Galicia. After half a year, more or less, the Polish military, in conflict with Ukraine, chases the Ukrainians out of Jezierna. Now Jezierna becomes a Polish city (with a short lapse, when in the year 1920 Bolshevik soldiers enter the city), until September 1939, when it is transferred to the Soviet Union. In July 1941, the Germans enter and remain until June 1944. Then the Soviet government returns.

During the Austrian era, the town was part of the Zloczow province; then from October 1, 1904, part of the Zborow county that was established at that time. That is how it remained in the days of Poland. In time, the larger administrative union, to which the Zborow county belonged, became the Tarnopol province. Under the Soviets, the town itself became the center of the region (formerly the province).

Demographic Details:

The number of residents in the city:[5]

Year	General	Number of Jews	% of Jews
1880	4.713	955	20.3%
1890	5.275	1,164	22.1%
1900	5.843	1,195	20.5%
1921	5.578	813	14.6%
1931	6.026	700	11.6% *****
1939	——	——	——%

The first three numbers are from the time that Jezierna belonged to Austria–Hungary; the rest are from the time that the town already belonged to Poland.[6]

We see from these numbers that between the years 1880–1900 the settlement grew: both the general population grew by 1,130 people (almost 19.4%), as well as the Jewish population by 240 people (that means more than 20%). The growth of the Jewish population becomes more impressive for this period if we take into consideration for the years 1880–1900 not the numbers in the general population, but the number of non–Jews and compare them with the number of Jews. In that case, for the year 1880 there were 3,758 non–Jews, and for 1900 there were 4,648; the increase in the non–Jewish population was about 890 people – that is, 19.1%.

It is worth noting that the general (non–Jewish) population in that first decade (1880–1890) grew by 562 people, almost the same number that it grew in the next decade (1890–1900) with 568 people – that is a normal rate. On the other hand, there is a great jump in numbers in the Jewish population. In that first decade, the Jewish population grew by 209 people, and in the next decade by only 31. These numbers are understandably not a result of a natural, normal biological increase, but only because of the incoming Jews from foreign parts, primarily from nearby areas. The majority of the Jews from the villages moved to the cities – a typical "Jewish" phenomenon.

In the year 1890, the Jews in the city reached their relative peak at 22.1% of the general population.

These were "normal" times that were exceptional because of the rise in emigration by the impoverished population of Galicia. Jews and Ukrainians alike, who left their homeland to go primarily to "America" (those who went to the United States were mainly Jews) and to Canada (mainly Ukrainians). This includes part of the natural increase and so the settlement did not grow proportionally as the natural increase would indicate, but in the later years it all took the form of an apparent increase.

However, when we look at the numbers of 1900–1921, a span of about 20 years, we see a different picture:

The non–Jewish population grew as follows: in 1921 – 4,765 (813–5,578); in 1900 – 4,648 (1,195–5,843), having grown by only 117 people, this is less than the natural increase would be, but nonetheless, there was growth.

On the other hand, the Jewish population dropped significantly by 382 people (1,195–813), not considering the normal increase that would have taken place over these more than 20 years – at least 50 people. The number of Jews was decreasing both in absolute and relative terms – in relation to the non–Jewish population, from 20.5% to 14.6%. These are the results of the war vis–à–vis the Jews. In other words, we suffered from the war (1914–1920) in a much more significant way than the non–Jews.

What in truth we have to admit is that among the Jews, at the beginning of the war and during the fighting around Jezierna (the Austrian–Russian conflict, then after that the Polish–Ukrainian conflict and the Polish–Soviet conflict), more Jews than non–Jews left the town (we don't have exact numbers), but overall the emigrations involved so few that they could cope with the dropping numbers – 382 people plus the natural growth from 1900–1914 in normal times; and the smaller increase from 1915–1921 in the abnormal war times!

And so, because of World War One, Jezierna lost 450 individuals. These were actually war victims (those who died in battle, soldiers and civilians, and those who died from epidemics, from famine and from need), and those who, willingly or not willingly (were chased out, were afraid of pogroms, etc.), had left the city and run away to distant Vienna (in Austria), or to the larger cities (to be among Jews – to Zloczow, Tarnopol, eventually Lemberg, etc.). A small number of Jews returned after the end of the war that lasted longer here than in the West.

For the later years, we do not have official data, particularly about the Jews, but the number of Jews certainly did not increase. The natural growth that decreased significantly, particularly for the Jews, after World War One, both because of the poverty of the Jewish population and because of the changing lifestyles, more modernization, fewer children, etc. – certainly included the emigration of Jews from Jezierna who settled in other, larger cities in Poland, or who left for foreign countries (America … and Eretz Yisrael).

Incidentally, in 1921, Jezierna still had 14.6% Jews, as opposed to the other cities – in total – from Zborow county, to which Jezierna also belonged, where the number of Jews was only 5.8% (down from 14.2% in 1881).

What is relevant is that in the year 1921, the natural increase of Jews in Zborow county was 1,000 – 31.1 births, 13.0 deaths, that is 18.1 (per thousand); that comes to 5.5% of the general population, while the percent of Jews in the county was 5.8%; that means that Jews decreased by 0.3% from the general non–Jewish population. The reason is understandable – Jews were more "big city"; more modernized, more thoughtful about … the future. So, the economic situation for the Jews was certainly worse than that of the non–Jews who lived on their lands (peasants and farmers), and those who enjoyed the state's support (officers, etc.).

According to the religious profile, in the year 1921, the town was comprised of:

2,496	Roman Catholics
2,269	Greek Catholics (Uniates)
813	Jews (followers of Mosaic Law
5,578	Total

According to nationality:

3,635	Poles
1,634	Ruthenians[7]
309	Jews[8]
5,578	Total

The large number of Poles according to nationality is remarkable. This is a result of the census method used in 1921. The Polish Commission of Statistics was especially interested that in that year, when Eastern Galicia had not yet been recognized as part of Poland, the number of Poles should be high. So they did not ask everyone about their nationality and they wrote whatever they wished. Secondly, not all the Jews, especially the Jews that did not know any Polish, paid attention to the questions of religion and nationality, and especially about their citizenship. For the ordinary Jew, it was important that he was just a Jew, that means a believing Jew, the rest did not interest him.

It is still not possible that in a city such as Jezierna 504 Jews (more than half) were actually assimilated, spoke Polish, considered themselves as Poles, etc.

To the above-mentioned statistic of the year 1921, you have to add the number of people who lived on the estates of the owners of the city, called in Polish "*obszary dworskie*" (court areas). With time, they established an independent administrative unit.

On the estate, (that means those who worked for the landowners), there were 106 people: among them were 61 Poles, 23 Russians and 22 Jews. According to religion there were: 24 Roman Catholics and 60 Greek Catholics, and we know that the Greek Catholics were primarily Ukrainian. This was how the Polish census looked at that time.

We have to add these 22 Jews to the numbers of the shtetl. They belonged to the Jewish community just as much as the other Jews did. The fact that they belonged to the estate shows that their work only involved agriculture (in a relatively large number): estate stewards, record keepers, guards, distillers, foresters, etc. At the beginning of the war, in September 1939, according to certain non–official calculations (taken from Jewish sources), there were only 700 Jews. A decrease compared to the year 1921 – of 113 people.

How Did the Jews of Jezierna Make a Living?

With regard to the economic situation of the Jews of Jezierna, we can quote this, which Dr. Ch. D. Hurwitz wrote about the "Jewish Economy" in general, in the year 1902, in the "Jewish People's newspaper" (*Jiddische Volkszeitung*), Num. 1 (from June 13, 1902), published in Krakow, edited by M. Spektor and Ch. D. Hurwitz: "The Jewish situation (in Galicia in general) becomes more tragic, more terrible, from day to day, and even more so for our Jewish artisans..." Before, they had a peaceful life; they were not rich men, but they earned a living. The same was true for the merchants. "Only one thing is missing for the Jewish artisans today – that is a livelihood. He becomes somewhat of a salesman (goes to the fairs to sell his wares), but the merchants also become poorer each day."

In August 13, 1902, Yakov Shor wrote an article in the same newspaper entitled: "The Jews in Galicia – saying that Galicia is filled with capable people … and no one has a livelihood. Among the reasons for this difficult situation, the writer listed: "…the competition of the Polish and Ukrainian cooperatives, the Polish "Farmer", the Ukrainian "People's Trader", and also the legislation that was enacted against the Jews. Jewish shops were closed for two days a week: Saturday by their own choice, and Sunday because of the enforced law. The same was true for artisans, etc.

The situation did not change even in later times until the very end. On the contrary, the situation worsened considerably.

And when the general depression occurred all over Poland, it fell first on the shoulders of the Jews, and when the establishment of the government's anti–Semitic edicts: higher taxes, not permitting Jews to take government jobs, etc. It seemed better in the thirties, the situation for the Jews was relatively better than in other places, and that was because in Jezierna, the Jews were occupied primarily with agriculture. It's as if the words of the folksong (of Eliakum Zunser) came true, that "in the plow lies good fortune and blessing."

Of interest is the article by S. Gershoni, published in the "New Tomorrow" (*Neuer Morgen*) of November 3, 1932, under the heading "A Town in Galicia Where Jews Live from Working the Ground".

The correspondent had a lengthy discussion with population registrar M.M. (Markus Marder), and this is what he said – based on what he [Marder] knew about the distribution of "his" town; on the basis of the statistics of which he was officially in charge – he concluded that 90% of the Jewish population in the town are small plot-holders, (not "Land-Owners"!) Almost every Jew owns a small piece of field, animals (or at least some goats that also give milk), a garden – of fruits, vegetables. The majority of them work the land by themselves (an indication that the area is not large): the Jews sow and plow. They live modestly, primitively, and if they save a few pennies, they buy more land. And this provides, if not a complete livelihood (for everyone), at least a livelihood more or less.

Understandably, in the town there are also artisans and a larger number of merchants (small shopkeepers), but not all can make a living from this – and therefore, their numbers are decreasing. Because of this, they also occupy themselves with agriculture. The wife stays in the shop, the husband works the soil, the son…

(About this problem, see also the chapter about the Jewish bank and about the cooperative "Unia.")

In Jezierna, at the turn of the century from the 19th to the 20th century, there was the well–known Shloimele Charap who was like a Rebbi, to whom *Chassidim* [followers] would come from distant places. This also provided a livelihood for the innkeeper – the sexton and for the Rebbe himself.

Footnotes:
1. Hrusewski Michaela: Russian History – Ukraine; volume 8, page 196
2. Hrusewski, volume 9, page 273.
3. Hrusewski, volume 9, page 1091. "*Pid Ozierniew.*"
4. According to the Encyclopedia (first Polish general encyclopedia) published by a Jew, Shmuel Orgelbrand, in the 60's of the previous century [1860's] in Warsaw.
5. Jezierna in Old Poland and after that in Austria, was considered a city (a small town was called "*miasteczko*"), and in independent Poland it was for the first time considered a "city settlement" ("*osada miejska*") and later as the location for the collective municipality ("*gmina zbiorowa*") to which only villages belonged.
6. These numbers for the years 1880, 1890, 1900, are taken from: Dr. St. Gnunski: *Materyali de kwestii zydowskiej w Galicyi*, Lwow 1910.
   The numbers for the year 1921 are according to: *Statistisches Gemeindeverzeichnes*, Berlin 1939, page 98.
   The numbers for the year 1931 are taken from: Bogdan Wasitynski: *Ludnosc zydowska w Polscew XIX, XX wieku*.
   The numbers for September 1, 1939, are taken from: *Bletter Fahr Geshichte*, Warsaw, 1953, Volume 6, book 3, table 11, page 132.
7. From the Polish "*Russini.*" The Polish administration was not eager to use the national "Ukrainian" descriptions.
8. According to the files in Yad Vashem.

Jezierna, miasteczko w pow. złoczowskim, 40 kil. na płd.-wschód od Złoczowa. Zajmuje ono płd.-wsch. narożnik powiatu, przypierający wschodnią krawędzią o tarnopolski, zach. o brzeżański powiat, i leży m. 49°35' a 49°40' płn. szer., 42°55' a 43°5' wsch. dług. od Ferro. Na półn. leżą Daniłowice i Ostaszowce, na wschód Isypowce, Seredyńce i Cebrów, na płd. Pokropiwna, Kozłów, Cewry i Płaucza wielka, na zachód Jarczowce. Przez środek mka płynie od półn.-zach. na płd.-wschód pot. Wosuszka (dopływ Strypy). Wchodzi on tu z Ostaszowiec, zaraz na wstępie tworzy stawek i zabiera od prawego brzegu kilka dopływów. W dolinie potoku na prawym jego brzegu leżą zabudowania przeważnie drewniane (361 m., 350 m. koło stawu); na lewym brzegu Wosuszki, o 2 kil. od mka, leży folwark Opal, a o 3 kil. na płd.-zachód od mka karczma Odydra. Najwyżej (do 394 m.) wznosi się wzgórze Jezierna w płd.-zach. kącie, na granicy; o 2 kil. od mka na półn.-zach. wznosi się Mikota do 392 m, a o 3 kil. na płd.-wsch. od mka Za dubem do 388 m. Przez środek obszaru idzie gościniec od półn.-zach. na półn.-wschód (ze Złoczowa do Tarnopola) a w średniej odległości 2 kil. na półn. od niego kolej Karola Ludwika, mająca tu stacyą, na lewym brzegu Wosuszki, na płn. granicy (stacya między Zborowem a Hłubocekiem wielkim, o 108 kil. ode Lwowa). Własność większa ma roli ornej 2132, łąk i ogr. 451, pastw. 75, lasu 440; własn. mniej. roli ornej 6102, łąk i ogr. 971, pastwisk 110, lasu 16 mr. Wedle spisu z r. 1880 było 4713 mk. w gminie, 226 na obszarze dworskim; wedle szematyzmów z roku 1881 mk. obrz. rzym. kat. 1386, gr. kat. 1900. Par. rzym. kat. w miejscu, dek. Złoczów, arch. Lwów. Rok erekcyi 1636, fundatorem Jakób Sobieski. Par. gr. kat. w miejscu, dek. Zborów, archid. Lwów. J. należy do sądu pow. w Zborowie, urząd pocztowy, stacya kol. i telegraf są w miejscu. Jest tu cerkiew i kościół murowany, szkoła etatowa dwuklasowa. Kuropatnicki wspomina w Geogr. Galicyi, że nad stawem leży piękny dom; Celary zaś mówi o obronnym zamku. W czasie budowy kolei w r. 1870 odkopano w miejscu, gdzie dziś leży stacya kolejowa, grób pogański z popielnicą i kościotrupem. Narzędzia wojenne nowsze wydobywano rozmaitemi czasy. Mogiłki poniszczone całkiem. 2.) J., przysiołek Wiszenki w pow. jaworowskim. *Lu. Dz.*

Geographic details of Jezierna in a Polish Newspaper clipping

[Page 38]

The Jezierna Cooperative Bank
Translated from Yiddish by Ida Selavan–Schwarcz

The Jezierna Cooperative Bank (its official Polish name was Bank Ludowy Spoldzielczy [Cooperative Peoples Bank][11]) was established in 1930. At that time the general crisis in the country affected the Jews, especially Jewish artisans and small merchants. The bank had to help its members as far as possible with small loans and discounted exchange rates, so that working Jews would not go under. These Jews struggled mightily for their economic existence and did not want to be considered poor folks dependent on social welfare.

The bank quickly joined the Union of Jewish Cooperatives in Poland (Zwiazek Zydowskich Spoldzielni w Polsce) whose headquarters was in Warsaw with a branch in Lemberg for Little Poland. The central bank gave interest free loans to every cooperative bank when it was established, thus helping it become organized; it gave instructions, intervened with those in positions of power when necessary, etc. The central bank also received exact semi–annual reports from its members and its affiliates and published them. Thanks to them we have accurate information about the working of the bank in Jezierna.

The central bank also granted loans from the funds which it received from the CKB Centralna Kasa Bezprocentowa (Central Interest–free Bank), which was a branch of the JOINT [American Jewish Joint Distribution Committee].

The operation of the bank in Jezierna was very active. We see this from the fact that from its very establishment it was in close contact with the central agencies, while other larger banks from bigger cities were not; some were even liquidated with the passage of time. Secondly, the Jezierna bank sent delegates to the conferences of representatives of the banks to Warsaw and Lvov. At the last annual conference of the Jewish Cooperatives in Little Poland, which took place in Lemberg [Lvov] on April 30, 1939, there was a delegate from Jezierna, Marcus Marder. He was elected as one of the 29 ambassadors of Little Poland, who were supposed to participate with the plenipotentiaries of all of Poland, in Warsaw.

On the basis of these publications from that time, we can reconstruct the activities of the institution. At the beginning of 1931 the Cooperative Bank had only 117 members. During the first year of its existence 50 new members joined and not one member left – a rare event in those times and places; thus at the end of 1931, there were already 167 members out of 750–800 Jewish souls in town! Almost every head of a family joined the bank. It was truly a peoples' bank.

To which economic classes did the members of the bank belong? Here too, the reports give us the data.

There were 33 farmers(!); 96 merchants and manufacturers; 15 artisans, and 23 others. The large number of farmers in town is astounding.

Let us look at the last report we have from 1937 (published in Warsaw in 1938; this is the last report which was published). In that year there were 195 members in the bank (about 30 more than at the bank's founding). During the year 11 new people joined and ten left, probably left town. Thus, at the end of the year there were 196 members. When we compare the numbers to other small towns in Poland at the time, we see that first of all, people did not desert the bank; they had faith in it, it developed, even though at a very small pace, but it was, after all, a small town! And in those times running a Jewish bank was not easy. Moreover, as far as Jezierna is concerned, the Jewish population of Jezierna kept decreasing. Nevertheless, the bank grew, even if only a little bit, probably helped by its members.

These were the members in 1937: 48 farmers – 15 more than six years before! 95 merchants and manufacturers – one less than in the previous report; 13 artisans – two less; 4 government officials, a new category; and 36 miscellaneous – 23 in the past.

From these numbers we learn that the bank was now including people who had not participated in the past, because their situation had been secure, better. Now they were also in need of a short term loan, and a promissory note that could be discounted, etc.

The growing number of farmers shows, indirectly, that times were hard for Jewish small merchants and artisans in Poland. This was happening in the era of the rise of a Polish middle class, or so they said. Just a few years before the great catastrophe, Jewish artisans and others changed their calling and became farmers (either exclusively farmers or farmers – working also as artisans, etc.).

The dues of the members was 25 zloty. In addition every member of the bank was assessed for another 20 zloty. By the way, in the report for 1931 there were two salaried staff of the bank. In the report of 1937 they no longer appear. They were let go in order to save money. We see that in 1931 the salaried staff received a monthly payment, but the director worked voluntarily. While there was no paid staff in 1937, the manager of the bank did get paid – very little, it must be said. These are the signs of the times.

Here we present the headings of the reports for 1931 and 1937.

CREDITS (The amounts are in Polish zlotys)							
	Highest Loan Amount	Number of Loans Repaid	Amount Repaid	Discount and other credits	Total	Number of Borrowers for the year	Highest earned interest on the loans
1931	1,000	119	46,071	54,667	100,738	111	11%
1937	800	228	46,180	732	46,912	120	10%

DEPOSITS				
	Deposits	Withdrawals	Number of depositors	Interest paid on deposits
1931	32,812	20,491	31	5%
1937	3,686	3,553	12	5–5.5%

DOCUMENTS IN BANK		
	Number	Amount
1931	742	107,442
1937	466	66,556

EXPENSES							
	Handling and administrative expenses (total)	Awards to goodwill organizations	Paid to Personnel	Social insurance	Payment to the Union	Taxes	Miscellaneous expenses
1931	1635	–	665	45	132	–	793
1937	2,066	1,100		4	160	4	798

Held back for costs for capital turnover		
1931	4.2	
1937		

NET PROFIT			
	Amount	**Transferred to Reserve fund**	**Other Purposes**
1931	700	60	100
1937	–	–	–

EXPENSES AND ALLOCATION OF PROFIT					
	Handling and administrative expenses	**Provisional percent**	**Amortization**	**Net Profit**	**Total**
1931	1,635	2.710	11	700	5.056
1937	2066	1.168	16		3.250

ACTIVE									
	Cash on Hand	**Investments and *Benak*?**	**Financial Instruments**	**Loans Due**	**Current Assets**	**Discounts and other Credits**	**Other Accounts**	**Losses**	**Balance**
1931	939	208	65	28.050	97	31.008	204		58.965
1937	97	107	1,065	24.782	298	–	537	363	27.249

PASSIVE					
	Current Liabilities	**Reserve Fund**	**Customer Deposits**	**Special Funds**	**Loan Received from Center**
1931	5,323	601	20,869		5,400
1937	7,646	1,122	5,423	1,022	5,423

By comparing the two rows of numbers from two years, we can learn about the economic situation of the Jews in Jezierna. For example, if we take the number and size of the loans: in 1931, 119 people paid off their loans with a total of 46,071 zlotys; in 1937, a larger number 228 people (almost double) paid off almost the same amount, 46,180 zlotys. What does this mean? The loans were smaller, but the number of people who needed even small loans grew! Obviously loans were not taken simply for luxuries. The impoverishment of the Jews is also indicated in the amounts of the deposits of money in the bank (for interest): in 1931 the sum was 32,812 zlotys; in 1937, only 3,686 zlotys. From the deposits of 32,812 zlotys, 20,491 zlotys were withdrawn in the course of the year. At the end of 1931 there still remained 12,321 zlotys [on deposit], as opposed to the end of 1937 when only 133 zlotys remained on deposit.

In 1931 the bank had a profit of 700 zlotys; in 1937 no profit was shown. The expenses increased and losses grew (loans were not repaid) etc.

From another report of 1933, we see that the deposits of that year total 47,437.44 zlotys.[2] This was the largest amount reached by the bank in its short history! This was a year of prosperity!

Naturally there are recollections in the book about the activity of the bank, as well as mention of people who were involved in its work and deserve to be mentioned favorably. But even from the dry statistics we see how united the people of the shtetl were, how with little means they were able to create a mutual aid organization which assisted them in their difficult economic struggles during the last year before the war.

The manager of the bank, Marcus Marder, was also the Metrical Book registrar, [recorder of the population's births, marriages, deaths]. As was generally the case in such a small town as Jezierna, one person took care of all the communal affairs. And, as is known, the income of the population registrar was minimal – the population declined as the young people left; natural growth decreased catastrophically; so that the mainstay of his [Marder's] income was from ..the bank. This allowed him to manage the activities of the Zionist organization, etc. Finally, since the town was small in size as well as in population, it was good that one person was in charge of everything.

Unia

In Jezierna there was a cooperative of grain merchants, "Unia" (Unia Zbiorowa, Spoldzielnia zarejestrowana z ograniczona odpowiedzialnoscia). In number 12 of the Przeglad Spoldzielczy, dated 1.12.1929, we find a report of the year 1928.

Active: Merchandise –21,354 zl.; Debts –2,211.57 zl; Fixed Assets –634.50 zl.; Miscellaneous –84.34 zl.; Cash–on–hand –527.64 zl.; Total –24,812.05 zl.

Passive: Loans –19,812.03 zl.; Current Liabilities –3, 500; Current accounts –1, 500 zl.; Total –24,812.05 zl;

Profits from Merchandise –13,824.47 zl.; Miscellaneous –84.34 zl.; Total –13,908.81 zl.

Charges: Administrative expenses –13,588.31; Benefits –250 zl.; Current Assets –70.50 zl.; Total –13, 908. 81 zl.

There will probably be mention of the Unia in the memoirs of people who belonged to it when they were still in Jezierna.

Footnotes:

It's first name was Kasa Kredytowa Spoldzielnia z organiczona odpowiedzialnoscia w Jerziernie, which was changed in March 1933.

Przeglad Spoldzielczy number 1 from 1.1.34.

Editor's Note: Some financial data were not translated.

[Page 45]

Cultural and Political Life
Translated from Yiddish by Ida Selavan–Schwarcz

The 'Hatikva', founded by Schmaryahu Imber, the teacher, was the only Jewish society in Jezierna and lasted 40 years – until the outbreak of the Second World War. It had its own little house. People came there to read newspapers, to hear readings, hold discussions, and here, too, was the only Jewish library in town, with books in various languages, not only Yiddish.

For the 25th anniversary of the Jewish National Fund, a 'Tea–Event' was prepared by the JNF committee in the Hatikva house, of course. Yitzchak Charap gave a review of the story of the JNF. The program included songs, an orchestra and the main point…the event raised a nice income for the JNF. (Correspondence from S.I. in 'Haynt', dated 4.1.27.

The local community did not have a great role in town affairs. It concerned itself with communal functions, the religious institutions of generations: rabbi, ritual slaughterers, ritual bath, cemetery.

There was also an amateur theatrical circle, which presented a play from time to time, and the receipts went toward 'a worthwhile goal'. On the twentieth of Tammuz 1934, the anniversary of Theodore Herzl's death, there was a memorial meeting in the morning, a 'mourning ceremony' (at which Professor Sassower spoke) and in the evening the drama group performed Gordin's 'The Unknown', under the direction of Mrs. Fancia Blaustein. A great success morally, it also brought in a nice revenue as well ('for societal purposes', Chwila, Lemberg, 2.8.1924).

Jezierna had only one party, the Zionists – with its various shadings; at least so it appears from the newspaper correspondence from Jezierna. As far back as 1900 a Zionist organization existed there.[1] In 1905 the Jezierna Zionist Organization founded a club 'Dorshei Zion', under the chairmanship of Schmaryahu Imber, which joined the Lvov district. The well–known Zionist communal worker Ephraim Wasicz also came from Jezierna.[2]

At the time of the elections to the Zionist Congress in 1933, Jezierna voted for the various lists as follows:

World General Zionist Organization	17
Mizrahi and Tzeirei Mizrahi	17
Labor Eretz Yisrael (United Zionist Socialist Party, Hechalutz, Hashomer Hatzair, Gordonia)	63
Zionist Revisionist (Jabotinskyites)	89
Zionist Workers Party 'Hitachdut' (opponents of 'Ichud' group of Dr. Schwartz)	12
Total	275

('Nayer Morgen' [New Morning] 17.7.1933)

In July 1939, the number of votes was considerably less (List 1 = 16, 2 = 4) according to 'Haynt' of 26.7.39. It is possible that this was a printing error, which we cannot correct at present, unless there are Jezierners who remember those times.

In 1934 the local Zionists were busy collecting funds for the pioneers of the General Zionist organization who had settled in Kfar Ussishkin. Participating in this campaign were the head of the community, W. Klinger, Dr. Tenenbaum's wife, R. Shtrick and others.

The local General Zionist pioneers founded a brigade which tried to find work on a farm under the supervision of the most important community leaders in Jezierna, firstly from Mr. Klinger, who was also the manager of the farm, and Mr. Falk.

Before the war Jezierna had a Jewish mayor. In order to prevent this, after the war a Polish government commissioner was appointed, and along with him there was a council, shared according to an understanding among the three ethnic groups in Jezierna: Jews, Poles, and Ukrainians. In 1931 the Jews resigned from the office of mayor and took on the office of vice–mayor. They assumed that an elected mayor would be more interested in the welfare of the town than an appointed official. In the end, the Jews, that is the twelve Jewish representatives out of 48, resigned from the office of vice–mayor for the sake of peace, in favor of the Ukrainians.

But when there was an opening for a treasurer in the municipality, with a salary of 35 zloty a month (!) and the Jews requested that a Jew receive the position, the Poles united with Ukrainians and gave the job to a non–Jew. There was not one Jew among the personnel in the municipality, although the Jews paid the largest proportion of municipal taxes.

The Jews also gave up three classrooms in the former Baron Hirsch school to the government public school, for no remuneration. On the other hand, the Polish Community Center, which gave up a room for that purpose, was paid.

"That is a good lesson for the 'Moshkes' (assimilationists)" – with these words M.M. completed his correspondence, published in the Lemberg 'Chwila' on 16.3.1932.

Footnotes:

1. Dr. N.M. Gelber: The History of Zionism in Galicia. P. 432.

[Page 47]

The Baron Hirsch School
Translated from Yiddish by Ida Selavan–Schwarcz

When the first Baron Hirsch schools were founded in Galiciain Bukovina, in the last decades of the 19th century, they were opposed by almost all the sectors of the Jewish population. The wealthy, so–called intelligentsia, insofar as they were assimilated, had no use in particular for a Jewish school; on the contrary, knowledge, culture, were considered 'international' and they were ready to assimilate according to language to the Poles who ruled our region, or to the Germans, who were the *'crème de la crème'* and boasted of their capital Vienna, the Kaiser's court, etc.

The Jewish masses were mostly very religious and saw no need to leave the heder, yeshiva or bais midrash [study hall of the synagogue]. They considered the Baron Hirsch School as unfortunately leading to conversion. Of course they did everything in their power to prevent the schools from opening. And when they were nevertheless established, they did not send their children there. On the other hand, the children hated attending the general 'public' school where they had to sit bareheaded and look at the crucifix on the wall. The Baron Hirsch School had difficulties, struggling in Jezierna and other towns (Sasow, Zborow, Zalocse in the nearby area) until it succeeded in making a name for itself and was properly appreciated by the Jews, since it was recognized by the authorities from its founding.

Today, from the vantage point of over half a century, there is no Jewish historian or person involved in cultural activity who does not appreciate the great achievements of the school in all aspects of life. The school not only taught the children according to a set curriculum, it also nurtured and drew the Jewish child nearer to what was then called European culture. It also taught Yiddishkayt [Judaism] in the new nationalistic mode. It showed Jewish society new realms of educational activity such as gymnastics, sport, geography, agriculture and gardening. It also encouraged poor youths, after finishing school, to learn productive trades, so as not to be dependent on the poverty–stricken Jewish society.

The school opened its doors in the school year 1895–1896 with one teacher and 100 pupils who attended irregularly. By the second year, 1896–1897, it had its own building, which cost a not inconsiderable sum for those days: 21,759 Kronen and 65 Groshen.

***

From the frequency of attendance of the pupils we can see that there were ups and downs. Some pupils left and did not complete their schooling; others came so infrequently that were not classified; some were kept back in the same class for another year, the reasons being the parents' indifference to the school in general, pupils' illness, low social status, etc. It seems for example that from November 1, 1900 to July 1,1901, classes began two months late because of an epidemic of pox, so that there were 1,958 days lost; that is, almost 19 late days for each pupil during eight months of study. Also during this period 1,450 days were lost due to illness, that is, 14 days per pupil. Really, a difficult situation.

As far as the social status (employment) of the parents of the pupils, they may be divided into the following groups:

1.	Officials, teachers, lawyers, doctors	1
2.	Manufacturers and independent artisans	4
3.	Independent merchants	36
4.	Clerks, bookkeepers, workers in factories	5
5.	Journeymen	0
6.	Day laborers (paid on a daily basis)	23
7.	Occasionally employed	27
8.	Received charity	0
	Total	96

A really dreadful picture. More than half of the parents belonged to the lowest social classes (numbers 6 and 7 equal 50% of the 96), had no stable employment, and were even occasionally unemployed (more than < of all parents, 27.5%!) Only five parents belonged to the highest group (numbers 1 and 2) a bit more than 5%. The third group were called independent merchants, but they only had limited merchandise in hole–in–the–wall shops. It is hard to believe that they all actually made a living! This situation, as well as the state of the independent artisans, indicates indirectly the fact that there were no journeymen in the entire town, and only four workers in category four [table shows five]. In other words, the independent artisans (there were no real manufacturers in town) worked by themselves, all alone!

The table shows who sent their children to the Baron Hirsch School. It also shows the economic situation of the Jews in the whole town, since [there were] 106 children in the school, (the table shows only 96, because others who did not attend, were not classified, therefore the school had no data on them, but they certainly did not belong to the upper classes! There was no one in charge of these children, thus they were neglected.), probably out of all the school–aged Jewish children in the shtetl, which numbered about 1195 souls, at that time. Some children did not go to this school but were privately tutored, or went to other schools and belonged to the wealthy families in town. It is certain that the children of the most pious, the religious functionaries, did not attend this school at all; this is true as well for the poorest children, who had to help their parents earn a living, or who went house to house begging. These categories of parents were not represented in the school at all. Thus, the table more or less reflects the economic situation of all the Jews in town.

Another sad note. Among the 96 children there were seven without a father, two without a mother, and one without either parent. There was one child whose father was not concerned at all (he had abandoned the family!) Also a tragic situation – more than 10% were orphans.

This is also reflected in the distribution of material goods to the school–children that year: new winter coats and hats –30 (almost 1/3); shirts –80; summer outfits –56; used winter coats, repaired –48; altogether seventy–eight coats (for 96 children!); underwear –40; shoes –73; (19 new pairs, 54 used, repaired); handkerchiefs –120 (!!) About this last item it should be clarified: giving a cloth for the nose to such children – this was part of their education, to teach proper behavior (not to blow one's nose with one's fingers, as was customary).

The school concerned itself with the pupils' outward appearance, cleanliness, just as it concerned itself, according to the instructions of the trustees of the Baron Hirsch School–to protect the child from negative influences at home and in the street. Therefore, the children were kept in after classes; they were involved in sport, games in the playground and general discussions. There were reading groups, story hours, and even vacation activities when the school was officially closed. There were also trips outside of town, etc.

In the same way the child was protected from foul language. They wanted to teach the child a beautiful language – Polish, and the children were required to speak Polish only, even during recess and in the street.

The children were also fed. During the year 1900 –1901, 70 children received supplementary meals. They received meals during 79 learning–days (79 lunches). This also shows the low economic situation of the parents.

Besides that, 410 books, 100 sets of school supplies, 228 notebooks were provided for the 100 children in the school during that year

That means that the school not only taught Torah and good habits, but also helped the child, and thus the entire family, with clothing and school supplies, so that the parents would not have to spend money on these items. In addition, it fed the child because he came to school hungry.

The school's expenses differed from year to year, depending on the number of pupils, the teachers' salaries, which increased according to the number of working–years, etc.

Just as an example, we shall display some numbers so that one can get an idea of how the school budgeted its expenses.

The normal budget of the school was 2,500 –3,000 Kronen per year. Thus the cost for one pupil (in 1900–1901) was 56.61 Kronen.

For clothing, food, and so on, the total was 800 –900 Kronen, for the year; thus the cost for each pupil in that year was 15–16 Kronen. In those days this was a great deal of money.

***

There were a great many repeaters (33 as opposed to 73 non–repeaters) for irregular attendance, not preparing lessons, etc. The grade results are:

Class	Very Good	Good	Pass	Not Pass	Total
1	4	11	8	6	29 (21)
2	4	10	6	6	26 (27)
3	2	6	12	6	26 (29)
4	1	7	9	0	17 (19)

The remaining 8 students were completely unclassified.

Obviously, this is not an overly satisfactory picture. The fact that so many pupils were left back to repeat a year was not due to the stupidity of the pupils, but because they were often absent due to social reasons. The fact that they did not prepare their lessons was due to the same factors. The children were helping out at home or in the business, or working in a shop, etc.

In addition, the children were also attending classes in a heder or in a bais midrash [Jewish study hall], which their parents considered more important than the 'shkola'. The child had neither time nor energy to prepare lessons for the 'shkola'. In general, the attitude towards the 'shkola' was negative.

The school was visited annually by representatives of the Austrian school authorities and by the trustees of the Foundation. The results of the visitations were good, as manifest in the reports. This is evidenced in the fact that the school was officially recognized in 1902–1903.

The school was for boys only. But the Foundation was also concerned about education for girls. It opened evening classes (in one year there were 30 girls), but after a few years (in the school–year 1897–1898) the courses were closed because "the pupils did not attend regularly."

After completing school, some boys whose parents agreed, were apprenticed to artisans. The school management paid for this. The number of pupils who studied a trade was small, three or four a year. There was seldom a larger number. The pupils studied mainly in Jezierna, tailoring, shoe–making, carpentry, turning [working with a lathe], tin–smithery, etc. Some pupils were sent to Zalocse to study trades which were not available in Jezierna. This is stressed in the report of 1898–1899, that seven pupils who had completed the school in Jezierna, were in their second year of studying a trade in Zalocse, paid for by the school.

What the Pupils Learned in the School

Let us consider the subjects and the hours devoted to them, which remained unchanged during the course of all the years of the school's existence:

Religion (except Hebrew), Hebrew, Polish language instruction, reading and writing, German language, arithmetic, geometry, drawing, singing, gymnastics.

The number of hours per week: in first grade – 21; second grade – 23; third grade – 24 and fourth grade – 24. In addition they also studied Ruthenian for two hours a week.

The school, like the other schools of the Baron Hirsch Foundation, ceased functioning with the outbreak of World War One. After the war the foundations funds were lost. Other communal institutions took over the buildings. Some buildings were rented to private individuals and with the passage of time, the fact that these buildings had housed the Baron Hirsch School was forgotten.

In the report of 1900–1901 there are interesting details about the building which the Baron Hirsch Foundation had built for its school. There were five rooms, three for general studies, one for the staff (and for meetings) and one for the lunches which many pupils received there.

In addition, there was a four room residence for the school director (!)

Next to the school was a large courtyard (147.28 square meters) for gymnastic exercises and a playground for the children; a school–garden (350 square meters) where the pupils, under the supervision of the teachers, learned how to work the soil (gardening).

Who Were the Teachers?

The first (and only) teacher and also principal, was **Akiva Nagelberg**, who had graduated from a seminary and had a teaching certificate. He began working on December 31, 1893. The second teacher was **Shmaryahu Imber**, from October 1,1896. He taught Hebrew and was an assistant teacher with a monthly salary of 80 Kronen. From November 15, 1897, **Anna Osterzetzer** worked there. She had graduated from a seminary but was an intern. (She had not yet received her teaching certificate.)

Nagelberg left at the close of the school year 1896–1897 and his place was taken by **Yakov Blaustein**, who also became the principal. He had graduated from a seminary and had a teaching certificate (license). His annual salary in 1900 was 1,980 Kronen, not a small amount for that time.

There was a provisional assistant teacher for only one year, 1898–1899, who had not yet graduated from a seminary,

Yehuda Prezes. Before that he had taught in the Baron Hirsch School in Kolomaya.

Ab Steinbach, seminary graduate, was a provisional teacher from October 1, 1896, receiving a yearly sum of 1,080 Kronen.

Tsippa Baruch, a seminary graduate, worked from November 15, 1900. She taught part time and received 60 Kronen a month. (Later she taught full time)

These four teachers – three for "profane (general) knowledge" subjects, as named in the reports of the Baron Hirsch Schools, and one for Hebrew and religion – worked in Jezierna until the outbreak of World War One in 1914.

As for the ages of the four teachers; in 1900–1901 one was 25 years old; another was 25–30; another was 30–35; and one was 40–50.

Two were "single" and two were "legally married". In effect, 1 teacher worked the first year, 2 the fourth to fifth year and 1 the eighth to ninth year.

The outstanding teacher was certainly **Shmaryahu Imber**, who taught there from 1896–7 until the outbreak of the war. In 1915 he and his family escaped to Vienna, but after the war he came back to Galicia, settled in Cracow, but would visit Jezierna from time to time. He was so connected to the place!

Shmaryahu Imber was born in Zloczow in 1868. He was a younger brother of Naftali Herz Imber (born 1857), the lyricist of 'Hatikva'. His son was Shmuel Yaakov, a noted poet in Yiddish and Polish, who wrote a doctoral dissertation in English on Oscar Wilde. [Translator's note: The dissertation was written in Polish.] In the last years before the outbreak of World War Two, when antisemitism in Poland was growing, Imber (the son) published a periodical in elegant Polish, O*ko w Oko* (Eye to Eye), in which he wrote ironically and sarcastically about those Polish writers who accepted Hitler's teaching.

Some biographies [Lexicon of the New Yiddish Literature, Volume 1, New York: 1936] mention that he was born in Jezierna, but he was actually a child of seven or eight when his family settled in Jezierna, where he spent his childhood–school years. Shmaryahu Imber was a devoted Zionist who wrote for Hebrew and Yiddish periodicals: "Yiddishen Vokhnblat"; "The Carmel"; "Hamitspeh"; "Hatsefirah". He was involved in cultural and communal affairs. In Jezierna he founded a Zionist society with discussions and debates, was a delegate to the World Zionist Congress a number of times. From 1887 he taught Hebrew in a school (Safa Berura) supported by a cultural society in Zloczow. In 1888 he founded, in Zloczow, a Zionist society, "Degel Yeshurun" one of the first in Galicia.

In Zloczow in 1901 he published the Hebrew poems of his brother, Naftali Herz.

In 1887 he married Bella Miriam, the daughter of Yaakov Freud. She died in Cracow in 1933 and he left Poland that year and settled in Jerusalem. He re–married to Sarah, daughter of David Efrat, sister of poet Y. Efrat.

In Jezierna, Shmaryahu Imber founded the Zionist society "Hatikva". In 1927, for the 30th anniversary of the society, he made a special trip to Jezierna from Cracow, in order to participate in the celebration.

In 1939 his friends in Jezierna had him inscribed in the Golden Book (of the Jewish National Fund).

In the Land (Palestine), he published articles in 'Davar', 'Haboker' and ran a free–loan fund for new immigrants from Galicia.

He published a volume of his brother's poems with a long introduction about the life of Naftali Herz Imber.
Zalman Reizin – Lexicon of Yiddish Literature, Volume 1, Vilna: 1928   All the Poems of Naftali Hertz Imber, biography by Shmaryahu Imber, introduction by Dov Sadan. Published by M. Neuman, Tel Aviv: 1950)

Naturally such a teacher, (even though he was not "qualified", as emphasized in official reports, and therefore received less salary), did not teach the rules of Hebrew grammar in a dry manner. "He was the educator of a generation of children and his influence was felt in the entire town until his tragic end".

** Biographical Notes, Vilna 1928, Lexicon of Yiddish Poets by Zalman Reizen

On July 31, 1902, Shmaryahu Imber published an article in the 'Lemberger Togblat' on 'Hasidim and Melamdim', [Pious Ones and Teachers of Religion] where he analyzed these two words, what they meant to we Jews in the past and what they meant at present. Once upon a time the word "Hasid" was "a title in its own right". It had an important meaning, and needed no additional explanation, such as rabbi, etc. At present, "whoever wants to — considers himself a Hasid –What? – Torah? What? – scholarship? What? – piety? A trip to the *Rebbe* and you become a holy man!"

"The word "Melamed" has no better fate. It sickens one to see who our teachers are now. Simple ignoramuses, and we let such Jews educate our children. The rabbis, too, who should be concerned with the education of children, do not bother themselves with it. They are only concerned with ritual slaughter __*kashrut* __ and what is forbidden."

The author asserts that there should be a seminary opened for *melamdim* [Jewish studies teachers] and that the Eighth Zionist Congress, which was due to assemble then, should discuss this problem also.

In the article the author characterizes the conditions of the cheders in general and in Jezierna in particular. The rabbis and *melamdim* have remained unchanged, not altering their approach, their teaching methods, etc. They have not moved forward with the times. These arguments were made by another writer thirty years later, as we shall see.

This article by Shmaryahu Imber expresses the position of a *maskil* [enlightened person] at that time, as well as the point of view of a teacher in a modern Jewish school, a Baron Hirsch Foundation school.

Notes:
1. Encyclopedia of Pioneers and Builders of the Yishuv, by David Tidhar, Volume 4

2. Editor's Note: In 1927 in New York, Shmaryahu Yaakov Imber edited an Anthology of Modern Yiddish Poetry, under his English name, Samuel J. Imber. He wanted to share with the English speaking world his amazement. "The origin of the Yiddish language and the rise of a literature in it is one of the wonders in the history of the Jewish people".

Certificate of the Golden Book of Keren Kayemet L'Yisrael [Jewish National Fund] "Presented to Mr. Shmaryahu Imber by the Jezierna Chapter of "Hatikvah"

*A letter in Hebrew, dated Kracow, 2nd Nisan, 1924 written by Shmaryahu Imber to his
"Distinguished Friends (men and women)" He writes that he found their postcard …*

Translation of Shmaryahu Imber's letter
by Ornit Barkai

Krakow, month of Nissan 1924

My Distinguished Friends !

This week I returned from Vienna and found your postcard, and I was very happy to see that the memory of me has not yet vanished from your midst, and that you continue the work of revival, the revival of our people, our homeland, and our language, for which I have dedicated almost all my life. So please go ahead, my dear sisters and brothers, with your strength and your will, and together with all the faithful sons help build our homeland.

In the last few weeks I have received many packages of 'Ha'aretz'[Israeli newspaper] that for some reasons were delayed along the way, but I have not read them yet. I am sending to you, with Mr. Gottfried, 20 new issues as well as old ones, and I am truly bestowing on you the good fruits of 'Ha'aretz'.

Together with my greetings, also receive my thanks. Be sure that I too have not forgotten and will not forget you. It is indeed a wonder to me that to this day you have not yet implemented your decision of last year regarding the Golden Book ?? !!

With the joy of the holiday and the blessing of revival,
Shmaryahu Imber

[Page 58]

The Rabbis
Translated from Yiddish by Pamela Russ

At the beginning of the twentieth century, the rabbi in Jezierna was Rabbi Asher Zelig Aptowiczer. We find his name among those rabbis who signed the protest (a public protest) of the rabbis, totaling 100 persons, who had assembled in Sadowa Wisznia in the year 1907, at end of August– under the chairmanship of *Harav Hagaon* [The Gifted Rabbi] Sholom Mordechai Hakohen Schwadron, Chief Justice of the *Beis Din* [Rabbinic Court] of Berezhany, in order to protest against the rabbis who permitted riding the electric tramways on the Sabbath – "in the carriage that runs on mechanical power (steel tracks and the tramway) " – as it was expressed in the protest document. We are leaving out the original words and format. See the [newspaper] *"Kol Machzikei Hadas"* [Voice of Supporters of the Religion] that was published in Lemberg in Hebrew, on September 8, 1907.

The Rabbi was the son–in–law of Rabbi Chaim Leibish, head of the Rabbinic Court of Lopatyn, and was–as the son of Rabbi Yosef, head of the Rabbinic Court of Schterwicz [Szczurowice]. (1) Besides him, in that same period, there was Rabbi Levi Yitzchak Manson, born in 1843, a grandson of Yisroel Ruzhiner, of blessed memory, and a son–in–law of Rabbi Michel of Azipoli. Reb Levi Yitzchak was the author of a book on the *Torah*, *"Becha Yevoreich Yisroel"* [Through You Israel Will Be Blessed]. "He was a man great in *Torah*," said the writer of *"Sefer Oholei Shem"* [Book on the Tents of Shem]. An additional praiser adds: "He distributed a lot of money to support the *Yeshivas* [schools for religious studies] in the above mentioned cities."[2] And in truth, in the newspaper *"Kol Machzikei Hadas"* of December 12, 1905, we found an announcement that Rabbi Levi Yitzchak Manson donated 10 Kronor (Crowns) as *Chanuka–gelt* [Festival of Lights – gift of money] to the *yeshiva* in Berezhany, the first modern yeshiva in eastern Galicia.

It seems odd, such a small town and at the same time – for part of the time – two rabbis.

As can be seen from the title page of *"Sefer Becha Yevorach Yisroel,"*, Rabbi Levi Yitzchok Manson was a grandson of The Ruzhiner (Yisroel Friedman), who in the year 1840 moved from Russia to Austria (Galicia then settled in Sadigora (Bukovina). He was the founder of the dynasties of rabbis that branched out into separate rabbinic courts, such as Vizhnitz, Chortkow, Husiatyn, to mention only the more famous ones.

Manson was a true grandson. In my younger years – I remember – they spoke dismissively about "ordinary" grandchildren, because his mother Gitel was the Ruzhiner's daughter; (his father Yosef was an ordinary pious Jew who knew how to study Jewish texts).

The book consists of 61 pages in two columns – and is a commentary on the *Torah*. That is just the first section; the second "*Zahav Peninim*" ["Golden Pearls"], if I am not mistaken – does not appear in the printing.

In the introduction to the book the writer excuses himself, and asks that if the reader finds any printing errors, he is not to blame for them and that "G–d should protect me and give me long days so that I will have the merit to publish the second part."The book was compiled by "the young man Mordechai Leiter," a disciple of the rabbi, who actually lived in the rabbi's house – with the support of the notes that the rabbi wrote in the margins of the books about individual passages in the Torah.

In the epilogue, the writer explains, for the second time, that what he put in the book he had noted for himself while teaching. It is likely that he used the explanatory notes for the lectures that he delivered in the synagogue. He apologizes for "mistaken or incorrect ideas and also for other discussions that are already included in a book." He asks to be forgiven for this, he did not do this intentionally – but only because "my memory is failing or that I did not see that particular article." That means – there is no plagiarism.

In a later explanation, he says that during his whole life he suffered from "the pain of raising children" – it would be interesting to find out from the Jezierna Jews who still remember this time, what happened to the rabbi's son.

Did he leave to follow unapproved modern ways?! And aside from that, the rabbi was always sick. These are the external reasons that disturbed the writer during his work. To his critics, perhaps, he responded as follows: "It's easier to be a critic than to be an investigator." A classic phrase showing that Rabbi Manson was a clever Jew, not in the least bit an old–fashioned fanatic ("*khnyok*").

In the epilogue, the writer concludes very nicely: "It is forbidden to enjoy anything in this world without reciting a blessing, so therefore I will say the blessing appropriate to this particular item: Thank you God, for teaching me Your laws."

Such a Rabbi was certainly the glory of the town!

There are two additional pages to the book with names of the "subscribers," meaning those Jews who paid for the book even before it was sent to print, and that made it generally possible to publish the book. In those times, this was an accepted means used by writers who did not have their own funds to put out a book and did not have a publisher who would do this at his own expense.

Among the subscribers there are 44 Jezierna families. Understandably, these are the prominent ones of the city, who were not only able to study it, but could also permit themselves to acquire the book. The amount that they paid – is not disclosed. Everyone paid "according to his means." Among these names we find: The Holy Rabbi, our Teacher Mishal; the son of the holy *Admor* [master, teacher and rabbi], may he have long life; the large court of the Holy Rabbi, may he have long life; Administers Sholom Charap, Avraham Charap, Nuchem Charap, Zalman Winkler, etc.; names of families that played a role in the lives of the Jews of Jezierna. Besides these subscribers, we find names of people from other places, such as Azipoli (The Gifted Rabbi, our Teacher Yishaje Landau, Chief Justice), Amiszynce, Bodzanow, Brody, Tarnopol, Koprzywnica, Podhajce, and so on.

Footnotes:

1. The book Ohalei Shem contains all the genealogy and addresses of the rabbis, city by city and country by country. It was edited, organized, and published by Shmuel Noach, son of our teacher, the scholar, Rabbi Dov Ber Gottlieb, of blessed memory, of Pinsk, in 1912; page 385.

2. From the book Ohalei Shem. In addition, we will add that the writer received his biographical information from the questionnaires he sent to the individual cities.

Cover of Rabbi Manson's Book

שמות הפרענומעראנטען

אוזיערנא	אוזיערנא

List of subscribers from Jezierna and other towns

Personalities

Wasicz, Efraim (Fishel)

Born in Jezierna in the year 1879, completed middle–school in Zloczow and then university in Lemberg as a lawyer. He was one of the founders of the "Tagblatt." He actively participated in the Zionist movement (*Zeirei Zion*) and attended all the Zionist congresses. After the pogrom in Lemberg in 1918, he founded a Jewish military. After that he escaped to Vienna and later he settled in Israel (1919) and worked as a lawyer first in Haifa and then later in Jerusalem. He died in Jerusalem, on the 17th of Shevat, 5705 (1945).

(from *Pinkas* [record book] of Galicia, 1945, p.225/6)

Fuchs, Avraham Moshe

Born 1890 in Jezierna. As a child from a poor little *shtetl* and closely tied to the village, he absorbed all the healthy good–naturedness and simplicity of the hard–working Jews with their joys and pains, and had a silent love of nature. At age 16, he came to Lemberg and worked at many types of jobs. Here he became interested in the Workers Movement and with the activities of the Jewish Socialist Democratic Party, (the Galician "Bund. Later, he came to Tarnopol, and here he became popular. In 1911, he made his debut with sketches and stories in the "*Sanok People's Friend*," and then also wrote for the "*Tagblatt*" and "*Yiddishe Arbeiter*" [Jewish Workers] in Lemberg. In 1912, he published a collection of stories titled "*Einzame*" [Loners]. That same year he left for America then returned to Europe in 1914 and settled in Vienna. With time, he became a contributor to a whole array of daily newspapers, journals, and literary collections of narratives, and grew in his *belle–lettres* skills to artistic perfection. Some of his works have been translated into German. The majority of his narratives are about life in the poorer classes and the underworld. His protagonists are the unfortunates, depressed, blind, insane, prostitutes, murderers and suicidal, and he painted them boldly and colorfully, revealing to the reader with satirical cleverness the most concealed images of human struggles in their frailties and abandonment in life. Human suffering, poverty, depression, bitter confusion, and phenomena of fate were the material for his creations.

(from Pinkas Galicia, 1945, pages 241–242)

Conclusion:

For the historian of an existing settlement, a *kibbutz*, first there is a past that he endeavors to reconstruct on the basis of documents. Not for nothing have historians been called "prophets of yesterday." He looks backwards, not like a prophet who sees the future as well as the present (time–warp), which passes ceaselessly into the past. The future is not the subject for the historian; he leaves that for the politicians, the columnist, the writer who has imagination, who sees that which is still hidden from the harsh, scholarly eye. Therefore, history has no beginning – because who can dig until the actual 'beginning'? And it has no end, because who can fathom the final days of a living nation?

But in our history of the Jewish community in Jezierna – as in the other cities in those districts – we have come, because of the tremendous tragedy that we lived through during the days of Hitler, to the end of the chapter. The Jewish settlement in Jezierna ceased to exist. Of the Jewish town there remains only a memory of those whose origins are from there, who still carry the memories of the town. The memory of the past remains within the organizations that continue the 'golden chain' of the earlier settlement – in their memories, memorials and Yizkor Books.

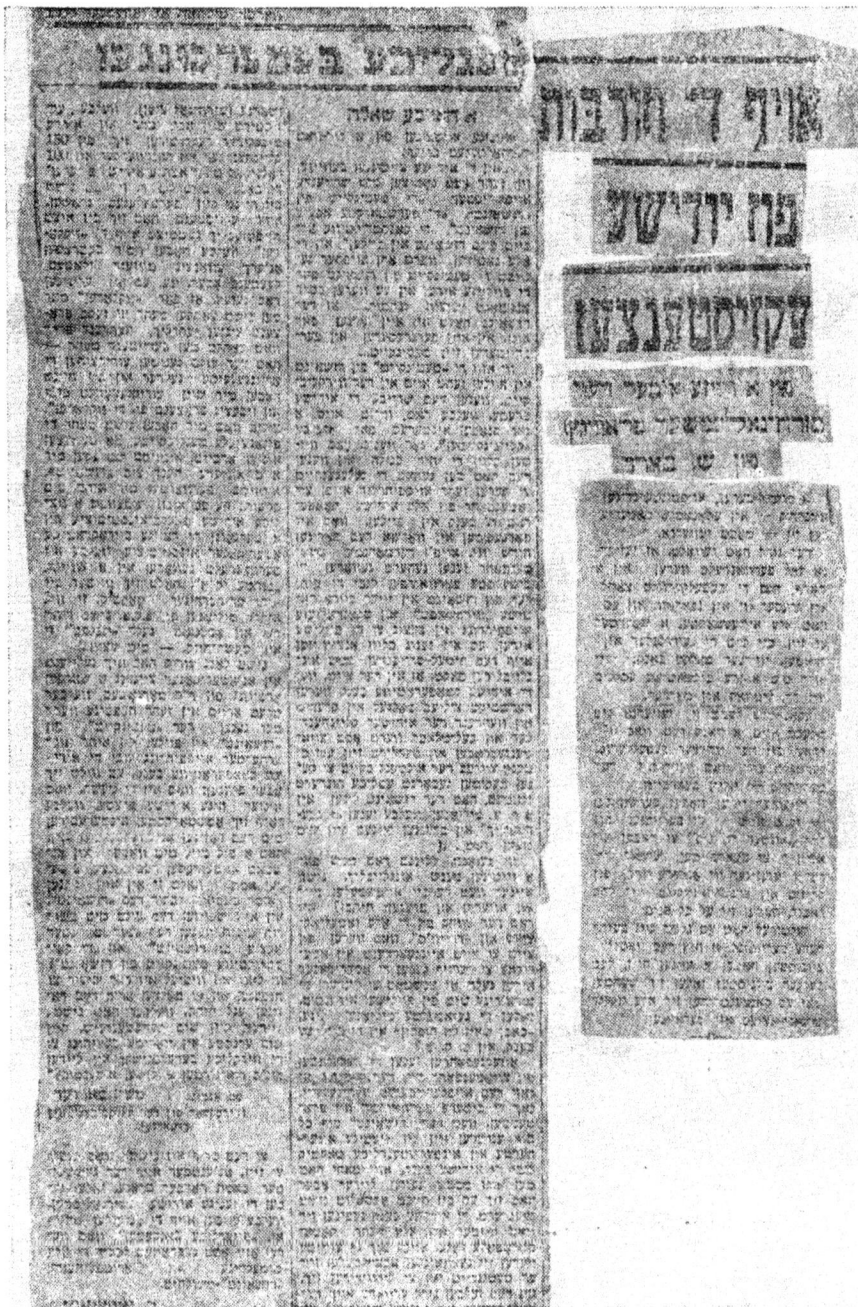

Articles about life in Jezierna, published in Jewish newspapers in Poland
Left side by: Mr. Barer - On the ruins of the Jewish existence - about a journey in east Galicia province
Right side by; Mordechai Marder - criticizing the activity of the "Joint" organization

Poem by Shmuel Yaakov Imber. Written in Israel between 1912-1915
Published 1918, Vienna

Title: Since I Saw

זינט כ'האב געזען

...

ש.י. אימבר

[Page 66]

זינט כ'האב געזען די ברידער וואס לאכן,
קאן איך נישט קלאגן שוין מער;
זינט כ'האב געזען מיין לאנד אין ערווכן,
האב איך קיין טרער חוץ פרייידנטרער.
זינט כ'האב געגזען דעם דור וואס קאן גלויבן,
קאן איך נישט גלויבן, אז גוט איז אונץ וייט;
זינט כ'האב מיין בליק צו דעם מזרח דערהויבן,
האב איך די נאכט אין די מערב זייט.
מתוך: "היים לידער", וינה 1918
נכתב בארץ ישראל

1912-1915

My Town As I Remember It
Shimon Kritz, Haifa
Translated From Yiddish by Ida Selavan Schwarcz

Years have gone by. There have been many changes in the world: nations have gone under, new ones have appeared, among them our state, the State of Israel. I myself am no longer young as in those times in Jezierna… I have children and grandchildren and they live in big houses and beautiful apartments. But when I remember the small town where I was born, the small house in which we lived, and in general, our way of life in those days, it seems to me that it was all a dream of years gone by…

Streets and Alleys

There is a long avenue on the way from Zborow to Tarnopol, and a long road from the train station to Tarnopol Avenue, and on both sides of the two long avenues, there were streets and alleys with small one–story houses, built of bricks in the front and covered with tin sheeting or roof tiles, with a few having thatched roofs. There were also modern houses with porches, surrounded by 'a living green fence', with benches where the family and invited guestsused to sit and breathe in the fresh evening air. Such houses belonged to Dr. Litvk, Dr. Tenenbaum, Moshe Heliczer,Zalman Scharer, Schlomo Glass, and others. There were no houses more than one story high in Jezierna

Further down from the avenues, in the narrow streets where the gentiles lived, most of the houses were built of clay and straw, with straw roofs. The houses which did not have any porches had small stoops. On Saturday the women and children would sit on the stoop and chat.

On Saturday and Sunday the *Ringplatz* would be cleaned, and there the children played the age–old games "King, King, send me a servant", *zemne*, ball and other games.

There were no paved streets yet in Jezierna in those days. On Zabramski Street, the long avenue and other small streets, where few or no Jews lived, each householder had an '*abaysczia*' that is – a hut, a barn, stalls for the cows and horses and a small sty for pigs, sometimes also stalls for a goat and chickens. They also had yards.

The *Ringplatz* was also the marketplace, and all around, in the form of the Hebrew letter–'ח', stood Jewish houses and shops. This was the business center. Jews also lived along the length of the two main avenues. The main avenue, Zborow–Tarnopol, which was called Kaiser Strasse, was well maintained, always repaired with '*szuter*' [gravel].

Originally the road from the town to the train station had been covered with wooden planks. Pools of water collected under the planks and quite often when a heavy wagon passed by, or even a horse and small wagon, the water would spurt out into the driver's face and drench the horses and passersby…Later this avenue was rebuilt. But the surrounding streets, you must understand, were not paved. In the fall, during the rainy season, or when the snow was melting, they, and even the street to the train station, were often covered with mud. Without high boots no one even had the "right" to walk there. If anyone attempted to walk there, even a little way, with galoshes on his shoes, he would often lose one of his galoshes. Even as late as Shavuot it was still necessary to wear high boots in a few side–streets. In order to cross the street from one side to another, stones were paced to make footpaths. It was almost impossible to go by foot from town to the estate.

The Little River

The river played an important role. In the spring and fall it looked like a great river; the water would overflow the banks and flood the surrounding fields and even reach the avenue. The women, especially the peasants, would do their laundry there, and beat the clothes well with a washing bat on a stone. The farmers would drive their horses and wagons into the river and wash the wagon wheels as well as the horses there. In the evening when the cows came home from pasture, they were also driven into the water, where they were washed and watered.

In the wintertime, when the surface of the river was frozen, the children used to skate on the ice, on one foot or on both. Along the snow–covered banks the boys would build forts or throw snowballs. For pious Jews the river had an additional role: On *Rosh Hashana* they would gather there for *Tashlikh* [cleansing of sin ceremony.] Men, women and also children would stand on the banks of the river, say the *Tashlikh* prayers, empty their pockets, and throw their sins of the whole year into the river, so they could swim away to the sea. "*Ve– tashlikh bi–metsulat yam*" ["and you will throw them into the depths of the sea" –Micah vii:19]. Before *Sukkot* [Festival of Booths], they would cut the branches of the willow trees which grew on the riverbanks, bring them home and sort them out; the longer and thicker branches were laid on top of the *sukkot* (and covered with straw or corn stalks) and the smaller ones were used for *hoshanas* [salvation prayer] for the *Hoshana Rabba* Festival.

In the summertime some of the men would go to the river in the early morning to bathe and on hot summer days the children would bathe there.

Water and Lighting

Water was pumped from wells. In the center of town there were wells with pumps and many householders would go out every day with buckets and pump water for their household needs, for drinking and cooking. The richer householders would buy water from male or female water–carriers. There was a water–carrier called "Fat Hersch"– a man with a beard, who would go around every day at dawn, with four buckets, two on a shoulder yoke and two in his hands. So burdened, he would sell water. But he had little income from this because his competitors were gentiles who also carried water but charged less. People were already saying that in the bigger towns there was indoor plumbing and people did not have to carry water… Meanwhile, we stayed with the old ways.

On the other hand, the illumination in town underwent an evolution. There had been times when the streets had not been illuminated at all. There was light only when the moon was shining… Later, some poles were put up in the center of town and kerosene lanterns were hung from the top. This happened during the celebration of Kaiser Franz Joseph's birthday. In autumn and winter time at dusk a policeman would go out with a can of kerosene, pour some into the lanterns, and light them. He was always surrounded by children who would stare at him with great curiosity. Most householders did not leave their homes at night, and those who had to go out carried lanterns. At first the lanterns used candles, but later they used kerosene. The tinsmith made the lanterns and he was always introducing new kinds. If someone brought a new lantern from Tarnopol or Zborow, the tinsmith would copy the newer model. The children even carried lanterns to cheyder.

Even greater progress was made by the introduction of gas–lamps in town. These lamps were also lit every evening by the policeman. When the gaslights were lit for the very first time, half the town, mainly children, came to look at the great wonder of the strong lights. "Oh, how light it is now in our town… the lamps shine like the moon!"…

Thanks to the Jewish mill–owner, Jezierna received electric lights. The town was modernized. The last institutions to use candles were the synagogues and the study halls. Long wax candles were used in the synagogues and regular candles were used in the houses of study.

The Marketplace

I want to devote some time to describing the marketplace. There were actually two marketplaces: one in the center of town, where the peasants brought for sale poultry, grain, greens, fruit, etc. and the second place outside the center, named "*tarhawicze*", which concentrated on the sale of horses and cattle. On fair–days both places were full of buyers and sellers, especially in the fall and wintertime when the peasants would bring out their wares to the fair.

At the marketplace in the center, there were many wagons loaded with poultry, grain, potatoes and fruit. Peasant women would sit on stools or stones with eggs, butter, cheese and smaller amounts of other products, and the wives of the householders would buy them. There were many retail dealers who would go from wagon to wagon, 'feeling' the bodies of the hens, ducks and geese, and finally buy a rooster. In the winter they would buy geese to fatten up for their *shmaltz* for Passover, and plums to make jam for the wintertime; because in winter the children's bread had to have something to spread on it – and what tasted better than plum jam?

At the *tarhawicze* market, as mentioned before, horses and cattle were sold. There one could buy or barter horses, cows, calves, goats, and pigs. There was a separate place for each kind of animal. The horse and cattle dealers did not disturb the pig dealers. Only gentiles dealt with the pigs. Every transaction was completed with a 'handshake' and a drink of *maharisz*. Land owners, land–leasers and farmers – Jews and gentiles – would buy, sell and barter cattle here. For each kind of animal there were experts who 'advised' the buyers and sellers as middlemen – and earned a living thereby. All kinds of specialists would be there – for cattle, Shevach Braun, Sanie Rosenfeld; for horses – Itsie Fuchs, Motje Fuchs and Leibusch Fuchs.

The butchers would buy all the supplies they would need for a week. There were also exporters of cattle and calves who had their agents in the small towns to buy what they needed. The exporters of eggs also had agents there, who would buy any number of eggs, as many as possible.

The Mischief Makers (or: A Merry Tale)

Five to six weeks before the induction of soldiers, which took place in Zborow, the drafted boys could not sleep. They would wander around all night and sing. They would walk to Zborow, Kozlow, Zalosce and request a glass of whiskey from every householder. This is what they would sing:

> "Give us a little glass of whiskey,
> We want to drink le–chayim;
> Wish us that we should remain Jews
> And from the Rebbe's table eat shirayim."

In more recent times the householders did not provide whiskey as in the past, but God helps, as–it–were, the drunkard and sends him the bitter drop.

And here is what happened. The *kloiz* [small synagogue] was built by Yehoschua Flamm, a rich man with a lot of property in Danilowicz, but he did not have any children. He had built the *kloiz* and donated a Torah scroll in his and his wife's names. The *gabai* [warden] was Yaakov Rosen, a dry–goods merchant, a respectable Jew, active in the congregation, who always had some bottles of 96 proof whiskey hidden in the Holy Ark. Every day after prayers he would give some of the men a '*le–chayim*' drink.

As we mischief–makers marched into the *kloiz* after Sabbath, we took out ten bottles of whiskey and replaced them with ten bottles of water… In the morning, when Rosen took out a bottle to drink '*le–chayim*' he saw that it was water. The founder of the *kloiz*, Yehoschua Flamm, wanted to inform the police. He suspected the writer of these lines. But some of the sons of *kloiz* members were also involved so the whole matter was hushed up.

Memorial Book of Jezierna

'Many homes had storage barns for animals and food. The food merchants stored unripened fruit in straw, to sell during winter months.'
[Photo from Rivka Ben Israel]

[Page 72]

How We Spent Our Childhood Years
Episodes from Jewish life in Jezierna at the beginning of the 20th Century
by Zvi Zmora
Translated from Yiddish by Tina Lunson

The Jewish settlement in Jezierna was considered a progressive one, and so it had the nickname "Philistine Jezierna". I came here as a boy from the village Ostaszowce, 3 kilometers distance from the town. But let us first talk a little about the village.

About 300 families lived in the village Ostaszowce, mostly of the Ruthenian–Ukrainian nationality. Poles lived there too, who in no way differentiated themselves from their Ukrainian neighbors. Among all these there were also 12 Jewish families, scattered around the village; the Jews lived very nicely with their non–Jewish neighbors. The Jews drew their livelihood from working a plot of land and from doing a little trade. There were even some who were in a good economic position – they had bigger plots of land and did more trade.

With such a small number of Jews it was not possible to create independent institutions, neither religious nor cultural – so the Jews belonged to the Jezierna Jewish community and it was from there that they reaped their intellectual and religious gratification. And if one wanted to send a boy to *cheder* [religious elementary school]– one sent him to Jezierna, where there were teachers of various categories, beginning with elementary teachers who taught the child the alphabet, up to Talmud teachers. A child studied with an elementary teacher until age 5. After that he moved on to a teacher of *Chumash and Rashi*, and later to a Talmud teacher. In Jezierna there was also a 4–grade Jewish public–school where they employed Jewish teachers – that was the Baron Hirsch School. It should be understood that many other villages in the vicinity with few Jewish families maintained the same contact with Jezierna.

***

Our family was among the earliest settlers in the village of Ostaszowce. My grandfather and probably my great–grandfather lived there from the beginning of the 19th century. The village Jews had lived peacefully together with the local people for generations. My father was one of the property owning Jews; he had his own field and also worked the priest's fields. He used to rent them from the local Ruthenian priest and every few years he renewed the contract. But as a Jew he was tied and bound to Jezierna. And when I became a bigger boy and the village teacher would no longer suffice, I began to go to study in Jezierna.

I went there each day by foot. In summer the way was very pleasant. I passed through green fields, bejeweled with little red flowers. The birds twittered… Crows flew overhead, making round circles and continually calling "kra–kra!" They made a few circuits in the air and then flew lower towards me. And when they recognized me, they cawed again and reckoned that they would not get any subsistence from this little Hershel... then they lifted off and settled a little further along, where a gentile was plowing the field, and where they pulled worms from the freshly–plowed earth and swallowed them hungrily... There were also green meadows with little streams along my way. Long–legged storks wandered through them, using their long beaks to search out frogs... they were not very agile movers on land. I would run to get closer – but the stork did not think for long before flying away... I was left standing there, looking after him and thinking, "If only I had wings..." I would look around, and it was already late, I should have been in school already, and started walking faster. But then, I might encounter a butterfly and I forgot school once again... And sometimes I would meet up with shepherds along the way. "Where are you going, boy?" they would ask. And I would answer, "What's up with you?", to which I would receive a few clods of dirt. Sometimes too I went with a horse–and–wagon, ours or a neighbor's – but in winter and autumn I stayed in Jezierna for the whole week; my father would take me home for the Sabbath.

***

In Jezierna I became familiar with the town. I remember her people from before the turn of the century, when I was just a young schoolboy. My first teacher was Reb Alter, Pinchus–the–ritual–slaughterer's son–in–law. The *cheder* was in the teacher's home; he ate and slept in the same room. In that crowded place the children sat at a table and studied from a prayer book. We would repeat after the teacher whatever he said. The pupils had respect for the Rebbi – that's what we called him – and always obeyed him. For disobedience, the Rebbi used several drastic, measures, the mildest of which was powerful.

In *cheder* several, shall–we–say, special events took place. Besides *Channuka* with its *dreydls* [spinning tops], which the Rebbi made with poured lead and gave out to the students; Purim with its *gragers* [noise–makers]; *Lag B'Oymer* when he led the *cheder* boys to 'Mount Sinai' with little rifles – there frequently took place a 'krishmelaynen' [reciting of the *Shema* (Hear O Israel prayer]. It was the custom that when a son was born and the child was a few days old, the father would invite a local teacher to come with his pupils to visit the convalescent mother. The woman, hidden behind a white sheet, together with the household members, awaited the guests. The Rebbi and the children came into the room and he immediately began to recite "*El Melech Ne'eman*" ("God is a faithful King" – the opening line of Shema) — and the children repeated after him with strong high–pitched voices. The children were honored with candies, the Rebbi got a shot of brandy and went merrily home with the children.

I remember my Talmud teacher too, Reb Yakov Biller, of blessed memory, a faithful human being who devoted himself to the children. For a certain time I also studied with Reb Chaim Lachman, who was not really a teacher, but a small merchant of charcoal. But when business was poor, and Reb Chaim was a knowledgeable Jew, he took in a few students and studied with them.

In 1898 I was enrolled in the Baron Hirsch School. There one studied according to the government plan. The language of instruction was Polish, but religion was taught in Hebrew. Some in the orthodox circles had no desire to send their children to that type of Jewish school because of the whiff of *apikorsos* [heresy] that they smelled from it... We did indeed study bare–headed in that place and the teachers were progressive people. The principal was Blaustein and the teachers were Imber, Feldman, the Misses Faust and Brik. After completing the 4 grades of the school, I of course went back to study in *cheders*.

***

The first years of the century. National consciousness began to develop among the Jewish youth and Zionism also arrived in Jezierna... Then a few Jews organized the first Zionist society. We used to meet in the home of Reb Josef Steiger (Yosi –Yizchok's); his low little house stood at the rear of the market square. There was a newspaper. We read and discussed world events and political Zionism. That was the only place where Jews used to gather, besides the synagogues. That same Yosi –Yizchok's was occupied with other community activities: along with other Jews he organized a *gemiles–chesed* [free–loan] society. If a poor Jew needed to buy some merchandise for the fair, he could borrow a little money there without interest; thus, he could earn money to buy food for the Sabbath. When Reb Josef passed away, the work was taken up by his son Luzer Steiger, who was murdered with all the Jews in the great Holocaust.

***

But politics one could hear about in other places, in particular the synagogue study hall. That was the era of the Russo–Japanese War, in 1904. The Jews in the Austrian Empire were then pro–Japanese and against tsarist Russia where antisemitism was rampant. It was that way in Jezierna too. We only debated the outcome of the war, we tossed it around ... we followed the battles as though we were generals. Reb Nuchim Schonhaut, Pinchus the–ritual–slaughterer's son, brought home a newspaper especially from Lemberg (one could not get such a thing in Jezierna...) and reading it, saw the whole strategy of the war. He had the map in front of him and he predicted that Japan would win. And when Japan did win – he got the nickname *Yapantshik*.

***

In those days there was this story: Scholem Francas, the son of the Rabbi's *gabai* [beadle], who sat day and night with the Rabbi in the small prayer house and studied, who wore long *peyos* [sidelocks], a long coat and velvet cap, disappeared one fine morning and showed up in the Austro–Hungarian capital– Vienna. There he put on modern clothing, shaved his beard and sidelocks and was accepted in a high school. He graduated and enrolled in the university and used to come home to his sister – his parents were no longer alive. He had changed so much that people did not recognize him. He later became a mathematics instructor in Tarnopol.

During that time the Jewish youth in Jezierna in general were eager to go to the larger cities. We wanted to be '*menschen*' [regular human beings]. There began to emerge Jewish officials, Jewish secondary schools, and the youth sought a purpose.

Community Leaders: M. Klinger, Itamar Katz and Moshe Shemesh
(Sherman) - attending to important community affairs

[Page 77]

My Shtetl
Autobiographical Notes
A. M. Fuchs
Translated by Lily Fox Shine and Cyril Fox

My hometown, the town of Jezierna, on the Lemberg-Tarnopol railway line in eastern Galicia was formerly part of the Austro-Hungarian monarchy, under the rule of Emperor Franz Joseph. After the First World War, in 1918-20, after the collapse of the monarchy, Jezierna, like the whole of eastern Galicia, belonged to the Republic of Ruthenia.

And then, when the Polaks won the war against the Ruthenians (1920), Jezierna belonged to Poland. Today, my hometown belongs to the Soviet Western Ukrainian Republic.

During World War I, the Jewish section of the Jezierna was destroyed. Later, during the Polish rule (for 20 years), the town was rebuilt.

At the beginning of the German-Russian war, Jezierna was occupied by the Soviets - from September 1939 until June 1941, when they left eastern Galicia. When the Hitler Germans entered Jezierna, in July 1941, they killed a large number of Jews.

***

We were 4 brothers; I'm the elder, then Yehoshua, Hersh and Itamar. The middle brother, Hersh z'l, was killed by the Germans in Zlochev, along with his wife Miriam and all the Jews of the city, in 1941.

My father's name was Chaim Fuchs, my mother was Feiga. My Zaida and Babba [grandparents] on my father's side, I did not know. (I am named after my grandfather.) I know that he was a retailer of products for the peasants on the gentile streets. He was a prayer-leader in the main hall of the town's largest synagogue. My grandmother Chana managed a dairy. In town, my father was nicknamed 'Chaim-Chana's smetankes'. My grandfather on my mother's side was named Sholom Fuchs. Babba was named Leika (Esther Leah). The families of both grandfathers were related. Grandfather Sholom was also a salesman with various products, and in the summer he rented fruit orchards in the villages of the area. Grandmother Leika ran a bakery with bread, cakes, rolls, cookies, billkes, salt-bagels, poppy-seed cookies and other baked goods in their big house. The customers were townspeople, the tenants of the villages and peasants . Every year before Passover, the Zaida and Bubba's large house was made kosher for Pesach. and matza was baked for the townspeople.

The families of my father's three brothers and two sisters from Jezierna all emigrated to America and England before the First World War. My two brothers also emigrated to London. My mother had three sisters and one brother with large families and many children in Jezierna. They were all killed by the Nazis. Only a very small number of them miraculously survived. Also from my maternal grandparents there were large families with many children, from brothers and sisters in Jezierna, in Zborov, in Tarnopol, in Lviv, in Chernivtsi. They all perished in the Hitler Holocaust.

In my childhood and adolescence, I was, of course, associated closely and uniquely with all the slain relatives, uncles, aunts, cousins with feelings of love. They all stand before my eyes with feelings of sorrow and heartache and bitterness. Among them were also friends of my youth, well-known, close people. All prematurely cut off from life by fire and blood and cruelly tortured and destroyed, with horrific deaths. All the beloved and pleasant, with their pure souls share in my inner cry of sorrow to heaven for their sanctified remembrance.

But along with the feelings of remembrance and sorrow, there also burns in my heart the fire of hatred and a death-curse on the German-murderer people, who ate Jacob and bathed in the sea of the innocent blood that was shed, of my beloved brother Hersh and all the relatives, and of all the multitudes of Jewish people and millions of Jewish people - that God should pour out His wrath on the Nazi murderers, that they should meet God's just punishment. There should not a man of them remain under heaven.

I descend from a line of simple Jews, decent, honest people, hard workers with broad shoulders and gifted hands; pious Jews with Godliness and with loud singing and shouting of the prayers in synagogue. They were good-natured people, with a sense of humor and equality, popular, friendly and light-hearted, willing to do good deeds such as running to the rescue at a fire, helping to pull out a horse drowning in a deep swamp, or accepting the faults of a righteous poor man. They were laborers, hired workers, artisans, carpenters, bakers, locksmiths, or traders in the market, deliverymen with fruit-dealers, peasant-traders with farm products, such as grain, flax, wheat, fleece, honey. Some had small horse-and-carriages to reach the villages and fairs. If a wagon was not available, they went by foot, with heavy sacks of goods on their shoulders - summer and winter. They earned their livelihood with hard labor on the weekdays. Only on Sabbath and Jewish holidays did they have a free day, an Oneg Shabbas. They and their families suffered more than enough hardship and trouble and bitterness. There were also joys, pleasures of children. The boys went to classes, studied with the Hebrew teacher, prayed and studied Chumash. Then they learned a trade. The daughters, the brides-to-be, learned Hebrew from the sidur [prayer book] and Yiddish from the Tzena-Urena [pious texts], with the Hebrew school assistant. The fathers had a hard time paying the teacher the two pure silver coins, for tuition.

At home, the daughters loved to sing Jewish folk songs. The two languages, Ukrainian and Polish they could speak well. They worked at their parents' premises until their marriage. They were decently and well educated and maintained purity and modesty. The mothers were pious. On Shabbat and on holidays they read the *Teich Chumash* [Yiddish translation of the Bible] and the prayer book. On the High-holy days they went to the women's shul to pray, praying to God with weeping and crying and hot tears, for a good year with a good 'kvittle' [inscription], for health and livelihood.

The people of my generation were happy and faithful, suffering hardships and giving of love. They raised their children 'to find favor in the sight of God and man' and they prepared their sons and daughters for successful marriages. They were honest folk, outgoing, their whole lives spent under the burden of work with honest conduct, believable and good-hearted. They honestly kept and observed the laws and customs of Judaism and humanity, with love of the Creator and human dignity, with respect and justice for man and beast. The men were well acquainted with the Jewish traditions from their early schooling, and spent Shabbat and Yomtov enjoying the pleasures of reading in Hebrew-Teich the lovely, wonderful Chumash stories of the holy Torah. Or, they would read with pleasure from a small old worn-out inherited book named Chayei Adam, or an Ein Ya'akov, or Shivchei Besh'T in Hebrew-Teich, or the beautiful stories and miracles of God, and pious practices of holy saints and Tana'im and 'lamed'vovniks', and rabbis of former times. One could also read a storybook, which could be bought for a 'gratzier' (coin) from a second-hand salesman in the marketplace. They loved to listen to someone tell a story, or even tell a story about themselves, about past events with robbers, and decrees against Jews, with Haidamaks and Hidukes (peasant revolutionaries) and evil fools, and miracles, and God's help. The people were not Hasidim, but they loved rabbis. There was a tradition among the pious Jezierners that every year, during mid-Pesach days, they would visit the popular Rebbe of Jezierna to ask for a blessing. They approached him with a kvittl (a note with names) and with a donation of money for charity, seeking their redemption from the Lord, and received a blessing, successfully.

3

The Jezierna Rabbi was famous in the neighboring towns, and attracted a large number of Hasidim (followers), who used to come to him for advice. There was a large walled courtyard with a study hall and students. His name was Rabbi Levi Yitzchak Manisohn, of the Rhziner dynasty. In my youth I saw the Rabbi many times. He was short and extremely slim in appearance, with a noble pale face, brown eyes, a short brown-silver beard, and short curly payot. (side-locks). On Saturdays and holidays he was dressed in a white satin green-striped robe, with a white-fitted belt and a large golden fur hat on his head, and white silk boots and socks. During the week he wore a round black velvet hat with a black silk trousers, velvet sleeves and small black shiny patent leather boots. I later heard say that the Rebbe had written a religious philosophical book. I just held in my hands and saw that I had such a printed Hebrew book, from another rabbi, perhaps a Chasid (I do not remember the name), with an introduction by the Ozerna rabbi. During World War I, 1914-18, the Rebbe's courtyard was destroyed, and the Rebbe himself and his son, Reb Moshele were refugees in Vienna. The Rebbe soon died in Vienna in 1915. Two years later, the Rebbe's son also died there.

Many years earlier, the Jezierna rabbi was Rabbi Shlomo. He was a native of the town, from the mid-19th century, when the Emperor Franz Joseph ascended the throne, and before the construction of the large stone synagogue, (the Germans - may their names be obliterated - burned it down in 1941). Rabbi Shlomo was very famous and revered by the Jews, including those from the neighboring towns, and also by the peasants of the area. The Jews considered him a holy, righteous and learned man. Many stories were told about him, of miracles and incredible happenings. He lived somewhere in an attic, and he was deaf and half-blind. He acted as a 'Shamash' (Beadle) and a teacher for young children. It was told that he used to go to the fair every Monday in Jezierna, carrying a bucket of fresh water from the well, and give it to the horses of the peasants' wagons to drink, in order to perform a mitzvah. Some peasants pitched him a small coin, in most cases nothing. The peasants called him "Spravidlivi Rabin" (True, honorable Rabbi Shlomo.) Once in my childhood, when I went with my father to the Ozezna cemetery, to visit the ancestral tomb during the month of Elul, I saw the tomb of the Rabbi, Reb' Shlomo. It was a small room with an old, crooked board-topped roof, overgrown with dark green moss, with dry twigs. The wall-boards were broken, and inside, in a dark shadow, stood a large memorial tombstone in the form of two tablets. It was engraved with the symbolic Kohanim hands with thin long fingers outstretched in blessing. Above it I saw the name: "Here is buried the righteous Rabbi Shlomo" inscribed large in the stone. The other inscribed words were already completely darkened and worn. I could no longer read them.

4

The main business and livelihood of my family during my youth was the wholesale fruit trade of Jezierna, which they operated every year during the summer. They rented orchards from the Polish gentry and land owners of the villages in the area, and harvested and sold the fruits. At first there were cherries, grapes for wine and later apples, pears, plums, and walnuts. The fruits were loaded all morning into boxes and sacks, then transported by horse-and-cart to Jezierna, for sale in the market and to the shopkeepers and townspeople, by weight and size. This work lasted all summer long - from the eve of Shavuot to Rosh Hashana. The profits were shared. This was also done with winter-fruit. The big green hard sour apples and hard big brown squashes that only ripened in the autumn, these unripened fruits were stored in sheds on straw and sold when fruit became scarce in winter and when the fruit became soft, sweet and juicy.

My father, too, was a trader with the peasants and a partner in the rented fruit-tree trade; and the whole summer he worked in this arrangement. At night he guarded the fruit trees against thieves, and did his part in harvesting the trees and collecting and transporting the mature fruit to the market for sale by horse and cart. Often my dad also had his own horse and wagon. Before that, he had a stall, selling spices and condiments on the side of the road to the town market, until one night, thieving village lads stole all the goods from the shelves and left them empty.

I remember from that time in my childhood, that we had a great misfortune at home with troubles and hardships and bitterness. My father, a noble quiet man, but weak from illness, was left without a livelihood and without the means to take care of himself. I remember that my mother then went to consult a special Rebbe Lazar in Tarnopol. The Rebbe Lazar gave a blessing and a good piece of advice - that my father should work in the fruit trade with the villages, in partnership with his father-in-law Shalom and brothers-in-law. Then, with God's help he would succeed and earn a living. He actually did that. I remember that my mother used to talk a lot about this, and tell the story of the Rebbe Lazar; that first God and then the Rebbe Lazar helped to save our family. She used to say this with a pious look on her face and with tears in her eyes.

My dad had a small lime pit in a hut that was covered with clay, at the corner of my grandfather's garden. From the front it was densely bordered with flowers boxes, shrubs, willow trees, thorny bushes, and tree branches which hung over from the very large courtyard of the Ruthenian Priest. There was a refuse bin and a lime pit in the large cattle, horse and pig market in the large square of the Trading Center, for the end of the market-year for pigs, horses and beasts. The large general-market square, with its Jewish dwellings and stands, was in the center of the town. Nearby was the old stone Shul, the Beit Midrash, the Rebbe's house and also the Polish and Ruthenian monastery, with the tall bell towers. The Hasidic Rabbi's courtyard, with a large garden, was on the stone-cobbled Kaiser Strasse, the main highway. The old stone brandy-distillery-bar was also located there, with a wide entrance for the horses and wagons of the peasants, the Polish gentry, and some of the wealthier Jews, who would gather there. There was also the old flour-mill, with a huge wooden water wheel by the side of the stream, a tributary that ran off the wide river, with tall willow-trees on the shores.

My grandfather Sholom Fuchs and my grandmother Leika died in 1910 in Jezierna. My father died, not of old age, in the year 1923, also in Jezierna. My mother moved to London with my two brothers, Joshua and Itamar. She died there of old age in the year 1943.

In my hometown, like all boys of the average Jewish families, I studied in the Baron-Hirsch School and completed 4 grades. The language of instruction was Polish. For Cheder (Jewish studies), I went to the teacher Rabbi Lazar Bick. I studied Hebrew, Chumash with Rashi and the beginning chapters and verses of Gemara, the Bible with Rashi and some Talmud. Later, I educated myself more deeply in Jewish subjects and secular culture.

In my early youth, at the age of 14, I left Jezierna for 'The Great World'. For a short time I lived in Lviv, for a short time in New York, for a long time - 24 years, in Vienna, for 10 years in London, and for a short time in Paris. In 1914, I enlisted in the Austrian army and served in World War I doing various military jobs, including in the of the city of Vienna in various military capacities and military work up to the border of Hungary.

5

From 1910 on, my permanent profession was as a Jewish writer in Vienna. Later in London I was a permanent editorial correspondent of the New York `Jewish Daily Forward' for 24 years. In Vienna I was a co-editor of the Jewish daily `Jewish Morning Post' and of the literary monthly `Critique'. I have been and continue to be a contributor to many Jewish newspapers and literary journals and anthologies in many countries, where I have published my short stories and literary articles. To date, 6 books of Yiddish short stories have been published; (2 books translated into Hebrew and many short stories translated into German, Polish and other languages). In Vienna I was a citizen of the new Austrian Republic. During the Hitler era, in Vienna in 1938, I was arrested, along with my wife Sonia and my daughter Lola, put in a prison, and then robbed of everything in my possession. A number of manuscripts of my stories and articles were also taken away by the German staff, during the ransacking of my apartment.* After that, my wife and daughter and I left Vienna for London.

6

I happened to be on a visit to my hometown Jezierna at the end of the first war, in 1919.

The Austrian and Russian warring armies passed through Jezierna, along the imperial highway, back and forth, from Lviv to the Russian border. There were many battles in the area. A large number of towns and villages were destroyed in the area. In Jezierna too, many dwellings were destroyed and burned. The Jews of Jezierna - and also the Jewish inhabitants of the surrounding villages - were forced to flee into Hungary via the roads of the Carpathian Mountains during the First World War. In a town in Hungary there was a camp with barracks full of Jewish refugees.

At the end of the war, in 1918-19, the Jewish refugees returned to Jezierna. A large number of their dwellings were destroyed, the shops were looted and burned. Livelihoods were destroyed and poverty and hardship prevailed. The rulers then were the Ruthenians. Ruthenian rule, however, was not stable. The Ruthenians then waged war with the Poles throughout the whole of Galicia. There was also the Civil War of Soviet Russia along the borders of Eastern Galicia (1919-20). The Petliura Soldiers' Heidamaks at that time massacred the Jewish population of Ukraine and also plundered and killed Jews in many border areas in eastern Galicia. The Russian Red Army protected the Jewish population and prevented Jews from being killed in pogroms. Parts of the Petliurian army, then parts of the Red Army of the Russian Bolsheviks, and then General Haller's Polish legionnaires passed through Jezierna. The Polish army killed Jews at that time in Lviv and other Galician cities. The battlefields were in the area of Zlochov. Eastern Galicia was occupied by the Ruthenian army and completely cut off from the outside world, with no postal services and no rail traffic for the civilian population. No one in Vienna received the sad news about the Petliura pogroms on the Jews in the cities of Ukraine and about the persecution and killings of Jews in Galicia.

At that time I lived in Vienna with my family, my wife and young daughter and I was an editorial writer of the Jewish daily newspaper "Wiener Morning News". I was then sent by the Jewish National paper in Vienna, and also by the "Wiener Morgenzeitung" to make a trip to Eastern Galicia to see the situation of the Jews there, in cities and other locations, and to bring the correct news to Vienna. My journey at the beginning of 1919 was very difficult. I had to travel for weeks by train across Hungary, through Budapest, Munkács, then through the Carpathian Mountains, until I arrived "downhill" in Galicia, through Stryi to Tarnopol. The large city of Tarnopol was half destroyed. The businesses were looted. Only a small number of Jews who returned from the refugee camps were in the city, poor, robbed, many of them with bowed heads from the beatings of the Petliura soldiers, who were the rulers in the city and who plundered and looted the Jews.

No train travel was possible then for civilians. I traveled through the areas, in the bitter cold and frost and stormy winds, using peasant sleighs, for high payment. At night wolves roared in the snow. The Jews in the areas were in the same bitter situation everywhere - poverty, plunder, persecution. People hardly survived the days and nights, with pain and fear.

The Jewish youth, soldiers returning from the Austrian war, tried to maintain their bravery, and with difficulty conducted small businesses in trades and crafts, and helped their broken parents with a small livelihood.

I, of course, soon traveled to Jezierna, to see my parents and family, who had also just returned from the flight to a refugee camp. During my trip in the Tarnopol region, I arrived in Pidvolochysk the border town of Galicia and Russia, where there were a small number of impoverished Jewish artisans. During my travels in those areas, I was arrested several times at the hands of the Petliura soldiers, Heydamakes, but I had good travel documents and newspaper documents from Vienna. Honorable Ruthenians, military officials, helped release me from custody.

The Jews were not conscripted to the Ruthenian military service, nor was there any civilian or military persecution by the Ruthenian government. The civil rights that the Jews had, from the dissolved Austrian monarchy, were valid. There had been isolated cases of looting, bullying and killings of Jews in some places, however the Ruthenian government had generally prevented murders or plots against Jews in eastern Galicia. However the pogroms and killing of Jews was widespread on the other side of the border, in the Russian Ukraine, from the bloody hands of the Petliura Heydamakn Army, who led the war against the Bolshevist Red Army, like in Kiev, Vinnytsia, Proskurov, Volochysk and other cities and places.

On February 18, 1919, I was in Tarnopol, and I learned from Austrian prisoners of war who had returned from Russia about the horrific pogrom of Jews in the large city of Proskurov, which had taken place on February 15. The Petliura soldiers-hooligans killed fifteen hundred Jews from Proskurov that day, after the Red Army lost the battle and left, and the Petliura army captured the city.

The hostility of Polish Nationalists from General Haller's army to the Jews in western Galicia as far as Lemberg and other cities and places to the east, was the same as the pogrom-like hatred of Ukrainian nationalist soldiers of the Petliurian army, as well as all of Poland. Reactive governors and politicians, in those dark times, took it upon themselves to accuse the Jews of agreeing with the Communists, that many Jews were leaders of the Communist revolution, such as Trotsky, Zinoviev, Yaffe, Radek and many others, such as the Jewish leader of the Communist revolution in Hungary, Bella Kun and others. It was generally named "Jewish Bolshevism", which is ostensibly the enemy of liberated bourgeois Poland and of nationalist Ukraine, and that they were waging war against "the Jews and the Communists".

It is true that in Soviet Russia and Hungary the Jewish intelligentsia and Jewish working masses were then integrated into the fighting ranks of the Communist Revolution. And also true is that the entire Jewish youth were some of the best soldier-fighters in the Red Army, and that in wartime they received the highest military honors, and that many Jewish fighters were lost on the battlefields.

The pogroms against the Jews in the cities and towns of Ukraine, which were carried out by gangs of soldiers-hooligans of the counter-revolutionary nationalist armies of the Tzarist generals Petliura, Denikin, Kalchak and others, turned into the river of blood. About half a million Jews in Ukraine and other parts of the world were killed, according to historical data and figures.

This is the sad news about the plight of the Jews in Eastern Galicia and about the pogrom in Proskurov, and the killings of Jews in other places in Ukraine, which I learned about during my journey in the regions of Eastern Galicia. I soon returned to Vienna and immediately wrote a number of articles which were published in the "Vienna Jewish Morning Newspaper" about the tragic events. My articles were reprinted in the Jewish newspapers in America, Poland, and other countries, so the local Jews learned details about the tragic events. After that, I also wrote a number of short stories on the subject of the disaster and the difficult life of the Jews in the Eastern Galician shtetls during the war, which were published in many newspapers, magazines and literary collections. *

We were living in London by 1937, where we survived World War II and the "Blitz" of the Hitler bombs. In 1950, we emigrated from London and settled in Israel, in Tel Aviv.

Note: Additional information below was contributed by Lily Fox Shine and Cyril Fox, niece and nephew of the author.

For 25 years A.M.Fox was the Vienna correspondent of the New York *Jewish Daily Forward.* He was also assistant editor of the *Jewish Morning Post* in Vienna and critic for a monthly journal, as well as contributing to many Jewish papers and books. He published six books of Yiddish stories, many about life in Jezierna. The articles about the pogroms for the *Vienna Jewish Daily News* were also translated and printed in America, Poland and other countries. Later he wrote stories with themes on the terrible breakdown and impoverished hard life of the Jews of Western Galicia at that time (1919). His books were translated into Hebrew, German, Polish and other languages and he received several literary prizes, including a major award in Israel late in his life.

* Primarily it was A.M.Fox's American Press Card that saved him from the Nazis in 1938.

Editor's Note: A translation of the original article by Lily Fox Shine and Cyril Fox, niece and nephew of the author was donated to the Yizkor Book by David Fielker. Part of this article was previously published in Shemot (JGS of Great Britain), September 1999

[Page 88]

The Yiddish Song
I. A. Lisky (formerly Fuchs)

דאָס ייִדישע ליד

י.א. ליסקי,לאָנדאָן

לערנט זיי לייַנען אייך א ליד --

א ליד געשריבן פון א ייד.

ניט א ליד מיט לידער גלייך --

וואָקסט אַרויס א ייִדיש ליד.

א ליד געשריבן פון אן ייד --

אויסגעצייטיקט האָט זיך אין געמיט.

עס איז דער ציטער אין דעם ליד -

דער איינציקער סימן פון א ייִדיש ליד.

מיט דעם כּוח פון זייַן לאַנד --

גייט אַרום דאָס ליד.

דאָס ליד געשריבן פון א ייד --

טראָגט דעם ציטער פון דעם נביא

אין געמיט.

געשריבן האָט דער נביא מיט א ברען

זייַן ליד --

עס איז דער ברען, דער כּוח פון

דעם ליד.

פון זיין ליד, דעם ברען און דעם

ציטער --

טראגט דער דיכטער, אין יעדן גליד.

דורכגעברענט דאס ליד אין זיין געמיט --

פארשרייבט דער דיכטער, דעם ציטער

פון זיין ליד.

(פון "געזאנגען צו מדינת ישראל"

לאנדאן 1968 ; ליסקי -- פריער פוקף)

(From "Song to the State of Israel London 1968)

Editor's Note: I. A. Lisky is the pseudonym of Yude-Itamar Fuchs, the brother of the writer A. M. Fuchs. He was born in Jezierna.

[Pages 89-90]

The Development of the Town
Lipa Fischer, Tel Aviv
Translated from Yiddish by Gloria Berkenstat Freund

The Jews contributed a great deal to the development of the *shtetl* Jezierna (Ozerna), starting with its external appearance. The houses that belonged to the Jews were distinguished by their nicer outer appearance, particularly the newly built ones. They were higher, built of brick on higher foundations; the roofs were covered with tin. The Jewish houses were also more beautiful inside. The floors were made of wood and the houses had large windows that opened. This had an influence on the non-Jewish population. New, small houses would appear that belonged to the non-Jews, with tin roofs instead of the former straw. The Jews had influence in other areas. For example, the best non-Jewish artisans were those who learned their trade from Jews…

In general, the Jewish settlement in Jezierna was deep-rooted; there already were Jews here in the time of the Polish King Sobieski, to whom the *shtetl* mainly belonged. Commerce was then in Jewish hands. The shops and inns were exclusively Jewish. In about 1860, the Jezierna estate of Count Lubomirski was transferred to the Jew, Mendil Yampoler; after the suppression of serfdom (the old feudalistic order), the Polish prince could not maintain his agrarian possessions and, as it is told, went bankrupt. Yampoler, on the other hand, adapted to the new conditions and created a blooming garden out of the abandoned fields.

And the Jezierna estate administered by a pious Jew became renowned in the area. There also was an alcohol factory on his estate. The factory was located in a modern building with a high chimney; when the factory was destroyed in 1915 by the retreating Russian Army, the chimney remained and stood for many years. A great significance for the economic development of the *shtetl* was the building of the first mechanical mill by Reb Wolf Fischer in the early years of the [20th] century, which served the Jezierna area.

Among the professionals were: Dr. Hirschhorn, who was the only medical doctor in the *shtetl* and the surrounding area until approximately 1910; the only apothecary was L. Mintz, a situation that existed until 1940. It appears that the above-mentioned, in general, were the first ones in the *shtetl* in their profession. They came to Jeziernia in the 1880's. There were also a few teachers from the Baron Hirsch School. There were more cultural leaders before the First World War, Yiddish writers, such as Shmuel Yakov Imber, A. M. Fuchs, whose names were known throughout the world. It should be understood that in these professional areas, Jews surpassed the non-Jewish residents.

Finally, there was the Jezierna *tzaddik* [righteous man], Reb Shlomale [Charap], who in his youth was a *dorfsgeyer* [village peddler] and was elevated to a higher level by the Peremyshlyaner Rebbe, Reb Meirl, as well as the well-known Rebbe, Reb Levi-Yitzhak Monson of the Rizhiner Dynasty. His court was renowned in the Hasidic world and drew many Hasidim from the Austro-Hungarian Empire to the *shtetl*. The non-Jewish population also showed the Rebbe great reverence. With the outbreak of the First World War, the Rebbe's escape to Vienna brought to an end the existence of the rabbinical dynasty in Jezierna.

[Page 90]

On My Grave
S. Y. Imber
Vienna 1921

זון מיינער, טאנץ אויף מיין גרוב, איך הער דיין געזאנג,
רוף מיך ביים נאמען און הויך קוש מיך אין שטילסטן געדאנק
און – זעץ דיך אנידער אין גראז – גראז איז דאך דא אויף מיין גרוב
טראכט, אז צווישן טויזנט האב איך אויך דיין ליב

ווינה,1921

c.1935. Courtesy of Talila Charap Friedman. Taken by Mordechai Marder.
[Photo not in original book]

[Pages 91-97]

Trade and Small Business in Jezierna
by Godel Fuchs
Translated from Yiddish by Pamela Russ

The Artisans

Jezierna did not lag behind other Jewish towns in Galicia and its many neighbors in anything; not in trade and not in crafts. There were artisans of all kinds: carpenters, tinsmiths, blacksmiths, masons, tailors, shoemakers, furriers, bakers, butchers, porters, and so on.

Eli Charap and his three sons were very well–known <u>builders</u>. They ran a large factory and worked for the entire region. All the work was done by hand–labor. **Yisroel Sokolski** was also prominent in the area – he was the best <u>smith</u>. Until the First World War, he worked in Korczyna along with his two sons. Many non–Jews acquired their skills by working for him. Jews and non–Jews alike had great respect for him. Also, the *chalutzim* [pioneers–in–training] learned their skills from him before making *aliyah* [moving] to the Land of Israel.

Naftaly was a fine <u>mason</u>. He was responsible for construction of private and government projects. He built the community house, the retaining stone–wall on the market street that supported the baths – from **Moshe Wieseltier's** up to **Jakob Pulwer's**. He also built two synagogues and a church.

There were a couple of Jewish <u>tinsmiths</u> in the town: **Yizchak Lechowicz** held a respected place in the artisan family. He was also a community worker, a member of the community council, and beadle in the synagogue. He also employed his son as well as other workers. **Getzel** the tinsmith was occupied solely with his daily life and constant work in order to support his large family. There was also **Majer Zilberberg**, **Avraham Kurzrok** and his brother **Shlomo**. This last mentioned, as an Austrian soldier, was taken prisoner in Russia (1915) and never returned. All of these were apprentices of **Yizchak Lechowicz**. Another one of his apprentices was **Yehoshua Fuchs**, who is now in London.

The <u>tailor</u> **Beril Bernstein** was a fine craftsman and also a conscientious person. He was the one who read the weekly Torah portion in the small synagogue. He also had respected children: one was a doctor, **Dr.Nisan Bernstein**; the second was a dentist and the third, **Moshe**, was a tailor.

There was also a <u>shoemaker</u> in Jezierna by the name of **Berl Bernstein**. He lived in the center of the city and was a reputable businessman. Journeymen would work for him, primarily non–Jews. There was also the shoemaker **Munye Blaustein**, who learned the trade under Berl.

It's important to mention the women who were <u>tailors</u>. **Batya Zilberberg** was known as a good ladies' dressmaker and employed a few young girls, both Jewish and non–Jewish, as <u>seamstresses</u>. Batya's sister, **Raizel Kurzrock**, also worked as a seamstress. Aside from those, there were also specialists for women's undergarments (lingerie makers) – the two sisters **Ruchel** and **Esther Braun**.

The <u>furrier</u> **Josef Okien** would sew fur coats and hats for the peasants from the best fur or from leather– that was the national dress for the local women. It was, so they say, a skill that used a special method. He would sell his products at the fairs.

In Jezierna, there were trades and tradesmen that were not so popular. For example, the <u>shingle layers</u> and the so–called 'printers'. The peasants would bring their own home–made fabric, and dye them for their personal needs. This would only be done on one side. This <u>dyer</u> and also the shingle layer (who would cover the roofs) were embodied in one and the same person – this was **Reb Yisroel Winter**. During the summers he would cover roofs and in the winter he would dye the fabric for summer clothing, primarily for the men in the villages.

The <u>butchers</u> held a respected place in the town. I remember a few butchers: **Hersch Katz, Shewach Baron, Gerschon Kurzrock, Avraham Czaczkes** and **Leibish Rosenfeld**. The last one left a generation of butchers – his three sons: **Yizchak, Juda–Hersch** and **Isak–Wolf**. Also **Natan Braun** considered himself one of the younger butchers in the town.

Grain Mills and Oil Presses

It's worth mentioning the small enterprises such as <u>grain mills</u> and <u>oil presses</u>; with the latter they would make oil from hemp seeds and flax. The peasants would bring the raw products and then grind them here. The grain mill they operated using 'their own' strength, and the same with the small oil machine. Each peasant who brought his grains, turned the mill–stone with his own hands… The owner of the mill would take a certain fee for the use of the machine; the owners would also work as <u>millers</u>. The owner maintained the mill so that the output of grain would be satisfactory. One could consider this type of miller as a craftsman.   In those times before World War I, these facilities were very primitive, but later the owners went on to modernize their enterprises. For example, the oil machine was a very simple thing, but in later years this was exchanged for another machine, which was factory–made, simplified the oil production, shortened labor time, and also improved the actual output.   In Jezierna, there were two or three such undertakings. **Zische Perlmutter** used to make flour and oil and from this he had a livelihood, together with his sons. **Schoel Goldberg** also had this type of enterprise; he set himself up with modern machinery. His oil machine was talked about in Jezierna and the surrounding area. It was the same for **Aron Kurzrock**.

The production seasons were before Passover and before Christmas. In general, the times before the holidays were periods of liveliness and commerce in all areas of the small businesses. The merchants and artisans would prepare themselves for these times, and look forward to the seasons with anticipation because their earnings for a few months depended on them.

Jewish Craftsmen before World War II

The percentage of Jewish artisans in Jezierna was practically unchanged before World War II, from the time of the First World War. Very few craftsmen remained from the time of the First World War, but later on there were many newcomers from other places also young ones, who learned the trade and worked independently.

The <u>metal-smith</u> **Yisroel Sokolsky** died in the 1930s; **Beril**, the <u>shoemaker</u>, returned from his flight [to safety], and managed his own workshop. He was already an older man and died in the 1920s. The <u>carpenters</u> didn't return from their flight at all after the First World War.

Yizchak Lahovitch, the tinsmith, left for America.

Before the outbreak of World War II, there remained from the older artisans **Beril Bernstein** the tailor, who worked together with his son **Moshe**. The other Jewish tailor was **Azriel Pollak**. **Michel Altman**, who also did tailoring, made *aliyah* to Eretz Yisrael in 1939, and today operates a tailoring business in Haifa. His brother, **Pesach Altman**, had a shoe–making workshop until the year 1937; he too made *aliyah* to Eretz Yisrael, and today runs a workshop in Haifa for orthopedic shoes and also has a shoe store. **Schmuel Altman**, a furniture maker, a friend from 'Gordonia', made *aliyah* to Eretz Yisrael in 1936. He runs a furniture factory there and is chairman of the Union of Craftsmen in Haifa. There were two tinsmiths: **Meier Zilberberg** and **Moshe Erdreich**; the latter was a newcomer. There was also a carpenter, a newcomer, by the name **Fink**. He lived in Jezierna for a few years. He was an authentic Jewish artisan type. He practiced the *mitzvos* [Torah commandments], wore a beard and side-locks, and worked hard to support his large family. He had six children – three of them I knew well. His oldest daughter, **Sarah**, was sixteen when the war broke out. His workshop was in the house where he lived. He would get up very early and work until the darkness of night set in. In general, the majority of Jewish artisans in town lived this way. The youth of that time, who wanted to make *aliyah* to the Land of Israel also learned a trade. **Yakov Kritz**, for example, learned a trade in Zborow and today is the manager of the 'Herut' company in Haifa.

Almost all of the artisans in the town worked alone, without employees, other than apprentices. However there were the exceptions who did hire workers, such as **Pesach Altman**. Besides apprentices, he also employed non–Jewish workers. In general, there were many non–Jewish apprentices who would learn under the Jewish experts. Once they finished learning the trade, they would consider themselves fine craftsmen. In general, the non–Jews who apprenticed under the Jews also paid more attention to their own work … they simply came more often.

Barbers in Jezierna were exclusively Jewish. There were two barbers, both of them newcomers. One was **Yehoshua Schwarz** from Tarnopol, and he worked with **Issa Blasser**. **Yehoshua Schwarz** was his step–father. Then came the second one, named **Berger**. He was the son–in–law of the teacher **Henzel Steiger**, of blessed memory. His barber shop was in the middle of the town and he had apprentices and even employees. The barbers in Jezierna were certified professionals.

Yehoshua Schwarz came to the place through Blasser; they used to call him 'doctor'. Aside from giving haircuts, he would do teeth extractions, apply *bankes* [cupping], and 'cure' the sick. There were also so–called 'midwives' or '*bubbes*'. These were **Chava Scherman** (Moshe the beadle's wife), **Salke** the Bubbe, and also the wife of Schwarz the barber. She also did cupping and 'cured' with 'modern' medicines: she would give aspirin and quinine.

There were two glaziers. **Shulim Bleich** had a small shop in the middle of the marketplace among the other community shops. The local residents and those from the villages in the area would bring him their windows to have panes put in. He would do bigger jobs for clients at their own locations. Reb Shulim was a Torah scholar. After a day's work he would go to learn Torah in the *Beis Midrash* [synagogue study hall]. The second glazier was Reb **Yizchok Kritz**, of blessed memory, the father of **Shimon** and **Yakov Kritz**, who conducted his work respectfully. He was a forward–thinking person and a nationalistic Jew. At the first opportunity, he sent his still young son Yakov to Eretz Yisrael. Several years later, 1935, he liquidated all his belongings and made *aliyah* to the Land of Israel along with his family, parents, and older son Shimon.

Bakeries

Before bakeries were established in Jezierna, Jewish women would bake cakes for stores and taverns. They would usually bake these in regular house ovens that existed in almost every home. Sometimes, the demand for baked goods was not very great – each homemaker would do her own baking for every Sabbath. Then, unexpectedly, a professional baker descended on Jezierna, by the name of Reb **Izak Mantel**. This was at the beginning of the century. He set up a modern bakery in the town, with mechanical equipment. To that end, according to the law of that time, he built a special building with several rooms. His business grew quickly and he had several workers. The baked goods were delivered by a special horse–and–wagon, not only to the local residents, but also to those in the surrounding villages. During the First World War, the bakery was destroyed, but later on, when life stabilized again, the business resumed its work.

In about the 1930s, another bakery opened in the town, with the owner **Leizer Zalcz**. He was from Lemberg. His bakery was also modern, with technical equipment, and run according to the regulations of hygiene. We must mention that these were the only bakeries in Jezierna and the surrounding area, which was not small. In the season of Christian holidays, especially Christmas, the bakeries were busy with work. This was the time of baking the *koylitches* (like small braided *challas*), and thousands were baked. There was not even one Christian family that did not have these loaves – that were baked in Jewish bakeries – for their holidays.

For Passover, they would make these bakeries kosher for baking matzo. In order to bake *shemura–matzo* [stringently guarded], the Rabbi would be personally involved.

The Inns

Jezierna was situated along the Tarnopol – Lemberg dirt road, near the intersection of the so–called 'Kaiser–Strasse' [highway]; thus the connection between the two major trade centers went through it. And since all means of communication before World War I was by horse–and–wagon, there were inns all along the entire length of the road. These were long houses which several horse–and–wagons could enter, all at the same time. The owner of this type of house also had, aside from his own home, a type of inn, where one could also have something to eat and drink, and spend the night.

In Jezierna itself, there were four inns; all of them were built close to the road so that the wagon drivers would not have to go far with their heavily–laden wagons. One of these lucrative operations belonged to Reb **Reuven Fischer**, the father of **Wolf**. All the owners of these inns were well off; summer and winter there were all kinds of people traveling on the road, merchants from all types of businesses, ordinary passengers on horse–and–wagon, that were protected with covers. *Chassidim* [followers] going to see their *Rebbe*, travelled long distances, more than once, and also patronized these same houses. Reb **Shlomo Charap** also owned such an inn. Generally, the *chassidim* who came to see their Rebbe stayed there. One of these inns, owned by **Yakov Czaczkes**, of blessed memory, remained standing until World War II, but it already served no purpose because of the modernization of communication. The tolls and the tollgates were also part of that period. At the entrance of the town, until the outbreak of World War I, there was this type of checkpoint, where they would take a certain payment from those entering the town from all different places. The toll was on the Tarnopol side before the bridge.

Watchmaker
– **Motel Byk**; his father was a teacher, **Bina Byk**.

Carriage drivers and wagon drivers:

Henik Feuerstein, Sanie Fuchs.

[Pages 98-99]

Commerce in Jezierna
Lipa Fischer, Tel Aviv
Translated from Yiddish by Pamela Russ

It is important to remember that just as in the other Galician towns, in Jezierna commerce rested in Jewish hands. This lasted until the 1930s. Even in those places that were entirely non–Jewish, also there the storekeeper was a Jew. It was the Jews who bought the farmers' products. There were Jewish buyers who went from village to village and bought the different products. The grain merchant traveled around with his horse and wagon and bought the grains from the farmers of the quarter–plots of land.

The government organizations did not present any particular difficulties and permitted trade to go on. You only needed to pay for the appropriate permits for this, and these were given out without any restrictions.

Various branches of commerce evolved in Jezierna. In first place stood the agricultural products. These products, which the dealers bought from the farmers, consisted of all types of grains, potatoes, beets, cattle, horses, flax, wool, honey, and chickens.

From all these items, the Jezierna area became a large marketing center. Major dealers were there shipping hundreds of wagon loads of all the products mentioned above from the Jezierna train station. Some of this was exported. These dealers would often buy these products from the smaller merchants, who, as already mentioned, bought them directly from the farmers.

During the war years of 1914–1918, commerce was destroyed and was only renewed with the rebuilding of Poland as it adjusted itself to the new age. After that, commerce grew to become even stronger.

***

There were no wholesale stores in Jezierna; there were only retail stores. Nevertheless, they were not all alike… There were large stores with a lot of merchandise, and small stores with only few items, and even these minimal items were few in number. There were also the so–called mixed–wares stores that sold textiles, leather ware, iron-works and radios, coal and lumber, taverns and restaurants, beer re-fillers, wood for building, etc.

There were also articles that one could not get in Jezierna, but had to travel to the bigger cities to buy. These were items such as ready–made clothing, fashionable shoes, etc. There was also no real bookstore in Jezierna. And for all kinds of building materials, one also had to travel to other cities.

In the 1930s, when the bus transportation began, some Jews established a transport company. The first bus that they bought was slightly used and didn't work for long... They exchanged it for a new one. It traveled along the main Tarnopol – Zloczow road. The driver was a Pole, brought in from somewhere.

***

Even years before the Second World War, a terrible propaganda campaign arose against the Jewish businesses, instigated by the leaders of the Polish and Ukrainian populations. They did not let any opportunity pass to show how the Jewish merchants were making a living at the expense of the non–Jewish residents. Besides the [Polish and Ukrainian] co–operatives, Christian merchants would gather on a daily basis to force the Jew out of business even before the Nazis, may their names be erased, showed how they wanted to physically eradicate them.

This was the so–called "regional politics."

[Pages 100-107]

Farmers, Merchants and Other Occupations
Compiled by: Lipa Fischer, Pesach Altmann, Azriel Zmora, Yizchak Charap, Shimon Kritz.
Translated from Yiddish by Pamela Russ

Unknown farm couple ploughing, c.1935. Courtesy of Talila Charap Friedman. Taken by Mordechai Marder.
[Photo not in original book]

*Farmers – Land Owners *

Mendel Jampoler, the estate owner from Jezierna, had over 2000 morg (approximately 2965 acres) of farmland, besides the forest and a water mill. He was a religious man, living and acting according to the Jewish traditions. His heirs, Jampoler and Jampolski, had already gone in another direction.

Wilhelm Klinger, an agronomist; in the last twenty years, was the administrator of the above–mentioned estates. He was also – independently – an instructor of the *chalutzim* [pioneers] who formed an agricultural group in Jezierna, in preparation for *aliyah*. The farmer – landowners in Jezierna and the surrounding areas would get advice from him and instructions on how to improve their economic situations.

Meir Falk was treasurer [of the estate]. His son was an officer in Poland. His daughter was murdered in the Nazi annihilation. Among the former employees were: **Aharon Helin, Hazelnuss, Daniel Bitterfeld, Rubenstein, Ostersezer.**

Mill Owner

Wolf Fischer, a refined Jew, a learned man, a skilled professional. He was the community representative and for a time also the head of the community. In later times, there were also partners in the mill.

Sumer (Itamar) Katz, a partner in the mill and also a land owner. A refined Jew, he was the cultural representative and also community representative. His two sons, **Aba** and **Munye**, were the first to make *aliyah* to Eretz Yisrael. His daughter lives abroad. Two of his grandchildren (Munye's sons) are officers in the *Tzahal* [Israeli army].

Jakob Danzer, a partner in the mill, a prominent Jew, a progressive individual. His son lives in Israel

Josef Kellman, **Wolf Fischer**'s son–in–law, was the manager of the mill. A scholar, a progressive man, a skilled bookkeeper. His son, **Dr. Reuven Kellman–Avineri**, lives in Israel. His second son lives in America. Theirs was an industrial mill. The farmers from Jezierna and the surrounding areas would also come there to grind their grains.

Smaller Landowners

Jehoshua Flamm, had many fields in Danilowicz. He was a religious man, strictly observing the tradition. He was childless – as a memorial he established a prayer court and gave a Torah in the names of his wife **Elke** and himself.

Chaim Steiger, also a grain merchant, a prominent businessman. Of his three sons, one was murdered in the Nazi destruction; the second, **Mundik**, was a fighter against the Nazis – and he died in Israel leaving a wife and child. The third son, **Bena**, fought in the Jewish Brigade [from Palestine] against the Nazis and lives in Rehovot.

Josef Byk, he also had a bank. The manager of the bank was his son **Avraham**. Three other sons, **Yankel, Naftoli,** and **Motl** were landowners and grain merchants.

David Blaustein, a major landowner, a prominent person. For a time he was head of the community, and community representative. His son **Tzina (Ben Zion)**, was a son–in–law of **Itche Lechowicz**. He was killed in the Holocaust. Tzina's daughter **Dozia** lives in America. David Blaustein's surviving daughter **Rivka** lives in Tel Aviv.

Shlomo Scharer, a respected Jew, a true farmer. He himself would do the ploughing, sowing, and harvesting of grain in the field.

Shimon Czaczkes, also a grain merchant, a religious man, was the collector for the Rabbi Meir Baal Ha'ness charity fund. His three sons, Motel, Henik, and Itzye worked along with him.

Avraham Pakiet, a respected and refined Jew. He prayed in the big synagogue. No one from his family survived. **Moshe Pakiet**, a landowner.

Nachum Fuchs, worked his fields on his own, and bought grain from the farmers and small merchants. A respected Jew, prayed in the Rebbe's court, a community volunteer, well–learned. His children: **Berchi, Moshe, Yosef, Chava, Chana, Dizia** – all live in America.

Mechil Fuchs, a respected Jew, a real farmer. Prayed in Flamm's court.

Mordechai Gottfried, a small landowner (around 200 morg) [approximately 280 acres] in Serwery. No one of his family survived.

Grain Merchants – Wholesale

Before World War I, the wholesale grain merchants were:

Wolf Fischer, Eli Gottfried and **Josef Heliczer**. After World War I, the trade increased greatly. **Shimon Heliczer** used to export wagon–loads of grain from Jezierna. His two sons, Moshe and Berchi, worked together with him.

Moshe Heliczer along with his brother Berchi ran an export trade. He bought the grain from the estate owners and land–lease holders. They had a large grain storehouse near the train station. A progressive man, he was the community delegate and cultural representative. His wife and two daughters survived. **Berchi Heliczer** was a dealer, in partnership with his brother Moshe.

Zalman Scharer, the son of Shlomo Scharer, was a trader, in partnership with his brother–in–law Shlomo Glas. Near the train station they had a large grain storehouse. In the two years before the destruction they, along with Wilhelm **Klinger,** were the lease–holders of the Jezierna estate. **Pepi**, the wife, survived, along with two daughters, **Bronya** and **Frieda**. They all live in Australia. **Shlomo Glas** – a businessman, worked in partnership with Zalman Scharer.

Yizchak Scharf, a partner with Scharer and Glass.

Avigdor Fuchs – was a purchaser and contractor for the **Heliczer** brothers.

Majer Zmora – was both a wood–dealer and agricultural products contractor. The son–in–law of **Berl Feiering**, son of Avraham Zamojre. A progressive individual, a skilled craftsman. A learned person. He was one of the first Zionists in town. His children, **Dvora Gottfried**, **Azriel** and **Munya Zmora** live in Israel.

Jakob Zamojre – Majer's brother. Together with his son–in–law **Josef Feuering**, he worked in partnership with Majer Zamojre.

As already described, the wholesale grain merchants had storehouses at the train station. Every Sunday, they would participate in the grain exchange in Lemberg.

Grain Small–Traders

Yekele (Jakob) Steiger – a brother of **Chaim** Steiger.

Chune Fuchs, son of **Mechil**. Survived the Holocaust, died in America.

Chaim Zottenberg, the grandfather of **Jehoshua Gliksman** was a grain merchant and also bought oakum and other products.

Jakob Katz, son of **Hirsch** Katz. An intelligent man, active in the community.

His brother, **Izio Katz**, lives in Brazil. **Majer Bien** – a partner of Jakob Katz.

Binye Gottfried and Jakob Gottfried, two sons of **Josef Gottfried**.

Jakob Byk – a son–in–law of **Sumer Katz**, an educated person; studious. He would lead the prayers. **Mordechai Byk** – the brother of **Jakob**.

Leib Fuchs – son of **Avigdor** – His two daughters live in Israel (Hadera)

Schmuel Bien – son of **Mosche Bien**.

Yizchak Halpern and Yechezkel Hoch – No one from their families survived.

Zalman Josef Frohlich – The children live in Canada.

Dudi Spindel – One of his sons was a pharmacist. Another son, a dentist. No one was left of this family.

Munye Pakiet – Moshe's son and Yossi Gottfried's son–in–law.

Scholom Fischer, from Zborow. A son of **Moshe Fischer**, the main tobacco processor.

Schlomo Feiering, Ostaszowce, a brother of **Yisroel Feiering**. His two sons live in Canada.

Efraim Rappaport from Nesterowce.

Avraham (Avromtze Eizik Uscher's) **Fuchs** with his son **Walke**.

Hersch Leifer, his son **Walke** came back from the war as a Polish subordinate–officer. Died in the Nazi destruction.

Josef Gottfried from Danilowicz. He and his sons made aliyah to Israel. One of his sons died during the illegal immigration; the second **Moshe**, lives in Afula the third, **Chaim**, in Moshav Herut.

Nute Hirschhorn, the son–in–law of **Schewach Baron**, was also a contractor for cattle.

Berisch Fuchs from Cebrow.

The buyers would go by horse–and–wagon into the villages. They had a scale with them, and that's how they earned their living.

Livestock Merchants

Wholesalers: (they would load wagons to go to Olmutz; they would also have stalls and kept animals there; raise and export them): **Avraham Kurzrok, Natan Rosenfeld, Hersch Fuchs** (from Cebrow), **Schewach Baron** (he was the main exporter).

Retailers: **Munye Rosenfeld, Izak Rosenfeld, Motye Rosenfeld, Aron Hirschhorn, Chaim Frenkel, Leizer Hirschhorn, Jakob Katz** (from Cebrow), **Yidel Katz** (his daughter **Chana** lives in Canada), **Jechiel Bien, Motye Katz, Boruch Fuchs, Josef Fuchs** (son of **Leibisch**), **Avraham Kosser, Mordechai Kurzrok**.

Egg Merchants

Export: **Aharon Bleich, Binyomin and Ire Kurzer** (two brothers),

Leib and Yidel Bleich. two sons of **Aron** Bleich

Egg Buyers: **Avraham Chaim Pakiet** (Tzirel Menye's), active in the community.

Mosche Rosenfeld; also worked with oakum. His son lives in West Germany.

Berl Rosenfeld. Jakob Ast, the son–in–law of Zottenberg. **Mendel Diamant.**

Zisia Pakiet (Eli Boruch's) the father of Avraham Chaim.

Fabrics, Food, and Sundry Articles

Scholom Charap with his sons **Simcha** and **Berisch**. Religious Jews; scholars. Lived by the Torah.

Leib Fischer – A well–to–do person, lived respectfully, highly regarded in town. His son **Lipa** lives in Israel.
Nachum Charap – a large flour store.
Leib Segal. His son **Yakov** Segal lives in Israel. His grandsons **Shmuel** and **Yossi Segal** – famous entertainers in Israel.
Abba Fuchs – a delicatessen store.
Yisroel Schapira, Bascha Rosenfeld, Mordechai Hecht.
Avraham Herzog. A grandson of the Sokoler Rav, the son–in–law of **Berl Feiering**. A gentle young man, a skilled artist. Would draw posters voluntarily for organizations. Of his two sons, one, **Motel**, survived and is living in America.
Berisch Baron – a fish merchant.
Henik Feuerstein – a haberdashery store. The daughter **Fruma**, her husband and two children live in Afula
Jakob Byk – the son of **Leizer** the teacher.
Luzer Steiger – also an egg buyer.
Mosche Wieseltier – an educated person, a Zionistic worker in the community.
Yisroel Feiering – also in the egg business. A respected businessman. His son **Leibisch** lives in America. His son–in–law **Yaabetz** was the Hebrew teacher.
Yizchak Wallach – seller of prayer and religious books. Lives in Israel.
Schulim Lachman, son of **Chaim** Lachman. A scholar and a fine prayer–leader. The son–in–law of **Berl Feiering**. Of his seven children, one survived, **Anschel**, and he lives in America.

Dry Goods Stores
Mosche Hochberg, the father of **Avromche**. A scholar. **Avraham Hochberg** – an intelligent person. Educated in a Jewish and worldly manner. A Zionist communal worker.
Mosche Bien – an educated Jew. **Zelig Bien** – the son of Moshe.
Shimon Schonhaut – the son of **Yankel**, the ritual slaughterer; the brother of **Shlomo** Schonhaut; a humble Jew, the son–in–law of **Sholom Lachman**.
Chana Katz – now in Toronto, Canada. Daughter of **Yidel** Katz.
Schmuel Reiss – was a respected Jew, a Torah scholar.
Leib Bleich – son of **Aron** Bleich. Son–in–law of **Mosche Bien**.
Dudi Pakiet – also a landowner.

Land Rent Collector
Jakob Rosen – a respected Jew, the gabai [beadle] in Flamm's court, a humorist, used to lead the prayers. **Naftali Charap** –son of **Scholom** Charap –a tailoring supply shop.

Leather Stores
Sholom Jaffe – **Josef** Jaffe, son of Sholom
Schmuel Korn, the son–in–law of Sholom Jaffe
Nuske (Natan) Paket, Yizchok Paket, the father of Nuske.
Schuli (Sholom) Fuchs

Ironworks Business
Zacharia Kaminker , Dovid Spindel.

Milk Merchants
Itche Fuchs- He would pick up the milk from the barnyard to make the dairy products for the Jews. His two sons and a daughter, **Schmuel, Jekel, and Rivka**, live in America.

Firewood and Coal Trade
Hirsch Katz, Scholom Lachman.

*Restaurants and Guesthouses *
Yukel (Jakob) Czaczkes and his son **Dudi;**
Scholom Eidel, Avraham Charap, Yukel (Jakob) Pulwer,

Schlomo Schwager, Itzie Katz, Olexyncer, the son–in–law of Itzie Katz;
Sumer (Itamar) Katz – an inn and tavern for the passengers who came by train and from the villages; Hirsch Katz – tavern. His two sons studied medicine in France.

Wood Trade
Hirsch Barer, a partner of Eli Gottfried. A learned Jew and also well–versed in worldly knowledge. His daughters, Leah and Raizel, live in Israel. The son–in–law, Nachum, an educated person, lives in Tel Aviv.
Majer Zmora – described above in the section on wholesale grain trade.
Eli Gottfried – a wealthy Jew. Also had a large farming business. His son Shloma lives in Israel , Leibish in Argentina. The daughter Devora died in Israel. His son Yoel died in the Holocaust.
Shlomo Willner– His son Zelig and daughter Tuni live in Buenos Aires.
Reuven Willner – son of Shloma.

Soda–water Production and Sales
Aba Katz; Manje Glass, the mother of Shlomo Glass.

Cigarette–Tobacco–Store
 Malka Lachman, the mother of Sholom and Moshe Lachman.

Mead Factory
Yisroel Zeidman, an honest and learned Jew.

Stocking Knitter
Mrs. Migden.

Fruit Merchants and Orchard Lease–holders
Meier Apter – leased orchards.
Pakiet Kasier – leased orchards and had sales stands.
Chaim Fuchs – leased orchards. father of the writers A.M. Fuchs, Y.A. Liski, and Yehoshua Fuchs
Chaim Schonhaut – salesman in a stall.

Agricultural Products Contractor
Berl Feiering – brother of Yisroel and Shlomo. A prominent person. Active in communal affairs, owned a quarry.
Majer Zmora; Hirsch Leifer; described under other occupations.

Watchmakers
Motel Byk, Moshe Byk.

Horse Traders
Yizchak Fuchs (Shpilkele), Motel Fuchs, Leibisch Fuchs, Pinchas Fuchs.

Beer Supplier
Schlomo Schwager.

Horse–and–Wagons – Carriage Drivers
Schimon Biller– His two daughters, Reizy and Chaya,live in Canada; Feige died in the Holocaust. Sanje Fuchs.

Dentists
Nuchem Kalafer, Nuni Heliczer, Bubek Spindel, Mechil Bernstein.

[Pages 108-110]

Zionist Activity after the First World War
by Yona (Taube) Fuchs-(Kurzrock), Ness Ziona
Translated from Yiddish by Pamela Russ

In the year 1918, we returned from our flight to Hungary; at the time I was a 10-year-old child. The houses were broken-down and in ruins. Livelihoods were also destroyed. The Austrian monarchy had fallen and the Ukrainian Republic was established, with its Haidamaks [Cossack paramilitary bands]. They were joined by the remains of the Petliura gangs who had fled the Soviet revolutionary forces, and Jewish population was scattered among them.

Zionist Youth Movements

Most of the refugees had already returned home. They received assistance from the Jezierna *landsleit* [compatriots] who lived in America, and Jewish life began to renew. A Zionist youth organization was founded by Chane Lechowicz, and the local members met at Pinye Paket's z'l. At the beginning, we were a small number of friends, mainly girls. We did this without any help from the adults.

First of all we had to equip the place with a table and several benches. We bought these with our own money. National cultural awareness activity was conducted. Chane Lechowicz held discussions. The first talk was about Dr. Herzl. We also sang songs and danced. Later on, the number of members increased and older members began to help us. Among them was Dvore Fuchs (sister of Sheve), Rifka Fuchs and Rina Czaczkes. Because of financial difficulties, the organization was officially closed a few months later, but the activity continued. From time to time, the leadership would meet and discuss current issues related to the Zionist organization. Activists were Fania Blaustein, the daughter of Avraham Paket who perished in the Holocaust, Chaje Charap, who went to Israel. Yakob Byk, Avraham Hochberg, Reine Czaczkes and others.

Hebrew Courses

In 1920, we organized Hebrew courses. The teacher of the first course was Shmaryahu Imber, the well-known teacher from the Baron Hirsch school staff. For a variety of reasons he found it difficult to get a place to stay, and rented a room from Itche Fuchs on the Railway Street; that is where the first course was held.

The number of students was small. I remember only a few names. In my age group there were only three: Lea Kurzrock, Schimon's daughter, Noske Feldman, the daughter of teacher Feldman, and myself. There were also older students, such as Basie Katz - Olexyncer with her sisters Reine and Sara, Rosa Lechowicz and others. The course lasted a year. The teacher, as already mentioned, was Imber, who was very devoted to the course, and thanks to this we each learned to read and write Hebrew. He himself was not in a good position, because his family had remained in Vienna. He arrived because he was sentimental about the Jews of Jezierna. But he had to return to Vienna. While he was in town, Dvora, daughter of Eli Gottfried, took a special interest in him.

I did not make much progress in studies, because at that time Yeshaya Yavetz, the son-in-law of Yisrael Feiering, who was a Hebrew teacher, returned to Jezierna. Yavetz influenced the young people to learn Hebrew. With the help of the Zionist Organization, they rented a new location at Chaye Gitel Mantel's, which was in the center of the town, which led to the flourishing of Hebrew studies. Most of the Jezierna youth began serious study of Hebrew. The book they learned from was *'Sfat Amenu'* [Language of our People], part one. There were Hebrew books in almost every Jewish household.

In the meantime, the Zionist Organization bought their own place named 'Hatikvah'; the courses were then moved to this location. At that time, the 'Tarbut' school was also established, and thanks to the teacher Yavetz the schools made progress in learning. Yavetz also organized a drama club, and from time to time performances were presented; the income was used for Zionistic purposes, such as buying books for the library.

Yavetz also organized a Bible study circle that attracted senior members of Hatikvah Association. There were discussions on current issues as well. The group existed until the 1930s. Yavetz left Jezierna, but he left behind a generation of students who knew Hebrew. They, in turn, made sure that the studies continued. And in fact Hebrew courses were taught until World War II. As a result, there was not a house in Jezierna where the children did not learn our language.

1935 - Zionist Youth Group with their supporters

[Pages 111-116]

Jewish Organizations in Jezierna
by Lipa Fischer
Translated from Yiddish by Ida Selavan Schwarcz

The twenty years during which Jezierna was under the rule of Poland, that is, the period between the two world wars, were years of lively development of organizational life for the Jews. This was a general phenomenon of the Jewish society in Poland, and Jezierna did not lag behind the other Jewish towns and *shtetlech*. This was the period of Schturm und Drang [Storm and Stress] among the Jezierna Jewish youth. All the Jewish organizations had, in general, a nationalistic character and belonged to the Zionist camp.

The "Hatikva" House

There was a Jewish National–House in Jezierna which belonged to the General Zionist Organization "Hatikva"; therefore the house was also called "Hatikva". The house was small and old, with clay walls and a thatched roof. It consisted of a large room and two small rooms. It was said that the owners of "Hatikva" bought the house before the First World War. It was in bad shape, like other Jewish houses; it was renovated somewhat – and the society began its activities. The plan was actually that, with the help of American landsleit [people from the same town], it would be possible to build a new modern house in place of the small one. But this plan was never realized and they remained with the small house, in which all of the movements found their places, and about which I will now write.

The main initiative to buy the house came from several Zionist activists, with the well–known teacher Schmaryahu Imber at their head. When he returned from his place of refuge along with the other Jews, he immediately began organizational activity, such as evenings of singing and dramatic presentations. The need for their own house was felt and so they decided to renovate the old house, and the money was collected from Jezierna's Jews. The whole thing was remarkable – that such a small Zionist organization could raise the funds and renovate its own house, while larger organizations in the neighboring towns and shtetlekh could not…

Library and Cultural Activity

They immediately started to organize a library. They managed to collect a few hundred books in Hebrew, Yiddish and Polish. They had the classic Yiddish works as well as works of outstanding writers of universal literature. Then they started other activities. Young and old came to the meeting hall of Hatikva; there they read newspapers, borrowed books, and discussed all kinds of Zionist problems.

Different points of view and philosophies of life appeared among the members of the society. The younger members leaned towards the pioneering camp, to Labor Eretz Yisrael; others tended towards Revisionism, which had begun to spread in the Jewish world. A third group remained among the ranks of the General Zionists, which lost some of its influence on social life in the shtetl.

Thus there were three groups: the General Zionists, the Leftists, and the Revisionists. There were quite often quarrels among the groups, especially during the thirties. New members, mostly young people, joined the organizations, and went through *hahshara* [preparation] hoping for the possibility of emigrating to Eretz Yisrael.

HaNo'ar HaTsiyoni

The first youth organization in Jezierna was "HaNo'ar HaTsiyoni" whose founders were Wolke Laufer, Ninke Katz, Yosef Fuchs, Helenke Fuchs, Chana Fuchs, Azriel Zmora, Chana Marder, Mosche Altman and others; the writer of these lines also belonged to this group. The organization then rented a meeting hall from Rifka Fischer (Trapik) and even started a small library. However, this meeting hall did not last long and was soon disbanded for financial reasons. (This applies only to the location, not the organization).

A "Circle for Culture and Science" was also established. It rented a meeting hall from Dudye Paket and was joined by a large number of members, among whom were people with refined cultural tastes. Since there were Revisionists, they influenced the choice of name, "Herzliah", and joined the Revisionist Organization. This was the seed of the movement in Jezierna. From that time on, there was a Revisionist Organization in Jezierna with widespread political activity among young and old. There were members of "Hatikva" who also held the Revisionist point of view. Among them were Avraham Hochberg and Yizchak Charap. "Herzliah" moved into one of the little rooms in "Hatikva House". They then organized a Betar and a "Brit ha–Hayal' movement with Lander at its head. At the same time some of the previous members of "HaNo'ar HaTsiyoni" moved into the room of the General Zionists.

The General Zionists then began to support the Zionist youth. They established the so–called "Apieka" which helped to reestablish "HaNo'ar HaTsiyoni". Mordechai Marder and Yakov Zamojre were especially active. They started a *hahshara* [preparation farm] for "HaNo'ar HaTsiyoni", which also included pioneers from surrounding *shtetlekh*.

Hitahdut – Po'ale Tsiyon

As was mentioned there had long been in Jezierna a leftist Zionist group; it was later called "Hitahdut" [unity]. This organization was in touch with the Lemberg [Lviv] center and from time to time various lecturers visited. Among the outstanding members of the branch were David Paket, Yosef Feiering, Yizchak Charap, Shmuel–David Shonhaut, Itche Paket and others. There was nobody under eighteen there. When the "Hitahdut" joined the "Po'ale Tsiyon" in 1930, and founded the "Ihud", some members left, but in general the branch became stronger.

The Ihud in Jezierna

The "Ihud" became a strong movement. In spite of the internal dissensions, many new members joined. At that time among the new members were Dr. Chune Litvak, Schule Fuchs, and many young members. The first chairman of the united party was Schimon Kritz.

First of all they organized the youth movement "Gordonia." For that purpose they rented two rooms in Yette Willner's house. That is where they had their meetings. The already mentioned Dr. Litvak helped bring in and activate the young people; he devoted himself to this goal, body and soul. "Gordonia" became very well–known and many young people from other organizations, influenced by the Zionist–Socialist ideals, joined. Somewhat later they left the rented quarters and moved into the third room of the "Hatikva" house. This was very hard because the room was in very bad shape and they had renovate it. This was carried out with difficulty. The same room used by "Gordonia" was also used by the "Ihud" organization, the "Ha–Po'el" sport club and the "League for Labor Eretz Yisrael". They also set up a new library, with modern new books, which quickly enrolled many readers. Many young members put great efforts into organizing the library. This library, along with the two other Jewish libraries, were confiscated at the beginning of the Soviet regime, in 1939. This library, along with the Polish and Ukrainian libraries, became a general municipal library, in the Polish "Dom Ludavii."

Emigration to Eretz Yisrael

The Zionist organizations were also involved, as mentioned previously, with emigration to Eretz Yisrael [Palestine]. In the shtetl, the importance of an organization was reckoned, and rightly so, with how many members it could give the possibility of emigrating to Eretz Yisrael. There was no lack of candidates; often, because of this, there was friction among the organizations, and even among the members of the same branch. The 'certificates' for emigration were scarce, and a small town like Jezierna received very few certificates. Nevertheless, members did emigrate from time to time. The first emigrants were Pesach Altman, Shimon Kritz, and their families. Munye Katz was the secretary of the "Ihud" but after a short time he also emigrated. Afterward Mosche Byk became secretary.

Elections

That was a turbulent period with conflict among the three parties. Each one wanted to spread its influence, especially at the time of elections to Congress [World Zionist Congress]. It was a time of "no holds barred," even the use of physical force, especially by the Revisionist side. I remember a public meeting at the time of the Congress elections organized by the "Ihud" in the synagogue. The guest speaker was Dr. Hornstein from Tarnopol. In the middle of his talk there was heard loud heckling. There was a tumult in the fully packed hall. The meeting was disrupted; the speaker barely escaped from the hall. The organizers were very upset and it led to personal quarrels and cursing.

The "Ihud" continued its struggle democratically. Moshe Byk wrote satires and pamphlets, in which he criticized the members of opposing parties; the opposition called the members of "Ihud" "Bolsheviks", "Stalinists", and the like. Nevertheless, it was the problem of *"aliyah"* [emigration to Palestine], which was at the forefront. When I was the last secretary of Ihud, from 1936–1939, I had to fight with the central organization in Lemberg [Lviv] for candidates for emigration. The party also devoted much effort to educating the young, the future of the party. There appeared posters in Polish, in which were printed articles and songs on actual problems. In later years the pioneering organization "Bosliya" joined the branch. It was particularly involved in agricultural training for its members.

***

One can say that in Jezierna, all the young people were involved in organizations. While they were in school, they were helped with their lessons, there were courses organized for them, although before the Second World War there was no longer a special teacher of Hebrew. The young people strove to advance their studies beyond the seven–grade public school, via the gymnasia [secondary schools], which were outside Jezierna, therefore neglecting the study of Hebrew.

There were national institutions where all three organizations worked together – Keren Kayemet L'Yisrael [Jewish National Fund], and the Keren Hayesod. Here as well there was friction and opposition. The Keren Kayemet activity was to collect funds in the Blue Boxes; every month two pairs of people would go around to empty the boxes and to distribute boxes where they had not yet been placed. During the 'holidays' people would announce donations to the Keren Hakayemet when they were called to the Torah in the synagogue or before the blessings for sick individuals. On the twentieth of Tammuz [*Yortsayt* of Herzl] there were assemblies and events in the streets.

Every Jewish house had a KKL box. Even if the father did not put in any coins, his children did. Often the older generation were not Zionists but the children were devoted members of the organizations.

The "Keren Hayesod" also had fund–raising activities, but these were managed by respected men of the shtetl and representatives of the organization. Such events occurred once a year.

A rival to the two national funds appeared in the Jewish street, the "Keren Tel Hai"; this was after the Revisionists left the General Zionist Organization.

In "Gordonia" there were "conversations." We danced and sang and did gymnastics and drills in Hebrew. It was often quite interesting. The participants wore identical shirts and it made a good impression.

The "Ha–Po'el" was actually a sport club. It bought necessary apparatus for soccer and handball and they played in … the market–place. They would set up two poles, spread a net, and play. There was a table–tennis table in the meeting hall. The "HaNo'ar HaTsiyoni" also had a ping–pong table.

[Page 117]

Various Shades of Zionism
by Azriel Zmora, Haifa
Translated from Yiddish by Zvi Greenberg

Almost all variations of the Zionist organization were represented in Jezierna.; Those which became active across the whole Yiddish world found themselves popular in Jezierna as well. Now I would like to list a few female and male members of the organizations.

HaNoar HaZioni [Zionist Youth] – Afeka Chapter

Mrs. Olexyncer Batya, Altman, Mrs. Glass, Mrs. Henia Heliczer, Mania Hazelnoss, Schlomo Glass, Mrs. Herzog, Hirschhorn, Gottfried, Mrs Zalz, Teacher Chermoni, Jacob Zmora, Tyncie Zmora, Dr. Tenenbaum and his wife, Mordechai Marder, Reize Marder, Neski Paket, Fuchs, Mrs. Fuchs, Mrs. Steiger, Pepi Scharer, Abraham Scharer and his wife, Nunke Kellman, Wilhelm Klinger.

Supervisory Committee of Zionist Activities
(Jewish National Fund – Keren HaYesod)
Zisel Goldberg, Chaya Charap, Eti Pakiet, Dora Fuchs, Rifka Fuchs

[Page 118]

Executive of The Jewish National Fund:

Among Others: Pepi Spindel, Rina Hochberg, Berisch Charap, Abba Katz, Tzila Rosen, Nunio Paket, Dora Fuchs, Feiering, Freida Spindel, Josef Feiering, Itzi Paket, Avigdor Fuchs, A. Lachman, Sarah Katz, Chaya Czaczkes.

[Page 119]

Revisionists, Herzlia, Betar:

Aaron Charap, Chaya Czaczkes. Malzia Schwager, Abraham Hochberg, Salke Fuchs, Nunke Kellman, Yekele Fuchs, Fruma Feierstein, Selma Schenhod, Jacob Paket, Josef Zilberman, Reize Paket, Helenka Fuchs, Nachum Katz, Pulwer, Gusta Hazelnoss, N.Fuchs, Chonke Fuchs.

[Page 120]

The Revisionists in Jezierna were a large active group

[Page 121]

United Poalei Zion, Ihud, Gordonia:

David Paket, Josef Feiering, Schmuel David Schonhaut, Itzie Paket, Dr. Chana Litwak, Schule Fuchs, Schimon Kritz (the first president).

Members, among others: Muni Blasser, Etil Pulwer, Latte Marder, Lusi Fuchs, Lipa Fischer, Jakob Fuchs, Avraham-Chaim Paket, Pesach Altman, Moshe Byk, Schmuel Bien, Moti Katz, Dezioni Zamojre.

[Page 122]

Gordonia Executive:
Lipa Fischer, Avraham-Chaim Paket, Pesach
Altman, Mosche Byk, Latte Marder, Etil Pulwer

A group of members of the executive of
"Gordonia" and "Hapoel"
A. Falk, Lipa Fischer, Nunke Kellman, Mosche Byk

[Page 123]

M. Kalafer, N. Kellman, P. Lander

The "Hatikva" organization in Jezierna celebrates its 25th anniversary

Yitzchak Zilfe, Jakob Fuchs, Heinich Czaczkes, Pesach Altman, Avigdor Fuchs, Avraham Herzog, Schimon Kritz, Wolf Fuchs, Zelig Feiering, Ire Kurzrok, Yitzchak Charap, Olexyncer, Jakob Zmora, Mordechai Marder, Schmaryahu Imber, Avraham Hochberg, Schmuel-David Schonhaut, Nute Paket, David Czaczkes, Sender Shonhaut, Meir Paket, Avraham Danzer, and others.
(Photograph taken in 1929)

"Hapoel" and the League for workers of Eretz Yisrael in Jezierna:
M. Schapira, Sch. Bien, M. Byk, V. Gottfried, M. Altman, J. Fuchs, Z. Feiering, M. Harenstein, M.
Pulwer, Sch. Gottfried, Kenigsberg, M. Katz, M. Gottfried, Sch. Kritz, G. Fuchs, L. Fischer, Sch. Fuchs
(beside his young daughter), D. Gottfried, Dr. Ch. Litwak, L. Marder, A. Fuchs.
Holding the "Hapoel" sign: Michel Fuchs, Alesh Litwak

[Pages 124-125]

Pioneering Movements
Azriel Zmora
Translated from Yiddish by Zvi Greenberg

Pioneering and training movements played a large part in Jezierna. Despite the differences in political and cultural opinions that divided them, among Jezierna householders and youth there was no disagreement on the subjects of pioneering and *aliyah* [emigration to Palestine]. There was productive competition, in which each party and group wanted to have the most members and supporters emigrate to the Land of Israel.

In Jezierna, an agricultural training center was established on the estate, which was managed by the administrator and agronomist, Wilhelm Klinger.

Others who worked at the estate also helped the pioneers. From time to time, party member Berl Schtok (today Professor Dov Sadan) would visit from the central organization.

Not only about pioneering and training were all levels of Jezierna's society united. The same unity was also found in so-called 'local politics' - whenever there was an issue about anything relating to Jewish interests, whether economic or cultural.

The young people treated their elders with respect, whether they were religious or free-thinkers. They would even observe the traditions on their own, and more than once protested against negative trends on these matters.

A group of Pioneers
Mottel Byk, Naftali Charap, Sender Schonhaut, Avigdor Fuchs, Benzion Bleich, Leibusch Gottfried,
Jakob Schwamm, Shimon Kritz, Shlomhele Gottfried, Jakob Fuchs
They said farewell to the head of their group Yitzchak Charap on his departure to Eretz Yisrael (in the
year 1933)

Three pioneers, 1924. Left to right, Yitzchak Charap, Shmuel-David Schonhaut, Josef Feuering

A Curious Event with a Correspondent

His name was Naftali Charap and he wrote sensationalist articles for the 'Lemberg Tagblatt'. Sometimes they were about 'remarkable events', other times about 'women's topics', etc. All the stories supposedly took place in Jezierna. When there appeared to be too many sensational stories happening is such a small town, it was understood that Naftali had taken the stories about women and men from American newspapers and signed his name at the bottom. He just 'changed' New York to Jezierna....Thus the career of the correspondent was ended.

[Pages 126-128]

Schools in Jerzierna
Yizhak Charap, Haifa
Translated by Maya Avis, great–granddaughter

In Jezierna there were two schools; a public school and the Baron Hirsch school that was only for Jewish children. After its forced closure, only the public school was left.

In the town there was a thirst for knowledge. There wasn't a secondary school, but many Jewish youth took the "school–train" to Tarnopol to study at the gymnasium [high school] there.

There was also an attempt to organize enrichment courses of the type that prepared students for the gymnasium or for its entrance exams. These courses were organized by Grubber, a Jezierna secondary school graduate, who later became a pharmacist. His son emigrated to Israel after the war, and was killed in the War of Independence in 1948.

Every morning one would see many boys and girls at the train station. Their destination, as we have already said, was Tarnopol for their studies at the gymnasium. Thus, thanks to this, many youth in Jezierna gained both a secondary school education and also a university degree.

***

On the school–train that ran from Zborow to Tarnopol, there was one carriage that bore the sign "Jezierna". In this carriage the students from Jezierna would regularly travel, both girls and boys. Who were among these passengers? – Moshe Sharer, Motel Spindel, Yakov Katz–Fuchs, Aharon Charap, Leah Barer, Malcze Schwager, Lotte Marder, Andzi Marder, the Haselnuss sisters, Munya Steiger, Wolf Laufer, Nisan Katz, Nuchim Katz, Ezyo Gersten, Schmuel Gersten, Yossi Fuchs, Lipa Fischer, Rosenfeld, Kalafer, Natan Kellman, Moshe Altman, Margulies, Muni Katz, Shlomit Katz, Brania Scharer, Freda Scharer, Yosef Hoch, David Czaczkes and others. In the station at Tarnopol the two Heliczer sisters and Henia Klinger waited.

These people studied away from Jezierna: Beno Steiger, Munyo, Nisan Bernstein, Reuven Kellman and others. At the seminary [teacher's college] studied: Rena Katz, Devora Gottfried. A young woman, the daughter of the milk–seller Schonhaut, won a scholarship and studied in Lemberg (Lvov), at Doctor Klaften's Art School. There she married a teacher. They were both killed in Jezierna.

On Saturdays, everyone used to remain in Tarnopol, so as not to travel on Shabbat. At school they also refrained from writing on *Shabbat*.

***

The "Jezierna carriage" was full of life and laughter. It was customary to tell "secrets", daydream, sing and even, off in a corner, review words in Latin or prepare mathematics homework. The conductor would enter and greet the passengers: "Jin Dobreh, Jezierna" [Polish: Good morning Jezierna], and in chorus everyone would answer: "Jin Dobreh Pani Conductor!". He refrained from checking the tickets. He knew everyone – these were his daily commuters.

There were three public gymnasiums for boys in Tarnopol, and one (privately owned by Lenkewicz) for girls. The third gymnasium specialized in mathematics and physics, and the mathematicians studied there – the aim of these students was to become math teachers or engineers or economists. There was also a vocational school.

Each day conversation always turned to the teachers, especially the Jewish ones among them. The math teacher, Franczos, was once a *yeshiva* student and more than once would interrupt in a *gemara*–chant [sing–song]: "Landeh, Where's your X? "Landeh, Where's your Y?" Numerous students would write a little Yiddish in their German homework. The German teacher, Doctor Teiwim, would discover this and ask where the "Odessian Deutsch" came from.

***

Something about the *cheders* [Jewish supplementary schools] and their teachers: All the boys also learned in the *cheder*, so that after a hundred and twenty years [optimal lifetime], they would be able to say the *Kaddish* prayer, learn a passage from *mihnayos* [oral laws], and other traditional readings [recited after the death of a parent].

The rooms were cramped (the children already started to learn at age 3). There was a beginners' teacher, a *Chumash* and *Rashi* teacher [*Torah* and commentary], and a *Gemorah* [rabbinic discussions] teacher. The star pupils studied with the *Rabbi*, with diligent *Torah* scholars, or went to study at a *yeshiva*. There were Jewish scholars who struggled to earn a living and earned a bit more by teaching a couple of children.

The beginners' teachers were: Yakel Melamed, Henzel Steiger.

There were also assistants: Aharon–Yizhak, Izche Shorr and others. Their role was to carry the small children to the *cheder* on their shoulders.

The *Chumash* and *Rashi* teachers were: Binya Byk, Lazer Byk, Eliakum, Avraham Reis. The *Gemorah* teachers: Peretz Schwartz, Hirsch–Leib Stokhamer, and Yakov Schochet. They taught at the *Beis Ha–Midrash* [synagogue study hall] or in their own private homes.

In addition, Itzi Paket, a *yeshiva* graduate, taught the older students for free. Visiting teachers were also occasionally invited for a *zman* [semester] or two.

In the cramped *shtiebel* [little house] of the beginners' teacher, about twenty small children sat around the table; squashed and jostling one another. The teacher had a large *siddur* [prayer–book] for the children with extra–large fonts, such as are printed for the blessing of the moon prayer. Apart from this, he would search in the *siddur* for instances where the letters were especially large. The rebbi–teacher would say: "*kametz aleph, kametz beis*"– and the children would answer in chorus. The teacher and children "repeated the words again and again" – like it is said in the well–known song – until the teacher felt sure that the children knew the words.

The teachers obviously did not have pedagogical knowledge, but through experience they constructed their own methodology, (cheder–methods) from the group to the individual usage. Using a *titel* [wooden pointer], they would point to each letter. The *Chumash–Rashi* teacher also used this method, as well as another one. He would point with his finger from place to place, (called the 'nail method'). Every Sabbath the students would be taken to learned Jews, for a '*farheren*' [hearing]. This was to test the students' comprehension.

The *Gemorah* teachers had a different method. The student would read the text alone, as well as the interpretations, and the Rabbi would only help where it was required. Today this would be called 'independent learning'.

***

It should be mentioned that the first Hebrew teacher was Shmaryahu Imber, and after   him, for many years, the teachers were Yeshayahu Yavetz and David Chisdis, from Rovna. By the time they left Jezierna, there was already a group of their students who were able to replace them and continue their work until the start of the Second World War.

In 1924, there were *chalutzim* [pioneers], who came to Jezierna for *Hachshara* [pre-*Aliyah* agricultural training program]. They would also teach the children Hebrew. Among these was Zvi Hermoni (Weisselberg), who lives in Israel in Kibbutz Usha.

[Page 129]

A Few Memories from Our Town Jezierna
by Devora Gilad (nee Fuchs), Hadera, Israel
Translated from Hebrew by Ornit Barkai

Jezierna, which had about 180 Jewish families before the First World War, was reduced to 120 families after it. During WWI, which took place right along its perimeter, all the Jewish families moved to the center of the country, fearing the enemy troops who targeted primarily Jews. By the end of the war a number of the families were scattered around the world and the Jewish community was small.

In spite of these circumstances, our town was among the most developed, both in its level of education and especially for its Zionist movement, which was founded by Shmaryahu Imber, of blessed memory, whose brother wrote 'Hatikva'. An official Zionist association and a Hebrew school already existed prior WWI, at Imber's initiation. The association had the best people and youth working together for Zionists causes, and also owned a private function hall.

With the return of the Jews to Jezierna after WWI, the school was reopened and the activities of the Zionist association were renewed. I remember that during the war between Poland and the Ukrainians, when Petlura and his troops were encamped at Jezierna's train station, we established "Agudat Bnot Zion" (Daughters of Zion Association). On Saturdays the cultural elite and youth all gathered for readings of interesting Hebrew literature (which was illegal, of course). And there, at one of the meetings, the door opened – and in came a Petliura soldier... no words can describe how we felt at that moment... When he saw our fear and confusion he said: "Shalom, I am a Jew, I heard about you, and came to take part in this too"…At the end of the wars between the Ukrainians, the Bolsheviks and the Poles, and since the Poles had the upper hand, they slowly brought life back to normal, and we returned to our routine Zionist activities. We established a few committees, such as the Keren Kayemet (Jewish National Fund) committee, and the *Pikuach* (Supervising) committee. Every once in a while we held gala events and dedicated the funds we raised to Keren Kayemet (JNF). Later, after the Ukrainians built a large function hall, a drama club was organized under the helm of Fancia Blaustein. Our performances received rave reviews in a place where theater, or even a cinema, did not exist.

I remember that it was problematic to get a permit before each play. Of course, this had to be done under false pretenses, for the good of the charity organizations. Chaya Charap knew how to trick the authorities in order to obtain a license. The funds, of course, went to the Keren Kayemet for Israel. We should mention here the skirmishes with the Orthodox Jews who opposed the "moral looseness" — they dubbed us 'the comedians'. This caused bitter conflicts in many homes between the youth and their parents.

As I said, the Hebrew school already existed prior to WWI. I was among its first students. After teacher S. Imber, of blessed memory, left town, teacher Yaabetz of blessed memory replaced him. One of the top educators, he too left after a number of years, and then we – the senior students – took it upon ourselves to continue to manage the school until a new teacher arrived.

In 1924 a kibbutz group arrived in Jezierna for *hachshara* (training). A few local youth joined them. This inspired the youth to 'make *aliyah*' (move to Eretz Yisrael). Among the first *olim* (immigrants) was Aba Katz, who went as a tourist. Discussions started and inquiries began on how to make *aliyah*. At Fancia Blaustein's initiation, we decided to establish a group for girls, ten of us all together. Each of us had to put in a sum of money and then emigrate together as a cooperative. Out of the ten only three immigrated. Following our correspondence with the Aliyah Center we finally received our certificates. Chaya'le Charap went first. I, who was married by then, gave up my certificate, because my husband had received his at the same time and I was able to join him as his wife. It should be noted that it was very difficult to receive certificates at that time, due to the British desire to control our moves as much as possible and to prevent Jewish immigration to Eretz Israel.

Some staff of the Hebrew school in Jezierna

[Page 131]

The Jewish Youth of Jezierna Thirst for Education
by Lipa Fischer
Translated from Yiddish by Simon Godfrey

The Jewish youth of Jezierna thirsted for education, general education, not only in high school, but also in the university. As it was difficult to study in Poland because of various restrictions, many studied abroad.

Shalom Francas, a child from a religious school studied in Vienna. He graduated from the university (mathematics) and became a mathematics teacher in the high school. The two Jewish doctors in Jezierna were born in the neighbourhood. Dr. Chana Litvak came from Zborow, a village near Jezierna, studied medicine and settled as a doctor in Jezierna. Dr. Tennenbaum, who came from Polowce near Jezierna, completed his medical studies and settled in Jezierna. Dr. Nissan Bernstein graduated from the Jewish *Gymnasium* [upper school] in Lemberg [Lviv], completed his medical studies in France, obtained his license in Krakow and settled in Chenstakova [Czestochowa].

Others who studied in France: Aharon Charap (did not finish his studies), Yaakov Fuchs–Katz (textile technology), Moshe Katz (returned to Jezierna in 1935 and afterwards emigrated to Eretz Yisrael). Those who studied medicine: Walke Steiger, Nissan Katz, Lala (Yossi) Fuchs.

In Belgium studied: pharmacy – Moshe Scharer; he lived in Brussels. In Italy studied: medicine – Izio Gerstein, Doski Charap. In Germany: economics – Reuven Kellman; he received his doctorate and lives in Israel. In Czechoslovakia: pharmacy – Chana Klinger (Duhl), Sofia Heliczer (Anderman), B. Spindel. Medicine: Josef Mosczysker, grandson of David Blaustein. In Lemberg University: Malzia Schwager – humanities.

Those who completed high school but did not continue to study:

Azriel Zmora – emigrated to Eretz Yisrael; and is now supervisor of the department of mail and telephones. Yosef Fuchs – lives in the USA. Two Gottfried sisters, Zila Heliczer – now living in Switzerland; Manek Margulies, Leah Barer–Korngold – now in Haifa. Aimek Falk – now in Poland, a colonel. Nunke Kellman. Those who also studied medicine but did not finish: Walke Laufer and Mondek Steiger.
Azriel Zmora is an engineer at the postal company.

[Pages 132-133]

Our Theatre
Yizhak Charap, Haifa
Translated from Hebrew by Maya Avis, great–granddaughter

In the aftermath of the First World War, the youth began to dream about the development of a cultural life in our town. In addition to evening gatherings that included a diverse array of programs, they undertook to set up a drama club, and stage performances and the like.

Their project was successful. Droves of enthusiastic young men and women streamed to the club, chose a play and began their rehearsals. You should have seen the youth's dedication, their discipline, their precision, and their aspiration to perform the role to the best possible standard.

The theatre hall was always full. All the town's honorable citizens, their wives and children would be there to see their "home–grown artists".

The program included: "The Intelligent", "The Jewish King Lear", "Mirele Efrat", "Hasia the Orphan", "*Der Batlan* (Idler)", and we even attempted "The Dybbuk ". Our Jeziernans were impressed by our theatrical accomplishments.

Our performers were: Chaya Charap, Zisel Goldberg, Fansie Paket, Nuni Paket, Rivka Fuchs, Eti Paket, Dvora Fuchs, Dozi Czaczkes, Lotte Marder, Nusia Blaustein, Aron Charap, Yizhak Charap, Sara Marder, Sheva Fuchs, Chana Marder, Leibush Godfried, Yakov Fuchs, Yizhak Paket, Nusi Blaustein.

The directors were Fansie Blaustein and Yizhak Charap. The prompt was Dozi Czaczkes.

The Jewish Drama Club, c.1923.

The Jewish Drama Club, c.1925.

איך קום צו אייר מיר נעמען
וואס כ'האב בײַ אייך געלאזט
מיין חכמה שטיין פון קרעמען,
מיין שליסל, רויט פון ראסט
ווי גאלד איז מיין געליבטע.
איר אויג מיט גאלד צוגלייך.
און איך האב גאלד אין קאמער,
דער שליסל איז בײַ אייך.

S.Y. Imber

[Page 134-136].

Rebuilding of the Jezierna Synagogue and Its Final Destruction
by Lipa Fisher
Translated from Yiddish by Pamela Russ

At the time of the First World War, it is known that many Jewish properties were destroyed by fire at the hands of Russian soldiers; among these was the large *shul* [synagogue].

This was a two–story high structure, built of brick, with long Gothic–style windows. The roof was covered with zinc sheeting. The entrance was through a wide gate. Inside, there was a foyer that led off to two smaller chapels on both sides; adjacent to those was the entrance to the large *shul*-hall.

The hall was two stories high. Through the long windows, glazed with multi–colored bits of glass, light would stream in, and it was very bright. The walls were painted with pictures and verses from the Bible. In the center of the hall was a podium which one mounted via small steps, surrounded by an artistic metal railing. From the ceiling hung brass chandeliers made with elaborate artistry. The Holy Ark was filled with Torah scrolls. In the *shul* there were also many *Gemaras* [Talmud- books of rabbinic commentaries] and other holy books that rested on shelves that were built into the walls.

In 1916, when the Russian army took over the town for the second time, a great panic set in. All the Jews fled with the retreating Austrians and the Jewish homes remained empty. The *shul* was converted into a stable and later into a hospital where wounded Russian soldiers lay. When the Russian army once again retreated, they first did their "reckoning" with the Jewish buildings. They actually left in a great hurry, but did not forget to set fire to the large, beautiful *shul*.

***

When the Jews returned after their flight, the economic situation was very difficult and for a few years, the *shul* remained in its destroyed state. And when the times began to normalize – this was already under the Polish government – the small Jewish community undertook to rebuild the Jezierna *shul* that was originally built in the 1870s, so they said.

And it was not so easy for a community of this sort to reconstruct such a building. As they tell it, the Jewish landowner Mendel Jampoler participated greatly in the construction expenditures. There were also "common" people who did not scrimp on their last pennies for the construction. The main reconstruction in the first twenty years, I personally remember well. I remember how the money transactions took place; the community was active in this. The community leader, David Blaustein, of blessed memory, one of the wealthiest Jews in the town, also contributed a lot of money, and he donated bricks from his own brickyard. The walls actually still stood, but a lot of bricks were needed to fix them. When the walls were ready, they had to cover the roof; there was no sheet–metal to cover it … so they assembled the Jewish residents and each homeowner pledged to donate some sheeting; at that time my father gave six metal sheets.

The above–mentioned David Blaustein also sponsored the podium. He gave 600 dollars towards it. It is opportune at this point to mention other Jewish businessmen who were also active in the reconstruction of the *shul*, such as: Avraham Pakiet (Avrumtche), Sumer (Itamar) Katz, Itzy Lechowicz, Mendel Fischer, Chaim Zottenberg, Moshe Pakiet, and others.

When the *shul* was completed, there was a great celebration in the town. Jews began to study Torah and to pray there anew. The *shul* also served as the center for meetings and other cultural events, for Zionist speeches, and so on.

***

This time the *shul* remained standing for only eighteen years. In 1941, when the German murderers invaded the town, they burned down the *shul* along with all the holy books. This time, no one rebuilt it... In 1952, when I came to Jezierna from Siberia, in the place of the *shul* I found a little hill of grass. I walked around it with Azriel Pollak, as if encircling a shrine. A few years later, in 1955, the grasses too were gone. Some non–Jews were standing there pulling apart the foundation... The rocks were used to pave the roads that had been very neglected.

The Jezierna synagogue in 1938, postcard.

[Pages 137-142]

Poets, Writers, Intellectuals and Performers
Translated from Hebrew by Simon Godfrey
Translated from Yiddish by Ida Selavan–Schwarcz

Shmuel–Yaakov Imber: [Samuel–Jacob] 1889–1942, Yiddish poet, nephew of Naftali Hertz Imber, published a few collections of poems, including "Songs of the Homeland". The historical poem 'Esterke' is famous. He also published critical essays. He was murdered in Warsaw during the Holocaust of Israel.
Jewish Encyclopedia edited by Yaakov Pevzner, Jerusalem, 1966 - Page 30

Note M.D.: During the Holocaust I met Shmuel–Yaakov Imber in Jezierna a number of times. From Jezierna he went to Zolochev where he was murdered.

The first emigrant to Eretz Yisrael [Palestine] from Jezierna, in 1912, was the poet Shmuel Yaakov Imber. He lived in Palestine for a while and then returned to Jezierna. He wrote about his impressions of living in Eretz Yisrael in his "Heym Lieder" [Poems of Home] published in Vienna in 1918.

While still a youth, living with his father in Jezierna, he published a small volume, "Vos Ich Zing un Zog" [What I Sing and Say] in Lemberg [Lviv] 1909. The lengthy poem "Esterke" appeared 1911 in the publication "Bildung" [Education] of Stanislow.

In 1914 he published his book "Royznbleter" [Rose Petals], (Vilna: B.A. Kletzkin). In 1920 his book "Viktoria" was published by Neuland, Vienna.

Tsipora Yelin, Jerusalem. (sister of S.Y. Imber)

And When I Die...

And when I die, my brother,
And when I die, my friend,
Gather up my merry songs
Gather up today's songs.
And publish them in the nameless book
Poems which are easy to read …
Sell my books, my flowers
To all who are yet young.
Sell my flowers, my books
And put up a simple stone
Thus it will be overgrown quickly
And my bones will rest easy.

(S.Y. Imber)

Avraham Moshe Fuchs: Born 1890 in Galicia (Jezierna). Yiddish story writer and newspaper reporter. In Israel from 1950 wrote stories about the lives of simple folk in the Jewish villages. 'Alone', 'On the Hill Top', 'Jews in the Diaspora' and others.

The author A. M. Fuchs

Shlomo Shenhod (Schonhaut): Born 1912 in Galicia (Jezierna, M.D.). Yiddish and Hebrew poet. In Israel from 1936. Initially he wrote poetry in Yiddish and later in Hebrew and published poems in various magazines. Wrote a collection of poems entitled 'Songs of the Shining Sadness'. He translated several books from Yiddish. "A poet whose poems overflow and he composes them in two languages, which means – this is his emotional need. His internal world is not divided by chance, but by his own order and reason."

"A poet who witnesses these events, seeks means of defense. He seeks escape in stories of other realities, of dreams, to bypass these depths. And because he sees dreams as an escape from the fear and depression of people in our times, he sees it as a rational approach".

"Everything vanishes from sight and disappears from vision
Only the dream persists
All our extinguished melodies are reawakened again

Memorial Book of Jezierna

With things that will never return –
Exist in a dream.
And there is no permanence
And no life
And no existence
Only in lofty dreams"
(Quotation by Avraham Blatt in 'Paths of Poets', Menora Publications, T.A. 1967)

Editor's Note: Sh. Shenhod (Sheinhot) translated several articles in the book from Yiddish to Hebrew for the benefit of non-readers of Yiddish.

***

I. A. Lisky: Born in Jezierna; Yiddish poet; publisher of the weekly 'The Jewish People' in London.

"…thus Lisky writes poetry about *Yiddishkeit* [Jewishness] in Yiddish, and all his poems which delight the soul, raise it from the dust and give the reader an hour of enjoyment, of belief in a more beautiful and better tomorrow that we are marching toward, that great and peaceful day which the prophets had foretold. All the poems sparkle with love of Israel with the Land of Israel, with a call for redemption, with freeing ourselves from exile, as well as with love of humanity, of the stranger. "And you shall love the stranger"… Lisky had a profound belief that evil will be overcome, and if we are good and pious we will merit a world of goodness, a world of Sabbath, where the righteous ("and your people are all righteous") sit and enjoy the light of the Divine Presence, and the Land of Israel will be ours forever. "They will inherit the land forever."

(S. Z. Shragai)

Bestow Peace

My people raises the flag to you –
Bestow peace,
I stand like a beggar at your door.
I shall not leave empty–handed –
Bestow peace,
My eyes see clearly I am not dreaming.
My people raises the flag to you –
Bestow peace,
The heroes stand at the borders as before
Let the nations hear my cry –
Bestow peace,
My hand will be free of rebuke.
I call to enumerate the people
and the heroes will come from the Diaspora –
Bestow peace,
They will walk hand in hand with their
brothers from the kvutzot
My people goes to defend its land –
Bestow peace,
Give the enemy into its hand.
My people raises the flag to you –
Bestow peace,
I stand like a beggar at your door…
(I.A. Lisky)
***

Dr. Efraim Wasicz: born in Jezierna in 1879. Among the founders of the organization of high school students, 'Zionist Youth'; among the organizers of 'Bar Kochba' at the University of Vienna. From 1904–5 secretary of the regional committee of Krakow. In 1906 editor of the 'Tagblatt' [newspaper]. 1911–1913 editor of the 'Dror☐ in Lvov. 1912–1918 leader of the Scouts. In 1918 during the riots in Lvov, he was a member of the national committee in the city.

In Israel from 1919. Fulfilled important functions as a lawyer in the life of the *Yishuv* (pre–state Israel). 1920–1931 in Haifa. From 1931 he lived in Jerusalem. From 1930 he became one of the leaders in the Zionist–Revisionist party in Israel.

(Dr. B. Lubotzky: Life of a Zionist Fighter, Jerusalem 1947)

***

Dr. Reuven [Rubin] Avineri–Kellman: son of Joseph Kellman and grandson of Wolf Fischer - educated Jews. His father was the Chief of the Kasse Kredit Bank in Jezierna. Reuven studied Jewish studies and economics at the University of Berlin and received a doctorate in economics. Published a book on banking in Galicia. Made Aliya to Palestine in 1937. Served as headmaster of the University High School in Ramat Aviv.

Die ländlichen Kreditverhältnisse
im ehemaligen Galizien
und heutigen Polen
unter besonderer Berücksichtigung des ländlichen
Kreditgenossenschaftswesens.

Von
Dr. Rubin Kellmann
aus Jezierna (Polen)

Günthers Buchdruckerei, Saalfeld (Ostpr.)

Cover of the book written by   Dr. R. Kellman

***

Rabbi Levi Yitzhak Mansur, [Manson]: Wrote a book 'Israel will be Blessed Through You'.

***

Shmuel Segal, the actor. His choice of the stage as a profession was both adventurous and mischievous, as it involved a conflict with his parents and the surroundings in which he was raised and educated.(Segal's father was the first orthodox immigrant from Jezierna – M.D.) Shmuel Segal was a Y*eshiva* student, [in a school of higher religious studies], from a modern religious family, and the grandson of a rabbi who was head of a *Talmud–Torah* [religious elementary school] in the town of Zloczow in Poland. At the age of 5 years he and his family made *aliya* to Palestine and settled in Haifa. During the War of Independence Shmuel took an active role in organizing the Israeli army bands and was their guiding spirit. S. Segal traveled through Europe in 1955 and studied for a short while at the 'Central School' (of Music and Drama) in England, taking a special course in acting and voice development. S. Segal regularly performs on 'The Voice of Israel' [radio station] and his performances have been recorded on many gramophone records.

(Yehoshua Yafe–Nof, "Artists in Israel publisher 'Yesod', Tel Aviv)

Yossi Segal: the actor, is a recognized performer in Israelthe son of Yaakov Segal and brother of Shmuel.

Note: Chapter's Information was assembled by Professor Menachem Duhl

[Page 143]

An Episode
by I. A. Lisky
Translated from Hebrew by Ethelea Katzenell

During the Second *Aliyah*, I was visited in Vienna by Samuel–David Scheinhaut, son of Jacob, the *shohet* [ritual slaughterer] from Jezierna, while he was in the process of immigrating to Erets–Yisrael. It was the evening of Yom Kippur.

Living in Vienna at that time was Rebbi Moishele, the only son of the *tsadik* [righteous man], Reb Levi–Yitzchak, zts"l, [may his righteousness be remembered], the Rabbi of Jezierna. With the outbreak of the First World War in 1914, the *tsadik* had fled to Vienna, where he died in 1916 and was buried in the central cemetery in Vienna. A tent was constructed above his grave. The Rabbinate was taken over by his son, Moishele. He resided in the 20th district on Klastenberger Street, where he had many *hasidim* [followers] from Jezierna and surrounding villages.

Samuel–David had suggested that we attend Rebbi Moishele's ''Kol Nidre' service. When we arrived, we found the 'whole world' there. We went back there the next day, as well, on Yom Kippur morning, but then we found the whole house in deep mourning – the previous day, Rebbi Moishele had passed away! We became tongue–tied … One of the praying men approached us and said: "You are from Jezierna, so go over and sit near the deceased. Perform the *mitzvah* of true kindness [respect for the dead]."

We sat there for over an hour. Afterward, others took our places. We felt it had been a great privilege.

[Page 144]

Communal and Religious Leaders in Jezierna
by Pesach Altman, Haifa
Translated from Yiddish by Zvi Greenberg

Rabbi Lipa Schalita and Pharmacist Ludwig Mintz, Community Leader

Officials and Rabbis
Rabbi Shloymaleh Charap – born In Jezierna
Rabbi Yitzhak Levi Manson – his son was Reb Moshaleh – See more information in the book
Rabbi Zelig Aptowiczer – until 1916
Rabbi Eliezer Lipa Schalita – from 1918. Murdered in the Nazi destruction.

Mayor
Ludwig Mintz, Esquire – the Jezierna pharmacist. He was the only Jewish mayor in our time.

Community Leaders
The heads of the community would change after every election. Those who we remember were:
Wolfe Fischer, Abraham Paket, Wilhelm Klinger, David Blaustein

Ritual Slaughterers [*Shochets*]
The position of ritual slaughterer was inherited. **Shochet Pinchas (Schonhaut)** died in 1914; he received the position from **Shochet Yaakov (Schonhaut)** . After Pinchas, the position was given to **Benzion Sigall**, Yaakov's son–in–law. Jezierna also had another *shochet*, **Rav Mosche**, and after him, again through inheritance, the position was taken over by his son–in–law **Shochet Hirsch Leib Stokhammer.**

Synagogue Managers [*Shamas*]
Moses Shamas (Schormann) and **Nachum Yaffe** in the study hall,
Meir Shamas (in the prayer hall)

Prayer Leaders
Binum Charap, Shlomo Charap, Abraham Paket, Shalom Lachman, Nachum Fuchs,   Michael Fuchs, Jacob Bik and **Nahum Schonhaut**

Burial Society
Undertakers: **Berl Feiering, Itziye Lechowicz**, among others.
Grave Digger – **Meir Tzonis**

Representatives and Spokesmen at various times:
Itamar Katz, Abraham Paket, David Blaustein, Shlomo Charap, Isak Czaczkes, Ludwig Mintz, Wilhelm Klinger

Disciples /Hassidim
A large number of Jezierna Jews were followers of various rabbis:
The Rebbi of **Husiatyn** [Husyatyn], the Rebbi of **Czortkow** [Chortkiv] the Rebbi of **Bojan [Boyany]**,
the Rebbi of **Kopyczynce** [Kopychyntsi], and the Rebbi of **Jezierna,**

Jewish Study Halls [*Batai Midrash*]
The Large Synagogue (within which were 2 small *shuls* for artisans and Zionists)
A Study Hall (for disciples of Husiatyn)
A Synagogue (the Rabbi's [*Klois*] Court)
A *Klois* built by Yehoshua Flamm
A Minyan [prayer quorum] in the Rabbi's home
The worshipers in the various study halls and courts were divided according to which rabbi they adhered to.

Ritual Managers in the Synagogue [*Gabbayim*]
Jacob Razen, Eli Gottfried, Itamar Katz, Sholom Bleich, Berl Feiering

[Page 145]

To Future Generations
S.Y. Imber

צו די קומענדיקע

איר, וואס וועט קומען ווען איך וועל שוין נישט זיין,

איר, וואס וועט קומען אין לעבן אריין --

אין אייערע הערצער לאזט ליבן מיין ליד,

פאר אייך, אוי פאר אייך, האט דאס ליד מיינס געבליט.

איר, וואס וועט קומען נאך יארן אין טעג,

איר, וואס וועט קומען פול צארן און שרעק,

איר וואס וועט קומען פון גליקן באגלייט --

אייך אלע געקענט האט מיין פרייד און מיין ליד.

איר, וואס וועט קומען פון געטער געשיקט,

מיט לידער באגליט און מיט טרוימען באשטריקט -

ביי אייך וועט מיין גייסט אין טרויס-שעהן רוען,

א יעדער פון אייך איז מיין טייערסטער זון.

(ש. י. אימבער -- גיזאמלטע לידער).

[Pages 146-150]

A Page from a Book of Memories of Jezierna
Written in Yiddish by Lotta Marder–Frankel, New York

Years passed by, the children grew up and became adults, revolutionary historical events gave rise to demographic, scientific and political changes. The entire human civilization paid the price for these changes with millions of human victims. The largest sacrifice of all was paid by us – the Jewish Nation – six million martyrs for the mere fact of being Jews.

I am filled with memories of the town where I was born – Jezierna – even though it no longer exists. Father–Mother, family members, friends, all died in the Holocaust and are no more. They found their deaths in mass graves which they were forced to dig for themselves with their own hands. The small homes in which they lived, the synagogues in which they prayed – those too are no more. Nothing left.

I now live in the United States of America, among Jews, most of whom left their homes in the old world many years ago. All they know about the horrible holocaust is what they read in newspapers and books about the Holocaust, or from movies. Their social and economic life styles are much improved -to luxurious levels. When I attempt to pour my heart out and share my pain with them, to relieve myself a little – my pain increases due to their lack of comprehension of the depth and size of the disaster. When the pain and longings attack me in their presence, they try to sympathize with my sorrow, even sighing with me, but cannot reach down to the bottom of my crippled spirit. The feeling that I sit alone in my mourning makes my pain so much more difficult to bear.

I was raised and educated in a progressive – traditional Jewish home. My father was a mixture of traditions – education and progress, Judaism and humanity, Torah and general science. He was a brave fighter for justice and freedom in general and for the national home for the Jewish people in particular. In his rousing exhortations he always wanted to raise in his listeners' hearts the need to give thought to the historical lesson they must learn, that there is no chance for Jewish survival in the diaspora for generations. For thousands of years they had been chased, tortured and attacked, endured years of pogroms and being sacrificial offerings, guilt offerings for all the upheavals and changes of regimes that took place in countries not their own.

My father was an active Zionist, who served as the manager of the cooperative Jewish bank in the town. All his energy, all his free time was dedicated to activities for the national rebirth, revival and productivity of the people of Israel.

In this atmosphere we grew up, the three girls – the sisters: Sarah the eldest, myself the undersigned, and my baby sister Hanna. We were all imbued, in Abba and Imma's house, with love for the people of Israel and dedication and active service in the movement for a national revival. We all took active roles in the youth movements in town.

Sarah, a member of the drama club, was the first one to make aliyah to the Land. The first one to fulfill with her own body the ideal we preached. All her life she labored and worked in Israel (her husband too, who actually built the land as a construction worker); she raised two daughters – teachers in Israel, and she also died there, before her time.

When I raise that period in my mind's eye ... I see at the center of our small town a hill near–by the main road, and on top of that hill sits a small house, that was the Community Center called "HATIKVAH". Here in that house was centered all of the "Zionist life" of the town, especially of the local youth. Here they organized courses to study the Hebrew language and geography of Eretz Yisrael; here they had lectures and participated in heated debates, celebrated parties; here side–by–side were the "General Zionists", the "Noar ha'Zioni" and members of the "Gordonia" youth movement.

In 1930, under the initiative of Aharon Charap and Meltchi Schwager, may their memories be blessed, the "Revisionist Organization" was founded. Their club was situated in the home of David Fuchs. There too, there were lectures and debates. Our movement supported self–fulfillment, to physically participate in the building of a democratic, progressive Jewish state, and indeed many of us moved to Israel, myself included among those.

I clearly remember my friends in "Gordonia": Altman, Pulwer, Bik, Lipa Fischer and others; how deep their dedication and enthusiasm was for the ideal. Where are they now? Where are the two Pulwer sisters? Where is the head director of our movement Dr. Litwak? They were all murdered by the Nazis. Could there be a greater pain than that? A deeper sorrow than that?

I remember the 20th of the month of Tammuz** at our club–house. We decided to celebrate that day with the most extravagance. We wanted our club to look the best of them all and there was much excitement in the air. We decorated the place, each of us brought something special for that purpose. We hung posters, invited guests, had meetings in study halls, held lectures, recited poetry, composed and sang songs. It was a big holiday for us. The club was packed full, tens of people stayed outside, looking in through the windows for lack of more space. I remember the loud singing of Hatikva which burst out of the club and spread throughout the town. Even the non–Jews stood there in awe and listened. For a whole week later all were talking about our celebration of the 20th of Tammuz. The impression in town was great, and we were all so proud and satisfied.

Oh, our debates! So young we were and our debates were heated and exciting. And about what? What will be the appearance of the state to be established in the Land; how should it be built and what position it will hold in the advanced world? Each of us believed in his own plan and only the concept that we designed for the state would be the right and justified one, all the others have nothing to rely on, and the right one is his alone.

My father and I – we stood on opposite sides of the aisle politically speaking, with conflicting points of view. Between us there were also arguments where each tried to convince the other that he or she is right, but in the end, my father remained "Abba" and I, his daughter, kept the mitzvah of respecting my father.

Not all had the chance of making it, to live in the State of Israel. Their eyes did not see the realization of their dream, for which they fought and dreamt with the fire of their youth.

I believe and am also confident, that when they were led to their death, standing in front of the mass graves, they still believed that this dream of the rebirth and survival of the people of Israel in their own land would come true, that it would rise again, and they perished with that belief. May their memory be blessed in our hearts for ever.

**Note: Hebrew Date, 20 Tammuz marks the passing of Theodor Herzl in 1904

***English Translation donated by her son** Ami Steven Frankel*

Editor's Note: The article is printed twice in the book, both in Hebrew and Yiddish. The Yiddish was translated into Hebrew by Shaul Yardeni.

At Home and in the Area

A Few Memories
Yoel Schwam (Charap), Tel Aviv
Translated by Ornit Barkai

Four decades have passed since the day I left Jezierna. Quite some time!

In the meantime, the shtetl was destroyed by the Nazi enemy along with many other similar towns, and I was left only with memories of the good old days. I remember well our life in this small town, especially the group of youths I was a part of. After World War I, new winds swept through the youth in our town, but we did not let them affect our *Limudei Kodesh* [Judaic studies]. These lessons took place at Rabbi Shloimele's *Bet Midrash* [House of Study].

There we learned. Thanks to a bunch of young men who got together each day and studied *Gemara* [rabbinic commentaries]. Together with me studied Moshe Bik, Naftali Zeidman, Shimon Scheinhous and Abraham Danzer. Leading us was Itche Paket, David's son, who had just returned from his *yeshiva* [school for religious studies], where he had received his Rabbinic ordination. He taught us "not in order to receive a reward". His teaching contributed greatly to the enrichment of our knowledge.

I also remember very well our studies with the *shochet* [ritual butcher] Hersch Leib Stokheimer, of blessed memory. A few youths, we used to go to his home in the evenings to learn; we were given a very friendly reception in his home. His wife Ruchama, a modest woman, was happy that her husband was performing the *mitzvah* [good deed] of teaching *Torah* to young Jewish boys.

All the while, we did not neglect other activities; we were all members of the Zionist movement. The only youth organization was the "*Hit'achadut*", the pioneer movement. My group leader was Motl (Mordechai) Bik; he would direct the conversations toward pioneering education. It was also very interesting when members from the secretariat would come to talk to us. Sometimes Berl Stock (now known as Professor Dov Sadan) would come to talk about national liberation.

We actually, then and there, started doing physical labor tasks in preparation for implementing our pioneering aspirations.

[Page 152]

Peretz Melamed
by M. D.
Translated from Yiddish by Dorothy Wolfthal

His name was Peretz Schwartz, a learned Jew, a Talmudist. He had a phenomenal memory and was a '*melamed*', a teacher of *Gemora*. [Rabbinic commentary]
He taught several generations, among whom many delved deeply into the realm of Torah. Students treated him with respect; it was an honor for them to be in the presence of such a scholar. If someone forgot a father's or mother's *yahrzeit*–day [memorial date of death], they would ask Peretz – he remembered everything – a living calendar. And if someone got sick (caught an 'evil eye'), to whom would he turn, if not to Peretz, for an 'exorcising'. One could also come to him if they needed good advice. Every Rosh Hashana Peretz Melamed sent hand-written blessings to each of his students.

But a *melamed* could not live only on tuition fees – he needed additional ways to eke out a living. In those days there was nothing like social security, no pension, no health insurance and so forth. Truly, the old age of such a *melamed*, if he was unable to work, was bitter. Oh, how well we understand [the prayer] "Do not forsake us in our old age …"

***

These are the names of his grandchildren and great–grandchildren who live in Israel: Pesach, Michael and Samuel Altman; Devorah, Reisel and David Landsman; his son–in–law is a lieutenant colonel in the Israeli army.

Transcribed by Zeneth Eidel

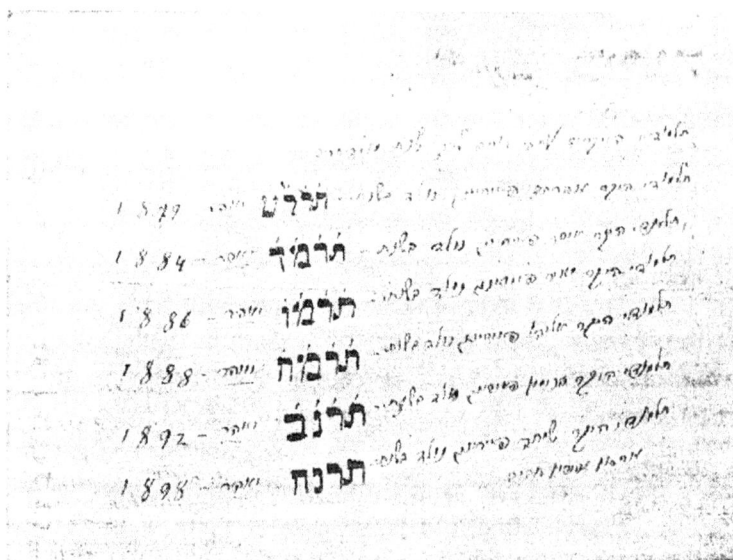

List of names and birth years of students from the Feiering family – 1879–1898

*Every Rosh Hashana Peretz Melamed sent hand-written
blessings to each of his students*

[Page 154]

In The Surrounding Villages
by Yisrael Schapira, Ashkelon
Translated from Yiddish by Dorothy Wolfthal

Within a circle of a few kilometers surrounding Jezierna lay the little villages and hamlets whose inhabitants were peasants – Ukranian/Ruthenian and Poles. And in this sea of *goyim* [gentiles] there were also a small number of Jews who had been there for generations, who lived their Jewish lives, though not unaware of worldly matters.

To the west of Jezierna were the villages of Polowce–Wielka and Polowce–Biala, Glinna and Krasne. These villages were about a kilometer apart, and within these settlements lived about forty Jewish families. The center was Polowce–Wielka where there was always a *minyan* (quorum for prayers) in Reb Schmelka Weissman's house, may his memory be blessed. It was he who led the prayers and read the Torah on the Sabbath and on holidays. This was the gathering place for people of the neighboring area. Also, at Jaeger's in little Polowce, *minyans* would come together.

The Jewish National Movement was not overlooked in the villages. The young people were active and would gather from time to time. And there would be discussions concerning problems in the Zionist Movement. The Keren Kayemet L'Yisrael committee was active under the leadership of Jakob Katz from the village of Krasne. The fund–collection job was widespread; in every household one could find a J.N.F. *pushke* (collection box).

The meetings would take place in members' homes, and when the weather permitted – in summer – also in nearby woods, in nature's bosom. This would usually happen on the Sabbath and on holidays. The surrounding meadows were adorned with colorful grasses and blossoms. At holiday times many of the young people would come home from the cities where they were studying or working, bringing fresh life into the community.

The neighboring gentiles treated us with respect; they knew that it was a holiday time for the Jews. They were busy with their work in the fields and they would look upon us and greet us like good neighbors.

Transcribed by Zeneth Eidel

[Page 155]

Jezierners In Various Armies
Compiled by Lipa Fischer, Yizhak Charap, Azriel Zmora
Translated from Yiddish by Dorothy Wolfthal

Jezierna was, throughout the years and periods, under the rule of various governments; and since some wandered away to other lands – it followed that Jezierna Jews served in various armies and participated in the wars of these countries. We are not able to list all of those who served in those armies or who fell in battle.

We will limit ourselves to a partial listing. In the mobilization of 1914 many Jezierna Jews were called up. I remember Corporal Gerschon Kurzrok with the *jingi–kop* (redhead), a gun over his shoulder. Also Aaron Blasser and others.

Listed among the fallen in the first World War are:

1. Buni Eidel, fallen as a hero; 2. Josef Fuchs, Elka's son; 3. Fuchs, Hencie's son; 4. Hirschhorn, Rivka's son; 5. Lotosky; 6. Mosche Bomze, Pinchus–the–shochet's grandson; 7. Blasser; 8. Bien, Moshe Bien's son; Pinchas Schapiro from Polowice.

Also Jews, even those who had been prisoners of war, enlisted in an army after the war. A few who had been in Italy joined the Polish army, even under General Haller (Schuli–Scholem Fuchs was a sergeant in Haller's army). A Jew as a 'Hallerchik'? This is shocking! The 'Hallerchiks' had authority to beat up Jews and cut off their beards.

Among the prisoners in Russia, I remember Leib Bleich and Ruben Willner – they lived through the revolution there.

Some who served in the Polish army: Yitzchak Charap, Godel Fuchs, Velvel Rosenfeld, Yisrael Hoch, Abraham Danzer, Aaron Charap, Motl Spindel, Mosche Scharer, Wolke Laufer.

Those in the Polish army who fought the Germans were: Hersch Spindel, Dovid Fuchs (fought in Warsaw), Wolf Laufer, and others.

At the outbreak of the Soviet–German war many Jews were conscripted into the Russian army and fought the Nazis: 1. Muni Steiger, Chaim's son; 2. Mosche Byk; 3. Chune Fuchs; 4. Mosche Wieseltier; 5. Muni Zamojre; 6. David Feiering; 7. Simcha Katz; 8. David Kurzrok; 9. Muni Blasser; 10. Yisroel Hoch; 11. Ejmek Falk; 12. Manek Margulies; 13. Muni Steiger, Yekil's son; 14. Yakov Kurzrock, Mosches son; 15. Schmuel Bien; 16. Yakov Broize; 17. Schmuel (Schmulik) Fuchs; 18. Mosche Kellman; 19. Hersch Rosen; 20. Dr. Heiman (medic); 21. Yisrael Schapira, Bina Fuchs' son–in–law; 22. Yehosche Gelbtoch; 23. Avraham Charap; 24. Feiwel Pollak.

Some died, some enlisted in the Polish army.

Those who fought in the [Jewish] Brigade: Itamar Caspi (Zilberman), Yakov Kritz, Beno Steiger.

Those who fought the Nazis in the American army: Joseph Fuchs (in Japan), Chunke Fuchs (Normandy); Arnold Lachman–Feiering (on the European front), and others.

At the outbreak of the Soviet–German war (1918), many Jews were conscripted into the Russian army and fought the Nazis: 1. Muni Steiger, Chaim's son; 2. Mosche Byk; 3. Chune Fuchs; 4. Mosche Wieseltier; 5. Muni Zamojre; 6. David Feiering; 7. Simcha Katz; 8. David Kurzrok; 9. Muni Blasser; 10. Yisroel Hoch; 11. Ejmek Falk; 12. Manek Margulies; 13. Muni Steiger, Yekil's son; 14. Yakov Kurzrock, Mosches son; 15. Schmuel Bien; 16. Yakov Broize; 17. Schmuel (Schmulik) Fuchs; 18. Mosche Kellman; 19. Hersch Rosen; 20. Dr. Heiman (medic); 21. Yisrael Schapira, Bina Fuchs' son–in–law; 22. Yehosche Gelbtoch; 23. Avraham Charap; 24. Feiwel Pollak.

Some died, some enlisted in the Polish army.

Those who fought in the [Jewish] Brigade: Itamar Caspi (Zilberman), Yakov Kritz, Beno Steiger.

[Page 155]

WWI foreign soldiers in Jezierna, 1916

[Page 156]

Bunio Eidel – fell in WW1, while serving in the Austrian army

In the Polish Army: Left to right: Izio Katz, Yizchak Charap, Leibusch Gottfried

Berchi Heliczer

1914–1918 Yaakov Charap

Memorial Book of Jezierna

Those who fought the Nazis in the American army: Joseph Fuchs (in Japan), Chunke Fuchs (Normandy); Arnold Lachman–Feiering (on the European front), and others.

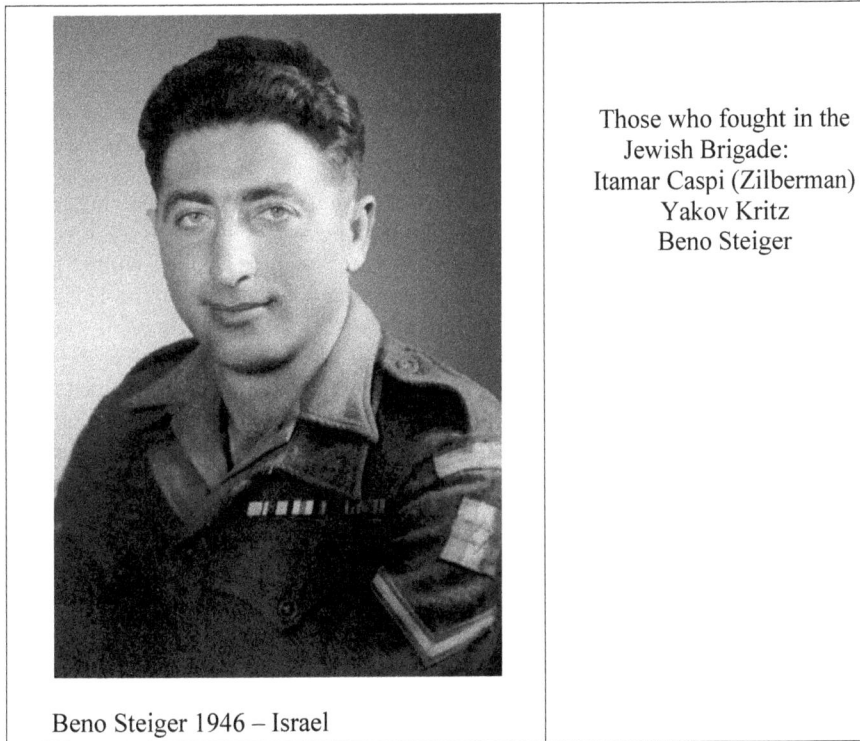

Those who fought in the Jewish Brigade:
Itamar Caspi (Zilberman)
Yakov Kritz
Beno Steiger

Beno Steiger 1946 – Israel

Beno Steiger in the uniform of the Jewish Brigade Group, Israel 1946

M. Katz, Polish Army.

M. Katz, Guard at the Dead Sea Works.

Yizchak Charap, Civil Guard

Transcribed by Zeneth Eidel

[Page 160]

In the Struggle Against the Nazis
by David Kurzrok, Toronto, Canada
Translated from Yiddish by Dorothy Wolfthal

By the month of June, 1941, the Soviets mobilized the Jews and Ukrainians of Jezierna into the army; I too was among them. And when the German–Soviet war broke out, June, 22, 1941, I was already a Soviet soldier. We were formed into units in Tarnopol; I was assigned to a tank unit and sent to the front.

Hitler's army attacked fiercely, from air and from land, and there was great confusion. Many Ukrainians ran back home to Jezierna. I stayed, but the Russians took the few who remained, loaded us into small railroad cars and sent us to Siberia. There we were formed into labor squads. The work was very hard. After a while I got a more responsible assignment and later they transferred me into the army, to the front. I was assigned to the Third Ukrainian Front.

My first battle was at Orsha, White Russia, and then further, in the direction of Lithuania. Severe battles took place there. I was a 'rozvyetchik' [combat intelligence]. Thirty–five of us went ahead to discover the strength of the enemy. In German territory we were discovered and shot at – thirty–two died and three of us escaped. We managed to make our way back to our unit. I was wounded and spent time in the hospital. Then I received a commendation.

In 1945 I demobilized myself and traveled to Jezierna. I longed to see my family. But I found no one there; they had all been done away with by the Nazi murderers.

My father Shimon and my mother Reisel were pious, industrious people who helped the poor and the sick. The older brother, Avraham–Chaim, the sisters, Leah and Chana, the youngest brother, Henik – I did not find them. All were murdered. I cannot forget them.

With a broken heart I left Jezierna and went out into the world.

Transcribed by Zeneth Eidel

David Kurzrok

[Page 161]

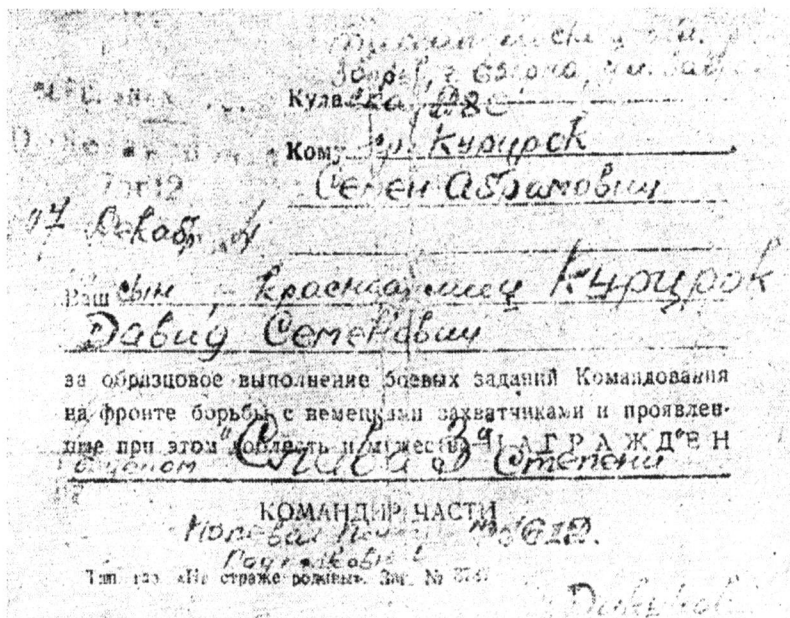

Russian notification of award for D. Kurzrok – a partial translation:

To: Kurzrok, Shimon, son of Abraham From: Colonel Dikurov Date: 07 December ...?
Message: Kurzrok, David, son of Shimon is awarded a Medal of Valor, third degree

[Page 162]

State of Israel
Ministry of Defense, Department of Rehabilitation
The Unit for Commemoration of the Soldier
24 April 1969, 6 Iyyar 5729
Number: 22/7/1289
Mr. Menahem Duhl
44a HaGalil St.
Haifa

Dear Sir,

Re: Edward Gruber z'l, 16872
In reply to your letter of 14 April 1969 we hereby inform you that our list shows an IDF fatality by the name of Edward Gruber z"l
Below are his personal details:
Parents' names: David and Helena
Date of Birth: 8 June 1925
Date of *Aliya*: Immigrated from Cyprus on 4 February 1948
Fell in battle near Manara, 23 October 1948.
Buried in the Haifa military cemetery.
We believe this is the deceased soldier that you referred to.

Respectfully,
Eliezer Leoni, Assistant to the Department Manager

Edward Gruber z"l
by Menahem Duhl
Translated from Yiddish by Dorothy Wolfthal

On the Jezierna estate almost all the skilled tradespeople were Jews, among them were Bitterfeld and Falk.

Bitterfeld had a son, David; Falk had two daughters, one was called Helena. David (he named himself Gruber) and Helena grew up together, and married. They had a son, Edward. This was in 1925.

Years passed. David owned a pharmacy. Edward was a student at the *gymnasia* (high school) until 1939. The war broke out. David died before the war and Helena was killed in the Shoah. Edward was homeless; wherever he spent the day, he did not stay the night; he wandered through woods and fields, and survived. In 1948 he left Europe and emigrated to Israel.

Edward fell in the War of Independence. In the cemetery in Haifa, among the headstones of other freedom fighters, one can find the grave of Edward Gruber.

Menahem Duhl

Transcribed by Zeneth Eidel

Men gather before prayers

c.1935. Courtesy of Talila Charap Friedman. Taken by Mordechai Marder.
[Photo not in original book]

[Page 165]

A Jewish Family
by Menahem Duhl
Translated from Yiddish by Pamela Russ

Horodyszcze [*Horodyshche in Yiddish*] – a village like all other villages in eastern Galicia – was populated by Ukrainian non-Jews and a few Jewish families. The Altman family – a husband, wife, and five young children, four boys and one girl, was one of those Jewish families. They had a hole-in-the-wall store, bought their products from the non-Jews, and lived their lives that way.

But at that time, even before World War One, incitement had already begun. Earning a livelihood became difficult, and in 1913 the husband went to America to look for a means of earning a living. Unfortunately, very soon the tragic news arrived that he was no longer alive. She – Fruma was her name – remained a widow with five children.

1914. The Austro-Russian war broke out. The village was taken over by the Russians and they ordered the Jews to leave the village, all the villages. Fruma and her children also had to leave Horodyszcze.

She harnessed their horse and wagon, took some provisions and some bed linen, put the children into the wagon, tied the cow to the wagon (so that they would at least have some milk while they were in a strange place), and they left. They abandoned their little hovel and tiny amount of merchandise. But where does one go? Only God knows!

The roads were filled with those who were fleeing, with horses and wagons that were filled with bundles, bed linen, men, women and children. People were going this way and that way, … and that's how they came to the town of Bursztyn. Here they were ordered to go back to Horodyszcze … and as they were en route, Fruma would always look at her young children to make sure no one was missing, heaven forbid, or that no one had fallen off. Very often she heard the voices of mothers and fathers as they were calling to their lost children.

As they arrived back in Horodyszcze, she no longer had anywhere to go with her children – everything had been burned down. There was nowhere to lay down one's head. So she had to keep going – to her father in Jezierna. Her father, Peretz the teacher, lived in a tiny house with his wife and daughter who had two children, and now this daughter Fruma came with her five children. And he still had to manage his *cheder* – he was a *Gemara* teacher and had many students.

1916. The Jews of Jezierna fled to Hungary and returned in 1918. The worries were the same. Fruma worked hard, day and night. She baked bread, rolls, challahs, and sold them herself. Money was very sparse – but she had one goal, that was to raise her children to be proper adults. The young boys studied in *cheder* and in school and later on each one studied a trade. The daughter helped Fruma in the beginning and then later got married.

The poor widow raised her children with lots of hard work but they grew to be fine adults. Three of her sons moved to Eretz Yisrael. Pesach became a shoemaker, an expert in his trade, and went to Israel in 1934. He has an orthopedic shoe store in Haifa. Shmuel learned carpentry and went to Israel in 1936; he has a furniture workshop in Haifa and is chairman of the Craftsmen's Association in Haifa. The third son, Michael, went to Israel in 1939 and has a tailoring shop in Haifa. The son Moishe and his family and the daughter Feige and her family were exterminated in the Holocaust, and Fruma herself, the elderly, exhausted mother, was murdered in Auschwitz in the year 1943.

Before her tragic end, she no doubt reviewed her life and thought about her three sons in Eretz Yisrael, who would never forget their mother, the E*shet Chayil* (Woman of Valor).

[Page 167]

In the Town
by Shlomo Warhaftig, Afula
Translated from Yiddish by Siri Jones-Rosen

Midway between Zborow and Tarnopol lies the *shtetl* [town] of Jezierna. I arrived there by chance, as my fate desired. I had gone there for the wedding of my cousin Yitzchok Spindel, and indeed there, I found my destined bride, the youngest daughter of the Rosenfeld-Bleich family. That is how Jezierna also became my home town.

It did not take me long to meet all the young people there, to join them every evening on the hill or in the field on Sabbath afternoons. Jezierna was actually a very small town, with few young people, but life was intellectually rich and all were good friends. For many of them their future lay in the Land of Israel, and in fact, percentage-wise, Jezierna sent more people to the Land of Israel than larger towns in Galicia.

Before I arrived in Jezierna there was a training-squad of pioneers, who worked on the farm managed by Klinger. For Klinger it was a big undertaking: to employ Jewish workers, pioneers, was not that easy. But from this we learn that Zionism influenced many levels of Jewish society.

The town consisted of only one main street and on both sides of it there were shops. Everyone existed in peace and calm and lived their lives without feeling what was awaiting them. But the Gentile townspeople already demonstrated antisemitism with their signs with slogans "Do not buy from Jews" and "Go to Palestine." - Meanwhile, life continued.

A wedding in the town was full of flavor. Before my eyes stands Aunt Basha in her joy, as she watched Uncle Berl coming back from the synagogue with a guest. A Jewish holiday in the town was a great pleasure... for the older folks - a quiet 'Shabbos' chat in the prayer hall courtyard, and for the young people – a hora dance in front

And over all this spread darkness and terrible fear. All the members of my family were deported to the camps, and not a one remained alive.

In the Great Synagogue

Right to Left: Zalmen Scharer, Meir Zmora, Avraham Fuchs, Sumer Katz, Moshe Heliczer, not recognized, Mendel Fischer, Yisrael Olexyncer, Yakov Zamojre, J. Hersch Rosenfeld, Meir Glazer

Cemetery in Jezierna
Yona Kurzrok and her sister beside the grave of their father Mordecai Kurzrock

[Page 169]

The Zilberman (Caspi) Family
by Sarah Klein, Haifa
Translated from Hebrew by Connie Edell Reisner

In November 1934, Michael Zilberman and his wife Tovah (nee Hochberg) immigrated to Israel from Jezierna with three of their children: 14-year old Yaakov, 12-year old Sarah, and 10-year old Itamar, and settled in Haifa. However, their eldest son, 18 year old Yosef, was prevented from joining them at that time and succeeded in doing so only after a year of intense effort on the part of the family.

When they arrived in Israel they were welcomed by Michael's parents, Shmuel and Rosia Zilberman and his three sisters, who had been living in Israel for the previous eight years, and also by two of his brothers, Pinchas and Moshe, who had made *aliyah* in 1920. (Yet another brother, Eliyahu, had succumbed to malaria in Israel in 1931.)

Michael, who had owned a fabric store in Jezierna, decided to work in Israel as a laborer, in order to physically help build the Land, as did his two idealistic brothers.

In January 1942, a great tragedy struck the family. Their son, Yaakov (Yankele), at that time aged 22, was killed while serving as a sailor on the merchant ship "Hatikvah".

Upon arriving in Israel, Yaakov studied to become an electrician. He began to work and joined *Ha-Noar haOved* (the Youth Labor Movement). In 1938, he went with a group of his young friends from the Movement for a year's training at Kibbutz Ashdot Yaakov. At the end of this training period, he and his friends joined the kibbutz Sdot Yam.

For a period of time at the kibbutz, he worked as a fisherman; this was a branch the kibbutz had begun to develop. During this period he developed a love and attachment to the sea. Nonetheless, by the end of 1940, Ya'akov decided to leave the kibbutz temporarily in order to help his parents, who were then having financial difficulty.

His parents urged him to find a city job in his original field, as an electrician, but Yaakov stubbornly insisted on boarding a ship; he had hopes of visiting different lands and of seeing the world. However, fate disappointed him. On his trip from Haifa to Turkey, not far from Lebanon's shore, a huge storm blew up; his ship was damaged and began to sink.

The crew of 21 men tried to save themselves in a life-boat, in an attempt to reach safe harbor, but huge waves overturned it. Sixteen men managed to swim ashore; five Jewish sailors drowned; three bodies were carried out to sea, among them the body of Yaakov z'l. This occurred on the fourth day of Shevat, 5702 (January 1942). He was buried in a Jewish cemetery in Beirut. This terrible disaster so horrified the family that it left scars for many years to come.

His father, Michael z'l, died suddenly on the first day of Adar Aleph, 5708 (February 1948), at age 58, at the height of the Israeli War of Independence. He was not destined to see the fulfillment of his Zionist dream, the establishment of the State of Israel. He was also not blessed with knowing his first granddaughter, Rachel, who was born one month after he passed away. Michael had been a man of faith, a man who observed the commandments, honored and loved by all who knew him.

His mother Tovah, after her husband's death, continued to live with her son, Yosef, even after he married, finding solace in her children and five grandchildren, born in the years that followed. Tovah died on the fourth of Tevet, 5722 (December 1961), after a severe illness. She was known to be a wise woman with a sense of humor and a good heart, devoted to her family and friends.

Yosef, their eldest son, during his first years in Israel worked as a builder and a stone-cutter until 1949, after which he became a clerk at the Israel Treasury Department, where he continued to work for the rest of his days. Not yet 50, Yosef died of a heart-attack on the thirtieth of Av, 5725 (August1965), leaving behind his wife Aliza and their 10-year old daughter Nurit. Yosef was remembered by all as an honest man, a seeker of justice, widely respected and admired by all who knew him.

Their daughter, Sarah, studied in an Israeli elementary and high-school. She married Joseph Klein and they raised two children--Rachel and Michael.

The youngest son, Itamar, first attended an Israeli elementary school, followed by studies at the Ben-Shemen Youth Village. He spent a year in a pioneer training group at Kibbutz Ginegar and, when he turned 18, he signed up for the Jewish Brigade in WWII. At the Italian front he was seriously wounded, and spent about a year there recuperating in various hospitals. Today he works at the 'Koor' steel plant in Haifa. He is married and the father of a daughter and son, Michal and Yaakov.

[Page 171]

Yaakov Caspi, The Fisherman
Translated from Hebrew by Hadas Greenberg

On December 28th, 1941 the ship "Tikva" sailed for the first time from the port of Haifa to Mersin, Turkey. After a heavy storm the ship reached Alexandretta. It remained anchored there from early January 1st, 1942 till January 19th. Then it sailed on to Port Said. At dawn, a big storm came up that worsened over two days, until the waves started to cover the decks and flood the engine rooms. The sea water extinguished the coal fire which reduced the steam. The overwhelming waves caused sections of the deck to fall apart one after another. The situation was terrible. All the workers, except the mechanic and the fire stoker, were on the deck for 50 hours with neither sleep nor food (the kitchen was flooded).

On the morning of the 22nd, it was decided to go down into the life–boats. They managed to lower only one boat, and all 21 people who were on board were lowered into it. The boat was a toy for the waves. Most of the oars were broken and lost. The people's spirits fell once they saw the rocky beach. A feeling of despair prevailed. They tried to sing in order to raise their spirits, but again they were silenced. Only Yaakov continued to sing: "Five went out ..." and in the middle of the song a huge wave flipped the boat upside down. The people were wearing life jackets and were seen bobbing, up and down, between the waves.

Here fate's judgment gave it's cruel sentence: five were smashed against the rocks and drowned. The water spit three corpses onto the beach; among them was Yaakov's. They were buried in the Jewish cemetery in Beirut.

By Anschel

For two and a half years you were with us; not a short time, yet not many succeeded in getting to know you intimately. Only a few of us came to know you closely and appreciate your spiritual qualities. You shared your concerns with few. You were among the very few who knew how to form a barrier between the accumulated bitterness of day–to–day concerns and personal characteristics. You knew how to remain good and be loyal.

You were able to take on, and indeed fulfill every assignment quietly, with reserve and humility. And hence, Fate chose you as his first sacrifice. Seemingly, you did not leave among us anything at all; an empty hole remained. But in that space the echo of your song was heard, an echo of the dream we all dreamed together for three years to the sound of your song, seated on the grass on moonlit nights. You knew how to sing, how to dream and how to realize.

Even facing death, you stood tall, accepting even it in song. Indeed you proved in your final moments, that you knew how to die quietly and bravely, and more than that, for what purpose and why. You expressed this in your last song: "Five went out to build a Homeland."

By Yiska

(Excerpt from the journal "Yaakov Caspi", published by Kibbutz Sdot–Yam)

Yaakov Caspi, of blessed memory

[Page 172]

The Fischer Family in Jezierna
by Lipa Fischer
Translated from Yiddish by Dorothy Wolfthal

In Jezierna there were two Fischer families, but their source was a single one. The founder was Yakov Fischer, who settled in the shtetl of Berch [Bircza] in the nineties of the nineteenth century. His three sons – Reuven, Yechiel and Mayer – founded three branches. My grandfather was Yechiel. Yechiel had three sons – Avigdor, Leib and Joel; Leib was my father.

My grandmother Yuteh was the daughter of Lipa Magierowicz; she was my father's mother; therefore my father called himself Fischer–Magierowicz.

As a twelve–year old boy my father and his parents came to Jezierna from Pluhov. My father, who had learned at all levels with Jewish studies teachers would, later in life, open a page of the *Gemara* and study, after his work. In his correspondence he would use the sacred tongue [Hebrew]. He was a model of industriousness, duty and integrity. In the First World War he served in the Austrian army.

My mother's name was Rachel, daughter of Shalom Shaps and Ester Balaban. She had two brothers and three sisters: Moshe, Chaim, Rivka, Rachel and Miriam. They all were killed by the Nazi murderers. The same fate overtook my father, mother and sister.

My mother was from Sasow, a village near Zloczow. She loyally observed Jewish customs and culture. On the Sabbath she would pray and read the *Teitsh–Chumash* [Yiddish translation of the Pentateuch].

My sister Reizel participated in the community life of the young people of Jezierna. She studied to become a dentist.

My father, mother and sister Reizel – they rest in the Jezierna common grave–pit. May their memory be sacred.

Transcribed by Zeneth Eidel

[Page 173]

David Blaustein
By Rebekah Blaustein-Shwalb, Tel-Aviv

The family Blaustein was one of the oldest settlers in Jezierna. They were always landowners. Jews who lived according to tradition; honest and respectable people.

My father, David Blaustein, was a landowner; he possessed great stretches of fields. He was also the owner and director of the "Bank Zaliatchkave". He was a philanthropist, giving alms to the poor and aiding them in their troubles; he was active in the social life of the town, at one time as the head of the community and also as a member of the city council.

When the population of Jezierna returned from their flight, after the first World War, and found their synagogue burned down – he helped financially in rebuilding it and donated a Holy Ark. He also donated a plot of land for the building of a Yeshiva.

We were five sisters and one brother. I live in Israel and so do my brother-in-law Teomim and his son, the engineer (architect). My son, who is a physician, lives in the United States, and so does my brother's daughter – Dusie (Dozia).

All other members of the family lost their lives during the great holocaust of the Second World War.

[Page 174]

The Charap Family
by Yitzhak Charap
Translated from Hebrew by T.C. Friedman

Shlomo Charap

The family Charap, was one of the largest families that resided in Jezierna for a long period of time. When they first settled there, who was the first, and where he came from – this I don't remember and I don't know. I do know that my grandfather's name A'H *(may he rest in peace),* was **Binum** Charap, and his brother was named **Yaakov**. **Binum** had three children: Shlomo, Avraham and Lantzi.

My father Shlomo Charap had five sons and one daughter: Hersch, Lipa, Yakel (Yaakov), Aharon, Haya, and me, writing these lines. Hersch had three children: Shlomo, Klara and Mindol. Lipa had two children: Yakel and Sarah. Only my father A'H, had the privilege of seeing three of his children emigrate to Eretz Israel– Aharon, Haya and me. Aharon passed away in Israel. My two daughters are teachers and they educate the young Israeli generation.My grandfather's brother **Yaakov** had 2 children: Shalom and Tova. Shalom had six children: Moshe, Naftali, Simcha, Berish, Reizel and Riva. Tova had two daughters: Ester-Malka and Babtche.

Indeed, it was a family with many branches, and much is recounted about it in this book.

Berl Feiering

From the time of Kaiser Franz–Josef
Seated: Berl and Eidel Feiering
Standing: Meir and Etel Zamojre, Zlata Lachman

Charap Family Tree

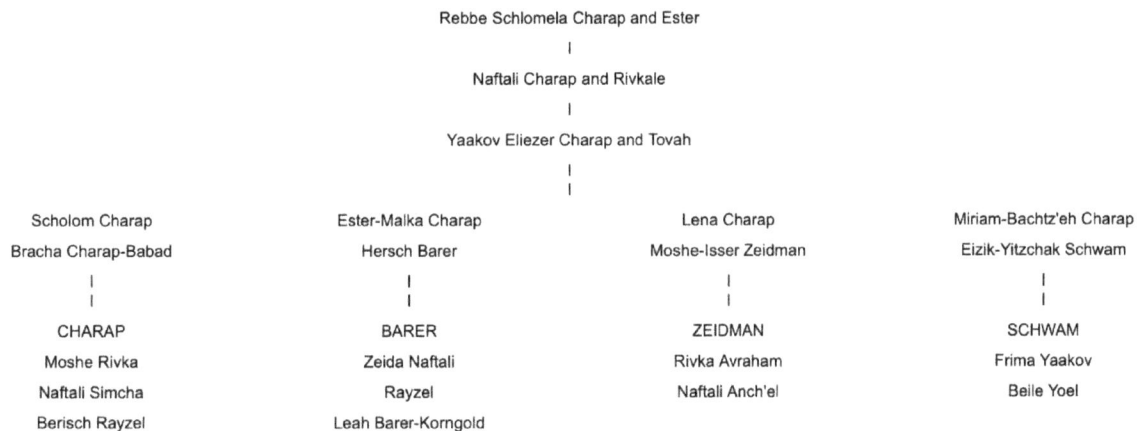

Rebbe Schlomela Charap and Ester

|

Naftali Charap and Rivkale

|

Yaakov Eliezer Charap and Tovah

|

|

Scholom Charap	Ester-Malka Charap	Lena Charap	Miriam-Bachtz'eh Charap
Bracha Charap-Babad	Hersch Barer	Moshe-Isser Zeidman	Eizik-Yitzchak Schwam
CHARAP	BARER	ZEIDMAN	SCHWAM
Moshe Rivka	Zeida Naftali	Rivka Avraham	Frima Yaakov
Naftali Simcha	Rayzel	Naftali Anch'el	Belle Yoel
Berisch Rayzel	Leah Barer-Korngold		

[Page 175]

Homesick and Yearning for My Town
by Azriel Zmora, Haifa
Translated from Hebrew by Simon Godfrey

Jezierna was a small town which, from the point of view of technological development, even in the context of the second decade of the century, was quite a failure. But for the people who lived in the town, breathed its air and grew up in its spiritual atmosphere and inter–personal relationships of the Jews there, this small town provided a wealth of experiences and deep connections at family, traditional and nationalistic levels.

For as long as I can remember, experiences and longings are intermingled as landmarks.

In 1914 the First World War broke out and most of the families of Jezierna and the surroundings dispersed ahead of the Russian invaders to various parts of the Austro–Hungarian Empire. My own family also moved to Hungary and afterward to Slovakia.

During their absence from the town they all hoped to return home. In fact, at the end of the war in 1918 the majority of families returned from all parts of the destroyed Empire to their origins – their town. Even those who had 'built their houses and settled' [quote from prophet Jeremiah], returned sooner or later.

My father Majer ben Avraham Zamojre, of blessed memory, an expert in trees, even though he had a good and secure income, did not want to remain in the foreign and intermixed environment of Slovakia. And despite the pleadings of my mother Etel, of blessed memory, and her six siblings, the children of Berl Feiering who had lived in America for many years – he did not want to follow in their footsteps and emigrate; he decided to return to the town in 1924 in order to ensure the Jewish education of his children.

Thus, despite growing up in Czechoslovakia from the age of one year, under favorable conditions, when I arrived in the small, dark and muddy town I immediately felt that I had returned home and was among my warm family. It was like a giant tree with all its branches and divisions comprising the families Feiering, Zamojre, Czaczkes, Gottfried, Lachman, Herzog and Pulwer who formed a substantial proportion of the local population. They mostly lived in Railway Street, 'Bahn Gaas', in houses adjacent to each other. At their head was my grandfather Reb Berl (Dov Ber Avraham) Feiering, of blessed memory, who was involved in public service, taking care of the poor, the sick and needy without rest, and who knew how to involve close and distant relatives to help the individual, the congregation and the public as a whole.

As a *gabai* [warden] in the synagogue, head of the burial society, sick visitation committee, fund for poor brides, righteous deeds charity, he knew how to involve not only his general business friends, but also his entire family in his charitable works. He was a traditional warmhearted Jew, honest and a lover of mankind. This legacy of love for his fellow man and performance of good deeds between men he managed to instill in all his children near and far.

My family, like most of the Jewish families of Eastern Europe at the start of the century, demonstrated within it all the same types of problems of those Jews. They were deeply rooted in traditional Judaism on the one hand and felt the attractions of modern America on the other hand – religious studies, manual labor and business side by side. Old and new did not always fit in with the gentile and hostile environment which was always present, and as time went by the Land of Israel became more of a factor. The young people in the town and some members of the family attempted to translate the Land of Israel of the Bible into that of the Zionist movement, that is, to the idea of Aliya and fulfillment. As a result of this, a small group was saved from the grasp of the Nazi murderers.

Another example of the unbroken connections of my Jezierna family in America is the way they formed a family society 'Feiering–Avner' and established joint ventures, the basis of which was mutual help among themselves and for those who remained in the town. In addition another two organizations of former Jezierna residents were established in New York.

I cannot forget the visit to the town of two of my uncles from America, my mother's brothers, Isser and Binyomin Feiering. They were very emotional about 'sitting together with their brothers' and remembered events from every corner of the town. It was a tradition of those who left the town to return to their former home and to give generously to the local institutions and to help the needy families.

We in Israel also united with all those who came from the town, which was manifest by meetings when they arrived on *Aliya*, to exchange memories of the past. The connections became stronger after the bitter fate which overtook all the families without distinction during the Second World War, which this book is modestly designed to echo. We hope that this echo will reach the ears and the hearts of the descendants of Jezierna in future generations.

***

The Feiring family was one of the largest in Jezierna. The great–grandfather of A.Z. – Avraham Feiering – had 16 children. They dispersed over the entire world they succeeded greatly in the United States, in Vienna and in Germany. In Israel – [Kibbutz] Bet Yitzhak is named in memory of Yitzhak Feiering.

Berel Feiering

[Page 178]

The Katz Family
Dina Katz, Bat-Yam, Israel
Translated from Hebrew by Ornit Barkai

May the following words be in commemoration of my father-in-law Somer (Itamar) Katz and his family who perished in Jezierna with the other Holocaust victims in town.

I was born in Warsaw, but became related to the Katz family in 1936 when I married one of his sons, Moshe (Munya) Katz, z"l, who came to Israel as an illegal immigrant. Also, I knew his sisters who immigrated to Israel earlier. From our many conversations I absorbed many details about the town in general and about my late husband in particular. omer (Itamar) Katz z"l was a wealthy real estate owner and among the town's most respectable folk. His home was open to many friends and he was known for helping the needy. He and his family held Jewish nationalistic views and were among the first in town to emigrate to Israel. The father himself came as a tourist to explore opportunities for settling in the country, but the raging war which started in 1939 severed all ties with Israel and prevented him from doing so.

In 1941 the German slaughterers entered Jezierna and annihilated most the town's Jews, including my father-in-law Somer and his three daughters, their husbands and children; the eldest daughter Sarah and her husband Yaakov Bik; the second daughter Sabina and the third one Adela and their husbands and children.

It was the tradition of nationalism in my father-in-law's home and the spirit in which the members of his household were all brought up that moved my late husband Moshe (Munya) Katz to come to Israel, build a family and teach his children to follow in his footsteps.

After arriving in Israel, he volunteered for guard duty in the Dead Sea area, which he performed for 12 years. He was injured twice while serving in this dangerous duty: in 1936 after the Arab disturbances against Jews broke out, and again in the 1948 War of Independence. As a result of his severe injuries, which caused prolonged suffering, he passed away at the age of 54.

His forefathers' legacy of patriotism took root in his sons' hearts as they continue their father's tradition to this day, serving in the Israeli army in protection of the country and the revival of Israel.

[Page 180]

An Appeal for Contributions
Translated from Yiddish by Pamela Russ

From the Building Committee of the Jewish Community House in Jezierna

To all our fellow Jezierners:

"If we want our youth to live with cultural independence …we must strive to build a Jewish Community Building, a Jewish meeting house.

We have decided to build a new Community House which will include a reading room and library, a sports room, a meeting room, a large hall for public meetings, and a small place for prayers.

Brothers! Remember! Without your assistance our plans will never materialize! "

In the name of the Building Committee:

Chairman: Pharmacist Ludwig Mintz; Vice Chairmen: Beryl Feiering, Shevach Baron, Beryl Bernstein. Members of the Building Committee: Nachum Fuchs, Itamar Katz, Avraham Fuchs, Ben-Zion Blaustein. In the name of the Community Management Committee: Avraham Paket, Head officer. Community Councilmen: Moishe Hochberg, Yakov Czaczkes, Mordechai Marder. In the name of the "Hatikva" Union: Avrohom Hochberg, Chairman. Committee Members: Shlojme Glas, Yakob Zmora, Yitzchok Charap, Wolf Fuchs, Shimon Kritz. In the name of the Merchants Union: Moishe Heliczer, Chairman. Committee Members: Michel Zilberman, Moishe Wieseltier, Yisroel Olexyncer.

December 1928.

DESTRUCTION and ANNIHILATION

Prof. Menachem Duhl participated in editing the Holocaust section

The Second World War
by Menachem Duhl
Translated from Yiddish by Gloria Berkenstat Freund

The Outbreak of the German–Polish War: The Reverberation in Jezierna

Hitler's Germany attacked Poland on the first of September 1939. Everyone believed that Poland was strong enough to not let itself be conquered and that the world would not allow this to happen, that Hitler would not swallow Poland. If the world helped, let Hitler rack his brains.

The Jezierna Jews, in particular the synagogue–politicians, maintained that Jezierna was far from the German border and close to the Russian one; one did not have to be afraid. The Germans would not come here. They listened particularly to the veterans of the First World War; their opinion was authoritative. However, automobiles full of people immediately began traveling through Jezierna. They were citizens who had escaped from western Poland, among them Jews. They said that the Germans had bombed their places of residence. The Polish Army was routed and was in retreat. Only individual military units were staging a resistance and they were waiting for aid from the western nations.

Civilian officials, small military units, individual officers, soldiers and citizens – all ran. A fear fell on the Jezierna Jews, who had been almost calm until now. They also were engulfed by an atmosphere of panic. Many automobiles stopped at the Jezierna marketplace. They were immediately surrounded by a cluster of Jews. They asked various questions, they wanted to learn from them what was happening, hoping to hear joyful news. But what could people who were escaping in panic to save themselves say? Here and there a Jew would stutter something and draw back at once. There was great fear. Almost everyone would exaggerate, although they did not want to spread panic. There was no shortage of stories and exaggerations then. It was said that the French would send help and would march into Germany… English airplanes would arrive in Poland… The Poles have recaptured Danzig, and many other preposterous rumors…

Then two automobiles full of people arrived at the marketplace; a captain, women and children were in each automobile. They came from Jaroslaw; they would surely know something – it was said – and they began to be questioned. They had escaped with their military automobiles driving their families to eastern Poland, bringing them to a safe place where the war definitely would not reach; they were traveling to Tostobaby, a village in the Podhajce [Pidhaytsi] district, which was inhabited by real Polish peasants. After securing their families, they would return to the war.

There was heavy movement on the main street; it was impossible to go through. Civilians, military men – everyone traveled in the direction of Zalischyky in order to reach Romania.

Now it also was clear in Jezierna that the Germans would arrive there in about a day or two. People began to buy whatever they could in the shops: food, textile goods, leather, and merchants hid some goods in order to have things to sell later or even to trade, if it was necessary. The older people still remembered how things were with food during the First World War in Ukraine and with the *Petlurawices*. [followers of Symon Petlura, commander in the Ukrainian People's Republic, who carried out numerous pogroms against the Jews] The tax office received an order to pay each state official their salary six months in advance; the Jezierna officials traveled to Zborow to receive their money and wanting to make sure of its value, they immediately spent it all. In general, they did not think of the danger; they only wanted to take care of their needs against hunger and want…

That is what Jezierna looked like during the first week of the war. At that time, when there was panic in the western Polish cities and *shtetlech* [towns], offices were closed and it was difficult to get food, (whoever had not bought bread from the bakery at dawn, did not have anything to eat for the entire day), there was paradise in Jezierna: bread and food were in abundance; for money one could have whatever the heart desired.

Jezierna Under Soviet Rule (1939–1941)

On the 17th of September 1939 the Red Army marched into Jezierna; the town became part of the Soviet Ukraine. The Ukrainians went around full of joy, everyone in holiday clothing. With song and dance they welcomed the Red Army and pelted them with flowers. The Soviet's slogans were that they had come "to redeem" their Ukrainian brothers from the Polish yoke. Even Kuzmin, the former Polish senator, and other rich Ukrainians celebrated and prepared to take over power. However, they immediately cooled off a little; the Soviets openly said that was not the meaning of the quote… They came to "redeem the wretched," the poor peasants, and not the rich, the '*kulaks*' [rich farmers].

The Poles were again dejected particularly those who belonged to the government circles, to B.B. [*Bezbartijny Blok* – non–party block, Jozef Pilsudski's party], to *Strzelec* [paramilitary organization – Riflemen] and the " *Owszem* Poles" [those taking part in an economic boycott of Jewish businesses]. The Jews, they were disoriented: the fear of the Germans was so great that they welcomed the entry of the Red Army with joy. In addition to this, the anti–Semites in Poland everywhere would always shout at meetings that the Jews were communists and the communists were all Jews; if true, of what do they have to be afraid? Killing, as the Germans do, they will not do, and if they do not kill, they would get by.

By then, there already were a large number of Jews in Jezierna. Refugees from western Poland had come here, in addition to the residents. A week after the army's march through, a party secretary arrived and began to organize the administration and the community council. The new people in power in Jezierna were almost all Ukrainians, employees, workers, artisans and small farmers. The Ukrainians considered themselves to be like the ruling Nazis; they incited against the Poles as their former oppressors and here and there also against the Jews, that is, only against the rich Jews, the 'bourgeois'. This they could still do.

The estate was parceled out immediately. Here a Jew was still the owner, and [they also divided] the fields of the rich farmers, the '*kulaks*'. They simultaneously also parceled out the fields that belonged to Jews themselves, with the claim that the Jews did not personally cultivate them, but employed non–Jews to do so. And although in Jezierna, Jews did work their lands themselves, this did not help, and as they possessed many fields, they were considered as '*kulaks*'. They also liquidated the Jewish shops and thus the Jews completely lost their income. However, when they opened cooperatives for trade, craft and industry, the former owners of the small shops received work as sellers in the state factories; the artisans – in their co–operatives. The owners of the larger shops and wholesalers, that is, the 'speculators', could only go to more difficult physical work.

Jews who were workers, artisans, had a good social status (*satz–pakazshenya*) – they received responsible positions and state posts. On one hand, Jews obtained state posts, many of whom had not been able to obtain them in Poland. On the other hand, however, this eradicated private trade and also destroyed the livelihood of many Jews...

The change in the regime brought with it social and economic changes to the *shtetl*. The regime strengthened from week to week, from month to month and there was progress in the Sovietization. The regime began to carry out a 'cleansing'. Former political activists, judges, prosecutors, policemen, property owners and landholders (*pamyeshtshykes*) and also Polish colonists (they called them "enemies of the Ukrainian people") – were deported to Siberia; to the white bear [polar region of Russia], "*bili nidshzvidi*" [unnoticed – people picked up by the police and forgotten], as they called it.

Almost all of the deported were Poles and also among them a few Jews. A number of Jews in this category hid and remained in Jezierna. This deportation, and particularly the manner of deportation, created a frightful impression. Winter at night, in a deep frost, they were taken out of their beds, loaded onto wagons, taken to the train station in Zborow and there they were loaded into cattle cars; this was how they were taken to Siberia (it meant that they made the *shtetlech* clean. The counter–revolutionaries and enemies of the regime were taken away). They traveled this way for weeks under guard in these small wagons. Many of them died en route, particularly the old and weak.

Jezierna really was a small *shtetel*; however, in addition to the small shops here, there were also large merchants, a Jewish property owner, Jewish farmers, a mill owner and also an intelligentsia. Like Jews generally in Poland, they also did not receive any state posts or municipal positions there; they were a national minority that was treated differently than the other two ethnic groups. The Jews played a certain role economically and agriculturally despite the extermination policies on the part of the *Owszemnikes* [followers of the economic boycott] in both ethnic groups

The new regime changed the situation. All of the ethnic groups were officially equal, excluding the non–productive elements. Jews actually felt like equal citizens; some of them were endowed with responsible positions and government posts. They took part animatedly in cultural life. There were Jewish teachers in the schools, as well as directors and inspectors. A Jew could be found in almost all of the offices. This was only one side of the coin.

There was another picture, as I already have mentioned. The liquidation of the Jewish shops led to a situation in which Jews remained without income. In addition, the newly organized shops did not have any goods; there was a shortage of some products. They would stand in line for hours for bread and other articles; sugar, soap – in general, were difficult to obtain. The same with manufactured goods, leather, shoes and clothing. The formerly great merchants lived in fear. They sold clothing, shoes and household articles and bought food. Bartering spread. Former state officials and former rich merchants stood in the market and sold "*alte zachn*" [usually old clothes or household goods]. There was great fear of arrest and exile to Siberia. The regime gave the feeling that there was hope, that the war would quickly end and everything would return to the way it was (the merchant would again be a merchant, the official – an official, the owner, an owner and the artisan, an artisan). However, before the arrival of salvation – the German–Soviet war broke out.

The German–Soviet War

On the 22nd of June 1941, the news that the war between Hitler–Germany and the Soviet Union had broken out, fell on the Jews like thunder. The Ukrainians again walked around joyfully; they hoped that Hitler would create an independent Ukraine for them in eastern Galicia and with that bring about their dream of 1918.

A retreat, a stampede, a panic began. The civilian administration and their wives and children, the military – everyone ran. They wanted to be quickly 'on the other side'. This also had an influence on the Jews. From towns and villages, Jews in small numbers also fled with the Red Army. Only a few Jews from Jezierna escaped with the Soviets, the majority remained on the spot. Leave their families, their homes, the shtetl where their father lived and run – to where? It was not a simple problem.

* * *

The Germans entered Jezierna and the great tragedy began. We have no historical source; therefore, we make use of the testimony of the survivors. The era of extermination, the experiences, persecutions and martyrology of the Jezierna Jews we will describe only in short strokes; exact descriptions will be given in the memories of others, individual survivors.

The path of the *Einsatz–GrupnS.S.* [*Einsatzgruppen Schutzstaffel* – paramilitary death squads], beginning in Przemysl, was marked with Jewish blood and tears along the entire march route. Pogroms, the dead in the streets – that was the picture. And the neighbors, the other residents of the cities and *shtetlech*, the gentiles – in Jezierna too – watched the Jewish tragedy with pleasure.

Right after the 'prologue' – the first pogrom in Jezierna – the Germans began to organize the administration: a Ukrainian and Polish Aid Committee and a *Judenrat* [Jewish council]. The names show that the committee had one role and the *Judenrat* another. Cynics would call the *Judenrat* "*Judenfarrat*" [Jewish betrayal], as a symbol of the roll of the council members. There was a local *Judenrat* in Jezierna and a county *Judenrat* in Zborow.

The organization of the *Judenrat* was the same everywhere: 1) the Chairman was responsible for all of the Jews; 2) the head of Labor–Supply had to provide workers at every request by the regime; 3) Welfare and Social Aid; 4) the Procurement department had to provide things of value, gold, money, at the request of the rulers, that is, every German and *Volks–Deutsch* [ethnic Germans]; 5) Postal department – a postal branch for Jews; 6) Liaison – the only one who had contact with the Jewish camps; 7) Metrical department that managed the documentation of the Jewish population, supplied certificates of identity for those who perished and those who survived; thus, the rulers knew, at any given time, how many Jews were still alive. 8) food distribution; 9) *Ordnungsdienst* [ghetto police] – Jewish militia; 10) *Leichendienst – chevra kadisha* [burial society]. In addition to this, there were *eilboten* – couriers, a sanitary committee, J.S.S. – Jewish social self–help. The *lumpensammler*, that is, the rag collectors occupied a respected place; they were men of aristocratic birth; they had the right to move freely and go into the gentile area

The Jezierna *Judenrat* would receive instructions from the Zborow county *Judenrat* and in them it was emphasized that there must be order! There must be a hierarchy! At the organization of the *Judenrats* no one will say: "What concern for people! Hygiene, self help, protection, their own postal system, shops with food and even … a burial society!"

Jezierna was not an exception. All anti–Jewish decrees and laws were also applied here. Here too, every Jew had to wear an armband with a *Mogen–Dovid* [Jewish star], was compelled to do forced labor, was not permitted to travel by train, to walk on the sidewalk, to buy products from non–Jews, was not allowed to leave home from evening to sunrise. There was a threat of the death penalty for each transgression of the directives. The non–Jewish population was threatened with severe punishment, including the death penalty, for helping Jews and for having contact with them.

The *Judenrat* in Jezierna

When the Germans organized the *Judenrat*, no one knew what kind of role they had set for it. It was thought that it would be like the former *kehilla* [organized Jewish community]. Therefore, there were candidates, even members of the clergy who wanted to be on the *Judenrat*. A merchant became a speaker, the owner of a leather shop became a postmaster, a *shoychet* [ritual slaughterer] a policeman, a student a police commandant (also coachman) and so on.

The Chairman of the *Judenrat* was named Lander. Originally from Kozlow, he married a Jezierna woman, had owned a fabric shop. As he had been an Austrian corporal during the First World War, he was a most acceptable candidate. The Contact Man was Nunya Paket, also an acceptable candidate. The provisions expert was Nuske Paket. There also was a postal chief, a metrical [vital records] expert, a labor and deployment expert, a finance expert, a storeroom man and members with roles and without roles.

The role of the man in charge of the storeroom was to gather the clothing of the murdered, to sort them after an *aktzia* [action, usually a deportation] – the best was given to the Germans – and to transfer the worn out [clothing]

to the local administrative official to sell to the peasants. The *ordnungdienst* [Jewish ghetto police] with the former student Wechsler as commandant was the implementation organ of the *Judenrat*. They did not have any weapons but whips, with which they would 'encourage' the camp–Jews as well as the locals.

The *chevra kadisha* [burial society] and the *chevra nosay hamita* [society of pallbearers] had their hands full with work and particularly after every *aktzia*. The two who served on the *Judenrat* were: Judge Tseimer and engineer Steinberg. As I have already noted, the *Judenrat* was responsible to the regime for the deeds of every Jew, for every crime, transgressions against the edicts (buying bread from a peasant was considered a crime). It also was the only representative of the Jews before the rulers. They alone were in contact with the chairman or the contact man; any other Jew did not have access. The *Judenrat* had to supply jewelry, gold, diamonds, money, coffee, vouchers, expensive men's and women's furs for each request. This, the *Judenrat* extracted from the Jews.

Every demand was accompanied by a threat that if they did not provide a contribution in a timely manner, they would be shot. Except for certain individuals, the *Judenrat* council members in Jezierna as well as the *ordnungdienst* men participated in the *aktzias*, seizing Jews and deporting them to Belzec. The members of the *Judenrat* in Jezierna also considered themselves better than the other Jews, a sort of 'ruling class'. They had access to the chief of the camp; the chief knew them; they would meet with other Germans, which a simple Jew would not be able to do; they spoke to the rulers without fear. Other Jews would escape and hide from the chief or from other Germans. However, a Gestapo–man or S.S.–man would often enter the *Judenrat* office and demand something and they immediately shrank, quickly complying with the demand and, as a thank you, they often received a few blows; this would even happen to the Chairman.

The Hitler regime demoralized the people. A Jew who was known as a respectable person changed. A religious official could sacrifice his family just to remain alive himself... The strong desire to remain alive led a person to act inhumanly without regard for others.

The Methods of Liquidation

The liquidation methods were the same everywhere: forced labor, deportations, imprisonment and labor camps, murder and gassing in the gas chambers. According to statistics, approximately 20,000 Jews were annihilated in Jezierna. The murderers systematically liquidated the *shtetl*. Heavy physical labor – 12–14 hours daily without food – typhus and other serious illnesses decreased the number of Jews. When the Jews of Jezierna were expelled to Zborow in July 1942, there were only about 1,000 Jews. I will yet write about the methods.

I already have stressed that an order arrived to drive out the Jews, confine them in a ghetto to be able to liquidate them more quickly. The murderers hurried; they had no time. The *Judenrat* in Jezierna spread the news that Chief Diga would intervene so that the decree would be rescinded, but it would cost 100,000 *zlotes*. This amount was quickly brought. The gold was taken, but the Jews were driven out. Our family too paid 5,000 *zlotes*, which were lost. In addition to the Jews in the labor camp of which Diga was the chief, 50 men and 50 women remained in two separate camps. They had paid very well for this.

From that time on the fate of the Jezierna Jews was bound to the fate of the Zborow Jews.

The Jezierna Jews in Zborow

The Jezierna Jews were housed five to six families in a room in Zborow. That came to about two square meters per person. Illnesses broke out in such density; people fell like flies. In addition, there were *aktzias* and hard physical labor; this all led to the final liquidation. Diga liquidated the Jews in the camps and from the two separate camps in Jezierna a few months later. Thus, Jezierna became *Judenrein* [clean of Jews].

The Labor Camp in Jezierna

Forced labor was one of the means of exterminating the Jews. However, it was easier to accomplish with the Jews who were imprisoned in the camps. The conditions created in the camps led more quickly to their objective. Slaughtering of the camp inmates, the heavy punishments, beatings, hunger, being shot for every trifle, all of this quickly brought the liquidation of the camp Jews. The camp was large in scope: the Jews from Borszczow [Borschiv], Czortkow [Chortkiv], Zaleszczyk [Zalischyky], Jagielnica [Yahil'nytsya], Monasterzyska [Monastyrys'ka], Podhajce [Pidhaitsi] as well as from the Jezierna area would be brought here. There were thousands of refugees in the cities and *shtetlech* then. Jezierna was widely known.

The camp was a unit unto itself. It had security officers, a cook, a *Chevra Kadisha* [burial society], an attic and a cellar and a post for a gallows outside. Diga would place several people in the cellar, others in the attic and they died there. He would hang some on the post and he would place some outside during the winter, naked in the frost, until they froze. And if one had particular merit, he beat him with a whip until he died.

Two groups in Jezierna made use of Jewish workers: the street–building group, "*Organizacion Tod*" [death organization] and the railroad–building group, whose leader in Jezierna was Engineer Jankowski, a Pole.

Dozens of Jews would die each day doing physically difficult work in the street and with the railroad, almost without food. Every day local Jews, that is non–camp Jews, also would go to work along with the camp Jews. The distribution of this work was done by the *Judenrat*. Every worker had an *arbet–ausweis* [labor identity card], but there was a separate labor identity card for Jews.

Diga, the camp chief, had a good income; he would receive gifts, money from the *Judenrat*, ransom money from rich Jews, who found themselves in the camp. He would arrange sprees, drinking and orgies. He left the *shtetl* after the liquidation of the camps in Jezierna.

Aktzias

The Inquisition, the pogroms and pogromists are well–known in our history. The times changed; the murderers also changed and with them also the methods and the terminology. New words (terms, concepts) were created: "Final Solution of the Jewish Question", "*Aktzionen*" [deportations], "gas chambers". However, the results remained the same.

Typhus, cholera, all sorts of other illnesses, heavy physical labor – all of this gave the *chevra kadisha* a great deal to do. However, the statistics show that the liquidation took place slowly. Jews fell like flies, but there still were many Jews and the murderers would hold *aktzias* from time to time without explanation: grab Jews on the street and simply shoot them. But there must be order! Therefore, before each *aktzia*, the murderers would inform the county *Judenrat* in Zborow as to what kind of consignment they needed, that is, according to the plan, how many Jews they intended to shoot to death, with a pretext that they were taking only those who had become a burden to society – the sick, the old, those incapable of work and small children. Then, the chairman or a delegate from the regional *Judenrat* would go with them, giving official notice to the local *Judenrat*, demanding that the members of the *Judenrat* and the *ordnungdienst* help them. Everyone immediately went out to grab Jews. What happened further is known. When they reached their consignment, they left the *shtetl*. After the *aktzia*, the murderers told them to pay for the bullets they had used and also for the trouble they took during the *aktzia*. Whoever could, and had a place, would hide either in a bunker or with a welcoming gentile, if they wanted to take him in, or ran away to the forest or into a field. There he would wait out the slaughter, not always succeeding. Each unfortunate one who fell into their hands would be shot on the spot or taken to a collection point, lead to the cemetery, where a mass grave had been prepared, stood naked in a row, each one shot with a bullet in the back, given a kick on the backside and thrown into the pit, not looking if someone was still alive or not. Thus, they often threw into the grave people who still were alive.

At the first *aktzias*, they would carry out selections before the shooting: healthy Jews capable of working, artisans and those protected by the *Judenrat* were freed. There were no selections at the later *aktzias*. Everyone who came into their hands was murdered. Here in Jezierna as in other cities and *shtetlech*, during the executions, local women would gather at the cemetery to watch as the naked Jews were shot. As I have mentioned, the *chevra kadisha* would gather the dead in the streets, take them to the cemetery, bury them in a communal grave and then one of them would say *Kaddish* [prayer for the dead].

The warehouse–keeper of the *Judenrat* would fill the warehouse with the clothing of those murdered. When the murderers fulfilled their consignment, they would stop the *aktzia* and inform the central [office] by telegraph. There were places where the *Judenrat* had specific work. It had a complete list of candidates for each *aktzia*. This truly was precise work. I do not know if the Jezierna *Judenrat* was completely precise [in their work]. I think not. In addition to this form of *aktzia*, there was another form. Murderers would come to the shtetl and grab Jews according to a designated consignment with the help of the local Jewish organizations – There must be order! – and they were sent to Belzec to be annihilated in the gas chambers there. The Jews caught in Jezierna would be taken to Zborow by auto. There was a collection point there for those grabbed throughout the area. At the train station they were crowded into waiting freight cars and sent to Belzec. Many of the deportees died on the way. There also were those who jumped from the trains in the middle of the ride and were either killed by the guard who shot at them or murdered by the Ukrainians. Chaim Steiger jumped out of the vehicle on the way to Zborow and although the policemen shot at him, he successfully escaped and returned to Jezierna. A truly courageous act! However, he perished in a later *aktzia*.

The final liquidation included all of the remaining Jews, even those who were in the camps. There were places where the Jews carried out a resistance. There also was an attempt at resistance against the murderers in Jezierna during the liquidation of the men's camp. The murderers entered the camp and dragged the Jews from it. They were taken to the cemetery and shot there. No one said *Kaddish* for them. Jewish Jezierna ceased to exist.

* * *

In June–July 1944 Jezierna became an important strategic position, during the great advance of the Soviet Army and during the retreat of the defeated German Army. Difficult battles took place here; the civilian population was evacuated and many Jezierna Poles went to Berezan to the Polish Aid Committee and did not know that Klinger's son–in–law had confirmed that they were Poles who had been expelled from Jezierna. Th

Editor's Note: Menachem Duhl wrote the original article in Yiddish. It was translated into Hebrew, with some alterations, by the Jezierna poet Shlomo Shenhod. Both the Yiddish and Hebrew versions are printed in the book.

* *

(*Eichah*) [Book of Lamentations]

[1:11] All her people are sighing [as] they search for bread; they gave away their treasures for food to revive the soul.

[2:11] My eyes are spent with tears, my innards burn; my heart is poured out in grief over the destruction of the daughter of my people, while infants and sucklings faint in the streets of the city.

****

[Pages 213-225]

A Chapter on Jezierna's Destruction
by Dora Mantel–Lempert, Nes Ziona
Translated from Yiddish by Ida Selavan Schwarcz

The First Terror

It happened on June 30, 1941. War had broken out between the Soviet Union and Hitler's Germany. The Russian army was in retreat. A bomb fell and caused a fire to break out – the houses of Hirsch Katz and Mosche Bien were burned down. The peasants of the surrounding villages and a few of the local gentiles roamed around carrying sacks and had already begun robbing shops and here and there some of the vacated homes.

On the second day, July 1, 1941, the streets were deserted, the houses shut– no one was visible; they waited to see what would happen. The Poles and Ukrainians put holy saints' pictures in their windows so it was possible to determine which houses belonged to Jews… News passed from one to another – the Germans have reached Lemberg… they are already in Zloczow … Jews are being murdered, etc. Soon there were loud noises. Germans came roaring by on motorcycles. These were the S.S. with the swastikas and the skull and crossbones. Jews were petrified. Then orders were proclaimed in three languages, German, Polish, and Ukrainian. They threatened anyone who helped Jews in any way with punishment by death. Yanke Vasilkovski told me about this and I was soon convinced that this was indeed true. I read the placards. On July 2, 1941, between five and six o'clock in the evening, masses of gentiles assembled on Dluga and Zarodzia Streets and along the highway. The Gestapo and the SS were there and were screaming that the Jews were killing Ukrainians in Kozlow. Obviously this was a provocation against Jews.

On July 3, 1941, at six a.m., a rainy day, the SS began their work. They went two by two from house to house and dragged out Jews, beating them and driving them along to the *towlyka* near Kozowyk's, where a pit had already been dug. The Jews who had dug the pit were the first to be shot and thrown into it. Afterward they arranged the captive Jews in a row, shot them, and threw them into the pit. This went on all day long. My brother Yaakov was one of the murdered pit diggers.

On that day several hundred Jews were shot. They were not only Jezierna Jews but also refugees who fled here from western Poland. On that day they also burned down the Houses of Study. The people were thrown into the pits, without verifying that they were dead. Among those murdered were: pharmacist Mintz, teacher Henzel Steiger, Schimon Kurzrok and his two sons. When the pharmacist's wife saw that her husband had been shot, she took poison. When Kurzrok and his sons were shot, his wife had to dig their grave.

The SS left the shtetl on Sunday July 5. The soldiers left behind wrote a placard in Ukrainian that the *Aktzia* had ended. The Jews who were left alive could go back to work and nothing would happen. Then they gathered the corpses and gave them a Jewish burial in a mass grave in the Jewish cemetery. The rabbi and the remaining Jews said *kaddish*. There was almost no family which had not suffered a loss that time. Among those who stood in the row to be shot was my cousin Zysie Fuchs, the son of Sonia; a young man who looked like a gentile. The SS man looked at him and said,

"Run away! You are not a Jew!" That day he survived. Also my brother–in–law, Schmuel Offenberger ran away and remained among the living that day. However, he was murdered in 1943.

Here I must mention something I cannot and must not overlook: the Germans treated the Russian prisoners–of–war horribly. They led them, half naked, to be shot one by one. Before shooting them, they beat them up murderously. I cannot forget it even though we had our own troubles at that time. Jewish blood ran like water. Dead bodies lay around in the streets. Women and children wept and mourned. Nevertheless the horrible attitude towards the prisoners affected me very strongly.

I have already mentioned this but I shall add details. On July 6, 1943, (1941) the Jews who remained alive requested permission to bury their dead in the Jewish cemetery. We were only ten persons, men and women, and we began to dig up the dead bodies. We dug with our hands; we removed everyone separately from the hole. The ground was soaked in blood; the work took a few days. Among us was the future Chairman of the *Judenrat* Lander, also Schlomo Glass and Chaim Steiger. Women, men and children stood by and tried to identify their relatives, but it was very painful. Every corpse that was uncovered evoked cries and tears, especially when a member of one's family was recognized. That is how we disinterred the bodies and reburied them in the Jewish cemetery.

While this work was going on, two cars full of Germans drove by and they asked us what we were doing. Meanwhile they photographed us. Lander did not tell them the truth, but Batya Olexyncer, whose husband was among the victims, told them the whole truth. "These are Jews, innocent Jews whom the SS shot a few days ago." She screamed and cursed the murderers. The officers calmed her and said that they were soldiers and had nothing to do with this.

Judenrat, Forced Labor and Mass Murders

A few days later the Germans organized the Jezierna *Judenrat* [Jewish Council]. They appointed Lander as Chairman and Nunya Paket, son of Avrum'che Paket, as Liaison. Naski Paket, son of Yitzchak, Abraham Hochberg and others were appointed to the appropriations department. They organized the *Ordnungsdienst* [security police] from among the younger men. These two organizations carried out the orders of the Gestapo. They helped with the *Aktzias* and with catching Jews to be sent to Belzec.

The Germans began to repair the main highway. Since they needed laborers for this, they put the Jews to work. They worked very hard, from dawn to dusk, breaking rocks to pave the highway. Jews were also taken to work for the train. Labor supply was one of the functions of the Judenrat. They sent Jews every time there was a demand for workers.

Richard Dyga, an SS man, came to Jezierna in November, 1941. He organized two labor camps, one for men and one for women. The men's camp was in the "Polish House" (Kulako Rolnicze). The women's camp was in Abba Katz's house. Around the men's camp there was a tall barbed wire fence that stretched up to the Polish church. There was a narrow entrance. The women's camp was similar to this. The Judenrat was responsible for the setting up and coordination of the camps. The first Jews in the camps came from the camps of Lemberg, Strij, etc. They were force–marched on foot, in the rain and mud. They were hungry, barefoot, with rags tied around their swollen feet, dressed in torn clothing. On the day after their arrival they were forced to work. Whoever could not work was immediately shot to death. Every day after work, dead bodies were brought back, of people who had expired while working. Dyga himself shot those who were weak or exhausted.

The Jews of Jezierna were able to avoid working by giving money to Lander which he gave to his chief. We, Jezierna residents, supposedly went out with the camp Jews but we actually stayed at home. The camp Jews used to tell us how Dyga behaved towards the Jews, killing some daily as a joke. Every day we noticed that many Jews were not coming back – they were already in the world to come.

At the train station a group of Jews from Jezierna worked under the supervision of the former train manager, Margolies. The work was hard with a high quota, which the Jews were unable to fulfill. Every day Margolies was threatened with punishment, even execution. He was required to beat the Jews and make them work harder. Margolies declared that he would not beat Jews – so he was beaten. Not being able to bear any more, Margolies resigned from his position. The next day he was found dead in his apartment – he had taken poison. This happened in March, 1942. The situation worsened from day to day. Jews were captured, some shot immediately, others sent to the camps. Once when they demanded contributions, the Judenrat, according to request, collected gold, jewelry, diamonds, furs, leather, and more. Lander and another two men, clothed respectably, went to Tarnopol to deliver the goods to the Gestapo. The Gestapo took the goods, counted them and said it was not enough. They chased the men out and threw Lander down the stairs.

The Judenrat did everything possible to meet the demands of the rulers. I remember the big *Aktzia* of Elul 16, 1942. The SS dragged Jews out of their homes and out of the bunkers. The Judenrat and Security Police assisted them.

Jews were shot in the streets. That day about 150 Jews were shot and about 200 were captured and sent to Belzec death camp. The house of Mendel Fischer was the assembly place. The captured Jews were held until the evening, then loaded onto trucks and taken to Zborow. There they were transferred into cattle–cars, which had been prepared in advance. Around 10,000 Jews were transported at that time; there were Jews from Zborow, from Jezierna, Kozow, Kozlow, also from Tarnopol and other places. Monya Czaczkes told me about this. She herself was among the captives, but because she did not look Jewish she was freed.

That day I had been at work and when I came back in the evening I could not find anyone from my family. The Judenrat took over the vacant homes and gathered the abandoned furnishings into their storehouse. They said that they gave the valuables to the Gestapo and sold the household goods or bartered them for food for the Jews in the camps. Some workers, men, were locked in the camps that day. Very few Jews remained in their homes.

The Expulsion

In July 1943 there was an order to expel the Jews of Jezierna to Zborow. There were only 50 men and 50 women left in the camps. The women laundered the clothes of the camp–Jews and the men worked. The Judenrat took over our bakery which baked bread for the camp–Jews. Every person received 100 grams of bread twice a day.

I was in the Zborow ghetto for only one month. Then, by Lander's request, I was return to Jezierna to supervise the bakery. Aside from the official baking, Lander used to supply me with flour, and secretly, at night, I would bake bread for the Jews of Jezierna who remained in the two camps. This went on for a few weeks, then I transferred the secret bakery to the home of my neighbor Vasilkovski. There, too, we baked at night.

The winter of 1942–1943 was very difficult. A typhus epidemic broke out in the camps. People died every day. Dyga showed his cruel character. He would put the half–naked sick people out on the street where they froze to death. If someone still breathed, he would beat him. I also caught typhus. We halted the baking and Vasilkovski drove me out at night when I had a 40 degree fever. I started walking in the direction of Zborow. It was freezing cold. Tired and hungry I lay down and stayed there until morning. A wagon with neighborly gentiles came by and they put me in the wagon and drove me to Zborow. There I went into the ghetto. After a week my fever broke, but I was very weak. I was put into a house full of people; there was no room to lie down, so I sat up the entire night. In the morning the militia men forced me out to work. We had almost no food; no bread at all. Twice a day we received some soup. So we became weaker and weaker, especially me, since I had been sick.

There were rumors of a new *Aktzia*. Once in a while, as we were working, gentiles would walk by, and seeing our terrible condition, they would bring us some food, a few potatoes or barley – not for free, heaven forbid, but in exchange for clothing. We would take off our last piece of clothing in exchange for food. After work we would return to the ghetto almost naked. This situation lasted until February 1943. The dreaded *Aktzia* did indeed arrive and about 12,000 Jews were killed. These were the ones who had remained from Zborow, Jezierna, Kozlow, Pomorzany, Zalosce and other places. In a field behind Zborow, the Jews themselves dug several large pits where the captured Jews were brought and shot. A small number of Jews survived. They had good bunkers in the ghetto itself. By chance I was in the bunker with the families of the Judenrat and so I survived.

As I have already mentioned, only a few families remained in the ghetto. Every day they would go out to work and be very much aware of what was happening around them. Jews would walk around mourning their murdered wives and children. Henoch Czaczkes, Berisch Baron, and others, were broken men, emotionally and physically. We could see that the final liquidation was not far off. Even Fuchs, Head of the Judenrat in Zborow, said that whoever could escape should do so. But whoever would survive, had the holy obligation to tell about the horrifying events.

A group of about 15 men from Jezierna, including me, decided to run away. Some went into the forest. I decided to go back to Jezierna, to my neighbor, Vasilkovski. Snow was falling, some of it freezing, so it was easier for me to walk. I walked with my last bit of strength and with great fear. I wanted to get to Jezierna as quickly as possible. There were rumors that there was a big *Aktzia* in Tarnopol and thousands of Jews were sent to Belzec. Some of the Jews jumped out of the wagons and ran away. Therefore I was afraid that when they searched for them I would be discovered. About halfway there, near the road sign for Yarchovtse, I heard a rider approaching. I thought that was probably the Gestapo Commander Muller. He used to ride a horse. I soon saw him. I knew that he was a horrible murderer, and that he would immediately kill me. Not far from me there was a wayside cross and an icon of the 'Divine Mother'. I went up to the icon, knelt, and put my face on the ground. Muller came along, saw a woman kneeling at the cross, looked and continued on his way. After a while I continued on my way to Jezierna.

Dead tired, almost completely exhausted, I came to our town. I sneaked through fields and gardens until I came to Vasilkovski's property. Willingly or unwillingly she used to take me in. This time she would not allow me to come in, so I hid in her pig sty without her knowledge. Every morning I would come and ask her for something to eat, without telling her where I was hiding. I managed to last a few months. She used to tell me what was happening in the camps and in town and Dyga's dreadful deeds. The women in the camps were forbidden to take their children with them.

Adela Katz hid her three–year–old child there. Dyga found out, took the child, and killed her in front of her mother. Then he gave the mother the dead body and said, "Now take her!"   \

My brother Marcus, who was also in the camp, used to visit me every week. This lasted for about three weeks. He told me that conditions there grew worse every day. Any day now there would be an *Aktzia* and everyone in the camp would be killed.

The End

And that is what really happened. Friday, May 23, 1943, the murderers surrounded the camp. Dyga gave the order for everyone to leave, but Lander countermanded the order and said that no one should move. The Jews set up a barricade. Dyga and the militia threw hand grenades into the camp and they started a fire. The policemen started dragging the Jews out. There were Ukrainian policemen on both sides forming a narrow corridor, and they beat the Jews with the butts of their rifles as they were hauled through. Half dead and bleeding, the Jews were taken to the cemetery, beaten, and thrown into a pit. This is how the men's camp of Jezierna was liquidated. The women's camp was liquidated on the same day. The women were taken to the cemetery, shot, and their bodies were burned. Thus Jezierna became Judenrein [free of Jews]. Dyga completed his work and left Jezierna.

Reuvele, the son of Berisch Heliczer, and Lander's son, hid and then ran away to a gentile named Valashin. But they were informed on and shot. Rozie Paket, Pinchas' daughter, hid at the home of Honya Berestetsky. But someone informed on her and the Ukrainian police shot her. I saw this with my own eyes, because I was hiding in the park, only a few meters away. First I heard her cry out and then I heard a shot. Since I was hiding not far from there, scared to death, I did not believe that I would survive, but luckily they left. Also Hejnoch Feuerstein's wife hid in the home of a Ukrainian; she was also informed on, taken to the Gestapo in Zborow, and shot there. This was around August, 1943.

I continued hiding in the pig sty without the knowledge of Vasilkovski. I begged for food from the neighbors and so managed to keep on living. Mrs. Kalanovski was very helpful. She brought me food to the sty, some boiled potatoes, crackers ,etc. 'Good news bearers' told me that Hitler was on all the fronts, killing Jews, and if this continued I would also not survive. But my will was stubborn – I suffered and held out. At night I would sneak into the park, pull up some greens, and pick some fruit from the trees. It was easier during the summer, but fall and winter were bad. When the rains and snow and cold would plague me and I could not remain in the pig sty, I went over to the cowshed and spent the winter there.

In December 1943, the peasant who had been hiding Baschie Ajken and her children betrayed them. They were taken to Zborow, tortured and shot. When questioned, the peasant said that the woman had paid him to hide them. The peasant could have received a death sentence but he was only required to pay a fine. When Mrs. Vasilkovski heard that the peasant was only fined, she calmed down and decided to help me. She allowed me to stay with her, but not to go out, so no one would see me. No one came to search. In this way a few more Jews were hidden, but our lives were bitter and we led dogs' lives.

***

Meanwhile changes were taking place. The war situation had changed. The Germans were withdrawing and the Russians kept getting closer. This situation affected the population. They started regretting that they had not helped the Jews. Those who had helped, were pleased. One of these was the old lady Kalanovski. As I have mentioned, she used to bring me food, with no charge. She used to say, "I do this for you and for God." The Kalanovski family also hid a Jewish refugee. Later he married their daughter.

The war came nearer to us. The Germans were packing and getting ready to leave town. We started feeling more secure, occasionally going out of our hiding places. I met Rosa Blaustein (Lechowitz) and her daughter Dozia, with Pepi Scharer and her daughter Frieda. We stayed together. We were all in the Vasilkovski cellar when Jezierna was bombed. A few days later the Germans evacuated the civilian population. Everyone took a bundle and under guard, were taken to Zborow. I, with Rosa Blaustein and her daughter remained in Popielow. From there we returned to Jezierna, back to our hiding place in the Valikovski cellar. We hid there for almost two weeks. There were fierce battles around us. We were saved by a miracle. The Wehrmacht, which was approaching, had us taken to Zborow. It was springtime 1944. There we were quartered with the local population. They were supposed to feed us. I, Blaustein and her daughter, and a few more Jews from Jezierna, eight people in all, stayed with a peasant who did not give us up. Schmuel Scherer, who stayed in Jezierna with his former maid, was found in Zborow and shot, just a few weeks before the Germans left Zborow. When the peasant who was hiding us heard about Scherer, he became frightened. He gave each of us a big piece of bread and a flask of milk and told us to leave. I parted from the Blausteins with a heavy heart. I tore my shawl into two pieces and gave them half so they could keep warm at night because they had no warm clothing.

I went to Ponevezh. The way was very difficult; I walked through the fields fearfully. Night came. Since I was very tired, I went to a gentile home and asked to spend the night. The owner of the house immediately realized whom he was dealing with and told me to wait; he told his wife to guard me so that I would not run away. He soon came back with two German soldiers holding revolvers. He told them I was a partisan so they searched me and took me to their captain. He saw that I was not a partisan, so he gave me some food and a place to spend the night. In the morning, after breakfast, he sent me to the field hospital, two kilometers away. The doctor and director there was his friend. I was a given a job as an aide. The hospital was full of wounded German soldiers and there was much groaning and moaning. I was disguised as a Polish woman.

Once, when the attendants were not available, I gave the wounded soldiers water to drink. The doctor saw this and it pleased him and he praised me in front of all the workers in the hospital. He said that the Poles had better characters than the Ukrainians. One of my acquaintances from Jezierna, a Ukrainian woman named Suretska, heard him. Until then she had helped me and confirmed that I was Polish. But this incident angered her and she shouted at the doctor that I was not a pure Pole, but a 'Mischling' [mixed breed] – that my father was a Pole and my mother was Jewish. The doctor reproached her but sent me to Pomorzany, to another hospital, at Count Potocki's former castle.

Two weeks later the Germans evacuated the hospital. Not having a place to stay in Pomorzany, I moved on with the hospital, believing that I would be safer there than with the Ukrainians. And that is how I reached Vienna. There I was freed, given documents, and could move freely. Vienna was full of fugitive Ukrainian fascists, so I moved to Vienna Neustadt. There I got a job in a munitions factory. All the workers were divided according to nationality, wore nationality badges, and were housed in separate barracks. I wore a Polish badge and stayed in the Polish barracks under the name of Maria Kriskov.

I was in Austria from August, 1944 until May 1945, until the entrance of the Red Army. I did not feel safe with my Polish housemates. They were friendly but suspected that I might be Jewish. Sometimes in my sleep I would call out Yiddish words, maybe mentioning "*Aktzias*" or pursuits, but they did not reveal this to anyone.

***

The Soviet Union freed us and allowed us to go wherever we wished. I went to Italy with a group of Jews. There we were in the charge of the Joint. [Joint Distribution Committee]. I was in Italy for about three years and when Israel became an independent Jewish state I came here, to the Land.

***

During the hardest time of the liquidations, Lander, the (Judenrat) Head of Jezierna, and Fuchs, the (Judenrat) Head of Zborow, instructed a group of Jews, that if any of them survived, they should tell the later generations the terrible tale of the time, the merciless dealings of the Nazi murderers, so that the world would know! And now, twenty five years after these gruesome events, I am telling the story, and thus fulfilling in part the testament of our Martyrs.

Editor's Note: Dora Lempert wrote the original article in Yiddish. It was translated into Hebrew by the Jezierna poet Shlomo Shenhod. Both the Yiddish and Hebrew versions are printed in the book.

[Page 226]

From Krakow to Jezierna
(Two Years in Jezierna: October 1939 until July 1941)
by Sh. Ch., Hadera
Translated from Yiddish by Pamela Russ

The German–Polish war had broken out. Many Jews left the Polish western provinces and went east. The eastern cities and towns were rife with refugees. When the Red Army annexed eastern Galicia up to the San River, the refugees stayed in this area. However, soon the issuing of passports began. Every refugee received a passport with a special section, according to which they were sent out of the larger cities; they were only permitted to live in the smaller towns. Several hundred refugee families also settled in Jezierna. I myself first settled in Tarnopol, but when I was forced out of there, I moved to Jezierna, where a relative of mine, Yisroel Hoch, lived. It was difficult to get a place to live here in town. It was even harder to find work. A large number of refugees moved into the abandoned stores that stood empty, because private businesses were shut down. Dudye Paket gave me his store and it became a "home" for me and my wife.

Before the war I lived in Krakow, owned a beautifully furnished home and a dentist's office. I left it all behind and went to live in Jezierna, in a small, narrow store, in order to save my life. After the outbreak of the German–Russian war, the population of Jewish refugees in Jezierna increased. Their living conditions became worse and worse. There was organized help given, but how much could the Jezierna Jews help, as their own lives were not much better after their livelihoods were also terminated. The living conditions of the local Jews helped a little in this, since almost every Jew owned his own cow — so he had a little milk for himself and sometimes even a few liters to sell.

After the completion of the refugee exchange between the Russians and the Germans, Jewish refugees were also able to return to their homes on the German side. There were men who had abandoned their wives and children and ran away from there. And when their situation was no longer tenable and their wives wrote that the situation at home had normalized, that Jews were living and were even doing business, it attracted them back. Here, men were struggling without work, suffering from hunger and deprivation, the families were far away, no friends and no rescuers; and over there were their wives and children, and life continued, so they wrote. How can one not go and register to return home to the German side? So, some of them actually did just that.

And now their real tragedy began. The government suspected them of being spies, enemies of the regime who wanted to leave their "Garden of Eden" and return to the Fascists, into Hitler's hell. These refugees now found themselves in a bitter situation – being neither here nor there; who could have understood this? And still, the refugees hoped that the Soviets would send them home to their families.

One Friday night, the Soviet military visited them in their "homes," accompanied by Ukrainians, as if searching for weapons. They told them to pack their most important belongings, and then these men were taken away. Under guard, they were loaded into wagons, and taken to the Zborow train station. Here they were forced into cargo trains and sent to Siberia. Those who had not registered to leave were very happy.

But fate turned out very differently. Almost all of those who had been sent to Siberia actually survived, and of those who remained, almost all were killed by the Fascist murderers.   And when the war between Hitler's Germany and Soviet Russia broke out, we were the innocent victims. The time that I spent in Jezierna, the experiences there, have been strongly etched in my memory.

* * *

End of June 1941. The Soviet units retreated, the Germans were advancing, when the first German military units marched in and behind them the SS troops appeared. There was terror in the town. There was shooting heard late into the night. There was a real slaughter in the town. I will never forget this. Many Jews were shot that day. Among them were Dr. Litvak, the pharmacist Mintz, the manager of the estate Klinger. The SS went from house to house and snatched out Jews wherever they found them. It was said that they had a list. Also, the Ukrainians revealed where the Jews lived and how many there were, and even where the Jews were hiding.

A rumor circulated that in each city and town the Ukrainian priest and a few respected Ukrainians had signed an act that they demanded revenge be taken on the Jews. They would find a reason.

Seeing the terror in the city, my wife and I left our "home," and ran away to Yechezkel Hoch on Zabramska Street. We thought that the murderers would not come there because there were only a few Jews living there. But we made a mistake. On the second day, early in the morning, the shooting began again. The murderers ran from house to house snatching out Jews. They were shown where to go and where to search. The shooting came closer and closer to us. There were already murderers on Zabramska Street. I went out of the house and into the stable to hide. Soon the murderers went into Yechezkel Hoch's house, dragged him out, and shot him in the doorway. The murderers were already intending to retreat, when their Ukrainian companions told them that there was still a son of Yechezkel's living here and they thought it was Yisroel Hoch, so the murderers went back and demanded that the women give up Yisroel. Even though they demanded this with some shooting, they did not succeed. So they ransacked the house, but in fact they did not find him.

I hid in the stable for a few days and was afraid to leave because the neighbors would inform on me. For one whole day, Yechezkel lay dead outside in front of his house and they were terrified to bring him inside. When the murderers left Jezierna, all the dead were taken to the cemetery. It was only then that I left the stable.

A great sadness enveloped the town. Women cried over their murdered husbands and children, fathers and grandfathers. There were hardly any people seen in the streets. Whoever did venture into the streets, went furtively with great fear.

* * *

One day, an acquaintance came to us and informed us that the Ukrainians were looking for my wife, probably because they wanted to hand her over to the Germans because she had been a teacher in a Ukrainian school during the Soviet occupation. We did not know that there was the death sentence for this; so then we decided to leave Jezierna. But it wasn't that simple. Jews were forbidden to go from town to town, and forbidden to have contact with non–Jews. All of these things were punishable by death. We found a Polish peasant, paid him well, and he undertook to take us to Tarnopol. We left disguised as peasants and we reached Tarnopol successfully. Here we tried to find ways to escape and get back to Krakow. In this we were also successful. In the Krakow area we merited to survive the horrific times and then to be saved.

[Pages 230-253]

A Year in Jezierna and Four Months
in Zborow with the Germans
by Menachem Duhl
Translated From Yiddish by Tina Lunson

Until September 1939 I lived with my family in Tarnobrzeg, where I was a professor of mathematics in the state high school. The war drove us from there; we fled with a great stream of others also forced to flee, and arrived in Jezierna, where my parents-in-law lived. Two or three weeks after the arrival of the Red Army in the town we were transferred to Złoczów, where I continued working as a mathematician in the middle-schools until the outbreak of the German-Soviet war. This is where we encountered Hitler's murderers.

In Złoczów

With the outbreak of the war there was chaos in Złoczów. The Soviets arrested the Ukrainian nationalists and a number of Jews were included in that group. The Germans bombed Złoczów; the houses in the center of town burned, people left their apartments and hid in the cellars. I was not at home during the bombing, and started running toward my wife and child. Coals were falling all around, buildings were burning, and the fires kept spreading – and I kept running. While running near the home of Dr. Hrastnik, their maid told me that they were fleeing and that their house was burning. When I did not find my wife and child in our home, I ran on to search for them and finally found them in the cellar of a two-story building that belonged to a Ukrainian, Dr. Vania. About 30 people were hiding there, among them about 20 Jews. The Ukrainians were going around with happy expressions and we had a deep sadness in our hearts.

On the first of July 1941, at eight o'clock in the morning, two SS-men with automatic weapons and hand-grenades in their hands, entered our cellar. I was the first one who fell into their hands, but soon other Jews were standing with me. We were meant to be the first victims, the 'blood-offering' for the *fuhrer*. Suddenly there was a noise; the Germans thought that there were also Russians in the cellar, and they shouted "Get out Jews!" and ran off in the direction of the noise. That was my first encounter with the murderers and I had won. My wife and child, seeing me with my hands in the air, had begun to cry and wail and other children burst out crying. With wailing and tears our children received the Germans – that was a sign of the times that had begun for us.

The Germans had bombed with incendiary bombs and on the street lay the burnt bodies of soldiers and, as though they were normal folk, scorched people were also walking around. When I had heard the shout "Out" I quickly escaped and along with my neighbor, the dentist Messing, went into a toilet, waited a little while and from there went into a hiding place that I had prepared ahead of time.

The situation got worse; the SS-men started snatching Jews off the street, dragging them out of houses – the pogrom had begun. The Ukrainians spread rumors that the Jews were guilty of everything. In the courtyard of the prison, at the castle, the bodies of several hundred murdered Ukrainians were exhumed. These were the people arrested in the last few days, who had been killed. Among the exhumed were also a few murdered Jews who had also been arrested, but that did not make any difference – only the Jews were guilty.

The SS-men with their horrible faces, those murderers, those wild animals, armed with automatics and hand-grenades, went from house to house and took every Jew that fell into their hands to the collection point at the castle; there a pit was already prepared for them. Their captors shot them and threw them into the pit.

Some of the Ukrainian population helped them. Peasants came from the villages, and also town folks with sacks, even with a horse and wagon, to plunder the shops and the Jewish homes, taking anything they could. There were even some who beat Jews with shovels and crowbars, while shouting "This is for our murdered husbands and children!" They killed quite a few that way, with the shovels and crowbars. Dead bodies lay in the street, blood ran, the screams reached up to the heavens. There were new reports all the time, as from a battlefield... The two Rattner brothers, high school teachers, were killed with shovels; the teacher Lifschitz was beaten to death. Streams of blood ran in the streets. As I described before, those captured were taken to the castle and shot; without looking to see whether they were alive or dead they were thrown into the pit. People who lived not far from the castle heard groaning and wailing in the night. Those were the voices of those not shot to death, who were dying in the pit. It was also said that two of the supposedly dead crawled out of the pit at night, rolled themselves away, and finally…fled. After that rumor, two Ukrainian policemen were posted at the pit day and night, so that no more corpses could run away…

My family and I were still in hiding. Our neighbor, Fraulein Gelber, a convert with a big cross around her neck, stood the entire time at the front of the house and told every German who inquired that no Jews lived there. My faculty colleague, the aged Professor Servanski, sent in bread for us every day so that we would not starve. Our child got sick in the hiding place. It was there also that the sad news reached us that my father-in-law Wilhelm Klinger was killed during the first pogrom in Jezierna.

The First Week in Jezierna

In Jezierna, as in all the cities and towns, soon after the troops marched in the SS-murderers arrived and began their craft. Wild animals, horribly murderous faces, ran from house to house and each captured Jew was taken to the common grave near the Kozowyk's, shot and thrown into the pit. That day in Jezierna some 200 Jews were shot, locals and refugees. Among those shot were Klinger and the pharmacist Mintz. Two of those captured that day were saved: Marcus Marder and Lander. Marder appealed to the young murderer and said, "If you have a father and a mother, brothers or sisters, call them to mind and do not kill a father of children." The murderer looked at him and said, "Get out of here you damned Jew", and indeed Marder slowly walked away. Lander also showed the murderer a document and a photograph to prove that during the First World War he was an Austrian officer, and he was allowed to go free. But Hitler's decree was not recalled, they were both killed later.

The murderers determined a horrible death for the community activist Dr. Litvak. They cut open his belly, pulled out his intestines, cut pieces off while his was alive until he breathed his last; then they shouted, "You damned Jew, you communist, you are to blame for the war!"

I have already mentioned the pharmacist Mintz. He, that tall old man with an aristocratic appearance, was in his pharmacy standing at the table in his white coat with a red cross on the arm and preparing prescriptions for sick people. Two murderers came in and took him out of the pharmacy, took him to the pit, shot him in the back, gave him a kick in the rear and threw him into the pit where the dead bodies of Klinger, Falk and others already lay. His wife followed him. When she saw that they had already shot him and that even the red cross had not helped him, she quickly ran home, swallowed a dose of poison and with the words "There is no God", died. Soon neighbors came into the house where she lay dead on the sofa and dragged the sofa out from under her, pulled the jewelry from her fingers and ears, took a watch from her arm and left. The poet Schmuel Yaakov Imber, Mintz' son-in-law, and his wife hid and were saved this time.

When my mother-in-law let us know that father-in-law had been killed, she sent us a wagon and we left Złoczów. Among the huge military transports that were traveling in the direction of Złoczów-Jezierna we were the only civilians. We heard how the Germans spoke among themselves, that these must be Jews traveling, but no one bothered us. In Jezierna we lived on the estate. I have already written about the *Judenrat*. It was the only agency that represented the Jews to the authorities. Through its organs it controlled the whole life of the Jews in town, even checking correspondence. The group that enabled this control was the *Ordnungsdienst,* their armed hands without weapons. Before each *aktzia*, the murderers who were to carry out the roundup and deportation of the Jews under the command of Gestapo Chief Miller, who was accompanied by a member of the provincial *Judenrat* in Zborow, announced their demands to the *Judenrat;* that is to say, how many victims they needed. That would take a few minutes, and with the help of the two Jewish institutions (*Judenrat* and *Ordnungsdienst*) the work would begin – snatching Jews and shooting them. After the *aktzia*, when they had obtained their quota, the *Judenrat* paid them for their trouble, gave them gifts, paid for the bullets fired and they left the town, satisfied. The number of Jews in the shtetl shrank. They would conduct those 'actions' from time to time and the number of Jews in Jezierna became smaller and smaller.

Contact with my Brother in the Pluhow Camp

In the spring of 1942 I received a letter through the *Judenrat* from my brother who was in the camp in Pluhow. Then the rumor spread that the Karaite's brother was in a work-camp in Pluhow; in Jezierna I was known as the Karaite.

My brother was an attorney in Czortkow, a community activist, chairman of the Revisionist Organization, taking part in the local and national conferences. In 1942 he had lived with his family in Stanislaw, in the Jewish quarter. There the Gestapo killed his wife and two children at the Rudolf Mill. He alone escaped and was caught along the road to Podhoretz, was brutally beaten and taken to the Jews' camp on Janowska Street in Lemberg. Here he was beaten again and when he fainted, they revived him and beat him more. They kept him there for two weeks then sent him to the work camp in Pluhow in terrible condition – with wounds oozing pus, unrecognizable as a human being.

In the Pluhow camp there was a secret organization under the leadership of the Revisionists; they knew him and protected him. But soon he came down with typhus, with a high fever, and in the heat of it cried out "Rozie, Rysiek,

Neutka (the names of his wife and children), where are you?" It seemed to him that they were calling for help. He could not reconcile to their fate. After that crisis with the illness he was very weak and could not go out to work. The friends protected him, and finally he obtained a task in the camp – he became a night-watchman.

He sent a message to Dr. Ritterman in Stanislaw, asking about the fate of his family and did not receive any reply. Now he was turning to me, so that I could ask Dr. Ritterman. I did so and received the sad news that the Gestapo had killed them. We corresponded for a while from Jezierna and also from Zborow. I wanted to draw him into my plans, but he did not come. The situation worsened; we could not wait; we left Zborow and disconnected all contacts; our illegal life on false papers did not allow for maintaining contact. In one of his letters he wrote that Petra Vandzura, a former school friend from Borszczow who lived in Stanislaw, had denounced them. He even asked that I remember it.

(After the war the number of saved Jews was small and the number of criminals large. The judges in the courts demanded witnesses and from where could I have known names? Those who could have given testimony were no longer alive. So a former friend, a fellow townsman, a denouncer, who delivered three Jewish souls into the hands of the Gestapo, he was able to walk around free.)

Aktzias in Jezierna

As I have already indicated, a great army with artillery, tanks and trucks marched through Jezierna. The roadway was destroyed, full of holes and it had to be repaired quickly; for that they needed a large number of workers. Also, the railway needed workers to build a second line – Jews had to do all of this work. They were a great unpaid labor force. The Germans established labor-camps for Jews along the whole length of the Zloczow-Skalat road, in the towns of Pluhow, Zborow, Jezierna, Borki Wielke. Each camp had a camp chief – a Gestapo officer – and his helpers were Ukrainian policemen.

The camp in Jezierna was in "*Dom Polski*". They fenced it around with barbed wire two meters high. This was intentional, because the Polish and Ukrainian churches were nearby. When the non-Jewish population went to church on Sunday, they could look upon the tattered, miserable, filthy Jews, now hardly comparable to living human beings, and take joy from it.

The first chief was Muller, the second Minkos, and the third, until liquidation of the Jews, was Richard Dyga. He was from Bytom, in Upper Silesia; he had been an overseer in a coal mine, and was a *Wasserpolak* [pre-war German resident of Polish descent]*,* who spoke good Polish. His family lived at number 2 Palatgasse. His wife visited him often and took home gifts that the Jews had given to their 'good Chief Dyga' as an expression of their gratitude. They were expensive gifts: the finest fabrics, leather, gold watches of the best brands, rings set with cut stones and diamonds, expensive ladies' coats, and the like.

The camp was opened in November 1941 and the first Jews in the camp were in fact from Jezierna, but almost all refugees. Next they brought in other Jews from camps and later finalized the area of the whole enclosure. There were Jews from Kozlow, Kozova, Borszczów, Chertkov, Monasterzyska, Podhoretz, Zaleszczyki, Tłuste, Jagielnica, Kopycznce. Thanks to the camp, Jezierna became famous… The living conditions in the camp, the hard work with hardly any food, quickly liquidated the camp Jews; the forced roundups and shipment to the extermination camps quickly liquidated any Jews who lived outside the camp. Dyga went around with his whip and struck Jews left and right, for no reason, more than once beating them to death.

Dr. Liebling writes in his book that in the Jezierna camp about 20,000 Jews were killed. Dyga was a typical murderer; he would beat and shoot Jews with a grimness, with a special satisfaction. I present a few facts:

In the center of town, in a lovely little house, lived the family of Mosche Heliczer, a respected family, wealthy people. The house fell to Dyga and he had it decorated for himself. He allowed the Heliczer family to live in the kitchen on the condition that his cook could cook there. His Gestapo fellows always came over, and wild parties often took place there, drunkenness, shouting, and more than once – wanting to give his guests an attraction to make them happy – he paraded out a Jew who had been held for hours, terrified by shooting, and his guests had a good laugh. Several times he called Mrs. Heliczer in the middle of the night, stood her against the wall and shot 10 or 20 centimeters over her head, threatening her with death. This spectacle went on for 2 or 3 hours. Then he released her, saying, "Go, you lousy Jew." Shocked almost to death, drained, trembling after such a scenario, she turned back to the kitchen.

When Dyga left his house with his whip all the Jews trembled, each letting others know and warning them. Whoever fell into his hands got a beating and more than once he confined them in the camp for a few days. When Dyga encountered a group of camp Jews who had been sent to the delousing shed – Jews who were weak, worn out, sick, shadows rather than people, who were dragging their feet, he would shout "Quickly, lousy-Jews!" and began hitting them until someone fell dead. The dead one was left lying where he fell and the group shuffled on. In   the winter, when there was a big freeze, Dyga would stand some naked camp Jews outside until they froze.

A book could be written with an endless range of Dyga's prosecutable murderous acts, but I will share just a few representative facts:

About 200 Jews went out of the camp under guard every day to work on the highway; about the same number went out to do rail-line work. The sick and those incapable of work, Dyga shot. Only he had been given the right from the *fuhrer* to shoot Jews – it was really a great honor!

Once, when my wife was passing near the camp at night during that time, when the workers were returning from their labor, she heard a voice: "Mrs. Hanya don't you recognize me? I am Magistrate Teiber from Tarnopol. See what the murderer Dyga has made of me. He has starved me, beaten me, sent me to work without food."

It was he, Magistrate Teiber from Tarnopol, but unrecognizable: hunched over, swollen, his feet wrapped in rags, barely able to stand on them. Dyga had him confined to the attic without food or water; he shouted, banged on the door of the attic and it did not help. The murderer kept him like that until he expired. Dyga ordered that his body be dragged out of the attic and given to the *Judenrat* to bury in the Jewish cemetery. Thus was murdered a good jurist, a father of children. Dyga drank a toast to the occasion and struck another name from the list of camp Jews. Order must be maintained!

From a shtetl near Czortkow they brought a group of Jews, among them a '*hekht*' [slang for 'big fish']. Dyga was happy, and the Chairman and liaison personnel from the *Judenrat* were also full of joy: they would get a large sum of ransom money for him, it was said as much as 20,000 *zlotys*. Dyga maintained that was not enough, that 'the fish' was worth more. They did not send him to work, they handled him like a fragile egg. But suddenly – oy vey! – the bird had flown the coop! They had believed him; he only slept in the camp, and spent all day sitting in the *Judenrat* chancellery; he ate in private, and this is how he pulled off the stunt, he just left! Incensed with anger, Dyga came into the camp and called together everyone who had any function in the camp and the *Judenrat* complex. He chose twelve youths 18 to 20 years old from the camp and ordered them strung up with their heads down and their feet in the air. One of the *Judenrat* members, who related this, wept. "It was a horrible execution," he said. Twelve young souls perished under horrible conditions, and Dyga stood there enjoying it and shouting, "So there, Jews!"

The Jewish doctor, Tenenbaum, an outstanding person in the town, was Dyga's house doctor. More than once he called him up in the middle of the night, and he sat with him all night. But when the liquidation of the camp began, Dyga before all else, shot Tenenbaum's daughter, and when Tenenbaum reacted to it Dyga shot him too. In fact Dyga was greatly in his debt, since he had saved him many times.

This very same murderer Dyga, who with such satisfaction shot and beat Jews, was a good and loyal father to his own family. In order to keep them secure, he had assembled a lot of possessions. He had to be concerned that he would have what to live on if Hitler lost the war. He received a weekly delivery from the *Judenrat*; wealthy Jews, who found themselves in the camp, gave him large sums of money to redeem themselves. Every two weeks he requested from the *Judenrat*, according to a list, gold-jewelry, diamonds, expensive textiles and other valuable things. He shipped all this to his family in Bytom. From time to time, when his wife Magda and their daughter Jaga came to Jezierna to visit, everything went off on wheels. Dyga. the good man and father, used to organize a nice week-end vacation for them. The *Judenrat* bought him a pair of handsome horses and a small open carriage on rubber wheels, and every day they drove out of town for an outing, and their coachman was none other than the honorable and respected commander of the Jewish police, the university student Weksler. He had merited being the driver for Mrs. Magda Dyga! Magda would come with empty cases and travel home packed full of gifts from the grateful Jezierna Jews.

Dyga made friends with the former mayor, the dentist Kowalski. He used to tell his friend what he did with the "*zydkes* in the camp", how he tortured them. Once he arrived at Kowalski's and reported with glee, "The *zydkes* will have a good lunch today, I found them a dead horse."

The director of the firm that was building the rail line was a Pole, a certain engineer Yankowski. Once I went to him, presenting myself as the former professor at the vocational school, and asked for work. His response was brief: for Jews I have only physical labor laying the railway. Yankowski and his family lived near the train station in Kastner's house. His wife went in to town to buy goods, accompanied by two Jews who carried her baskets; one of them was Kastner himself.

The assistant director at the firm was Kazimierz Argasinski. When the firm furnished its offices in November 1941, Argasinski went around the Jewish residences and requisitioned furniture. He came to us, too. With his whip in his hand he looked like a Gestapo man. He requisitioned a few things from us, tables, benches and armchairs. When my wife asked what right he had to do this, he answered, "Sit still, Jews, we will throw you out of this house too."

The furniture requisitioned from us was designated for engineer Yankowski's own office. A month later Argasinski stopped me, not far from the estate and asked me where my Jewish armband was. Argasinski used to beat and kill Jews. I saw such an incident myself: it was on the plaza near the train station, where he beat and killed an old Jew, a refugee from Tomaszow Lubelski. The reason – a day earlier he had missed work. Another time he had ordered an old Jew to climb up in a willow tree and tear off some branches; and when the Jew told him that he was old and could not do it, he beat him bloody.

The Last Weeks in Jezierna and the Expulsion

Conditions went from bad to worse and I saw that there were certain documents necessary for me to show at any time without fear and terror; no longer would I be able to move around so freely. That feeling in me was bolstered by my above-mentioned encounter with Argasinski. I soon found an opportunity. The Germans had a grain storehouse near the train station. The construction work had been carried out by the firm Suka-Silo-Construction. I did forced-labor for them. My boss was a German master craftsman who was not very intelligent. Once a week an engineer came to inspect the work. My chief had a seal and had a permit to travel every week to Tarnopol to collect provisions for the workers – but no one ever received any. He ate some of them and sold the rest. The *Judenrat* had assigned Chana Katz as his cook and he would say, "That Chana is a good cook".

One fine day he shouted an order at me, "You, Jew-pig deceiver! Thief... You stole my seal!" It was no help that he threatened to turn me over to the Gestapo. Without the seal he could not receive the provisions.

In sadness I walked around and could not even tell my wife what had happened. I could not get a new seal in Jezierna. I could not travel to Tarnopol – and the chief was threatening. While standing so worried, I hardly heard someone calling me: "Herr Professor!" It was the ticket seller calling me. He was a Pole who often gave me the news from the English radio and from the secret Polish radio station. He saw that I was depressed, asked what the reason was, and I told him the whole story and the danger I was in. He told me that just three kilometers from Jezierna, in a village, there was a peasant who could make seals and he sent me to him. The peasant made the seal for me. Two days later I gave the chief the new seal along with a gift to beg forgiveness. He accepted the reconciliation and I was out of danger.

That incident suggested the idea that the peasant could make me a round seal from a Karaite birth registry, and with that I could make a Karaite birth certificate. Among the gentiles in Jezierna it had been rumored for a long time that I was a Karaite. They did not even know what it meant, they said "Ukra-aimer". The communal secretary Petrischen even said that he thought exactly as they said, that Klinger's son-in-law was not a Jew, although our wedding was performed in Jezierna and the canopy ceremony and blessing was performed by the Jezierna Rabbi. I gave the peasant the form and the text for the seal; he brought the seal to me in three days; I paid him 25 zlotys. It was hard for me to check the text of the certificate, but I took my own advice. The only person to whom I could show the certificate was Markus Marder. He was an expert in certificates, and I wanted to hear his opinion. He held the opinion that it was in order, and that encouraged me. It was July1942. A decree arrived, stating that the Jews of Jezierna would be 'transported' to Zborow. The last date for evacuation was the 15th of July, 1942. Until that date people were allowed to travel alone or in groups.

In Jezierna Dyga laid out two camps – a men's camp and a women's camp, with 50 people in each. He himself selected the people, of course, and each one paid a large sum of money. It was said that he received 5,000 zlotys from each one. It was said, as everywhere, a tale, that the *fuhrer* himself did not want to kill all the Jews; a certain number, the best of them, he would keep alive. They, these 100 people, would be among the lucky ones, who must go on living (perhaps as the nucleus, so that the Jewish people would not vanish).

Our family was cursed. The *Judenrat* tried another trick: a rumor was spread that for 100,000 zlotys the chief Dyga would repeal the decree. The *Judenrat* certainly did collect money – unfortunate, naive Jews gave; we also gave 5,000 zlotys – how could one not give when everyone was giving, for calling off such a terrible decree? The money was taken, and the Jews were driven out.

Before we left Jezierna I prepared my documents. I needed original and current papers. The communal secretary Petrischin – who himself thought that at my wedding it was acknowledged that I was an "Ukra-aimer" – gave me a paper, written in German, in which he established that I was a Karaite. The statement carried the date of April 8, 1942, sealed with a big seal with Ukrainian text: "Ukrainian Revolutionary Committee Jezierna". In the center was a '*trizov*', the emblem of the Ukrainian 'Republic' from the year 1918, when eastern Galicia was a '*Samasteyne Ukrainia*'[province]. The Ukrainians used the seal from 1941 to 1944 for internal relations as a vestige of those times and as a symbol of their ambitions for the future. He also gave me two blank forms with a round seal and a swastika with the German text 'Collective Community Jezierna, Galicia District'. On one of the forms I attached my photograph and using a typewriter, I wrote an identification permit for myself and on the second form made one for my wife. It looked like an authentic document, although one given out by the town office. Eventually I had three new documents. After living under the Nazis for a year in Jezierna, we left the town.

Facts about Surviving in Jezierna

It is difficult to describe everything that we experienced. I will simply provide a few fragments:

It was August, 1941. I was chopping wood in the yard when I suddenly heard the steps of soldiers and voices speaking in German; they were Germans. The terror was great then, a few weeks after the slaughter. I went into the house and they followed me. Seeing that it was narrow, I went out through a window. They went into the building. At first they did not realize that they were in a Jewish home, but once they were oriented to where they were, they asked about the Jew who had been chopping wood outside. They continued through the whole building, searching for *shnapps* and creating havoc. One of them, a sergeant, put his revolver to my wife's head, threatening that he would shoot if she would not give up the Jew who had been in the yard. My father-in-law had also fled and only my wife and our child remained. The child was crying and they were shouting and threatening. They searched every corner. They found a bottle of 'batishe-visky' [home-brewed] liquor and they drank it and continued to shout and threaten. It was simply hell. That went on for about two hours. In the meantime, I ran to the regional commander and came back with a junior officer by the name of Heinz Lege. The junior officer requested that they leave the dwelling, and soon they did actually leave.

My wife remained standing, half dead, with the child in her arms. Lege directed the two sergeants out and came back alone to calm us down. He commiserated with us and regretted our fate. He sat with us for almost three hours, to protect us in case they tried to return. He visited us almost every day, ate with us sometimes and protected us.

When the troublemakers showed the sergeant the Omega watch which was left to me by my blessed father-in-law, he took it, laid out two *marks* and said, "Here is money for the watch. We Germans don't take things without paying." (I will write separately about the history of the watch.)

A week later I told Lege that they had taken the watch. He was very upset but could not help because the sergeant was on leave. A few days later Lege came to us as usual. During dinner he took out the watch, placed it on the table and related that by chance the sergeant had come back, he had forgotten something, and Lege used the chance to take the watch back.

Years have flown by; terrible events have altered the world map; we changed our residence several times, and more than once I have thought about Lege – whether he was alive, or had he been dragged down by the war. In December 1959, when we were already in Israel, I wrote to him even without an exact address. I remembered just one thing, that he was from Hamel, on the Vezer, and I wrote to him there. He received my letter and we began a correspondence. He wrote a lot, mentioning those terrible times, and he sent me his photograph. I have included the story of those two Germans as well as fragments of our correspondence in an article, *"The Fate of Watches and a Photograph"*.[Yizkor Book P.293]

In the first stage of the Soviet-German war, many Soviet prisoners fell into the hands of the Germans. At the end of November 1941 they brought about 500 Russian prisoners to Jezierna, as workers for the rail line. They were quartered in the estate, not far from our residence. Every day, when I went out to the well to get water, I encountered them – tattered, withdrawn, half naked, exhausted, their feet wrapped in rags. They also came to the well for water. They asked for a little salt. They worked very hard. Their keepers, the SS, beat them to the death for no reason, and shot them without mercy. More than once I heard them pleading, "Mr. German, have mercy, I have a wife and children, I want to live!" The SS-man would scream, "Swine!" and shoot him. One could also see that among the prisoners themselves, who came from various lands within the 'Red Union' – Russians, Ukrainians, Georgians, Tatars, Mongolians and so on there was no harmony or brotherhood. Every day they brought 10 or 15 bodies of shooting victims, lay them out in the yard, telephoned the chief of the camp to send a couple of Jews. He would send two or three Jews to dig a hole for the shooting victims. Afterward they would shoot the Jews too and throw them into the same hole. And so every day you could find in a common grave Russians, Ukrainians, Tatars, Georgians, soldiers of the 'Red Union', and two or three Jews – a real fraternity! They covered their common grave with fresh earth. The same thing was repeated every day. After a month only about 30 remained of the 500, and they were transferred to another camp.

Our neighbor was the Falk family, a mother and daughter; Falk himself had been among the first victims. From time to time I would visit them, and almost always I would encounter SS-men there, who were guards for the prisoners; I heard the names "Franz", "Willi", and I memorized the physiognomy of the Germans and their names. This came to be useful for me.

It was December 1941, the snow continued to fall, piled more than a meter high. Our home was almost completely covered and contact with the neighbors was almost cut off. In the middle of the night we heard a loud banging on the window: we heard "Open up!" in a German voice. Torn from sleep, we opened the door, full of fear. Two SS-men from the guard, wrapped in fur coats, came in. "Jews live here!", they began to declaim; "Jewish criminals! You are responsible for the war!" I recognized one of them – it was Franz, one of the regular visitors of the Falk family. I called to him, "Mr. Franz! What do you need?" Franz said to his partner, "These people know me," and they both quickly introduced themselves. Franz said, "I am Franz and this is my colleague Krulikowski. We are SS officers, the *furher's* elite!" and then they began the well-known song again: "Jews!" they shouted and threatened. But suddenly Krulikowski saw the photograph of my God-fearing father-in-law, in the uniform of an Austrian officer with many medals on his chest. He studied the photograph for a while and then asked who it was. We explained that it was Hania's father, just after the First World War, 1914 – 1918. He had fought against Russia and Italy along with the Germans, was commended and then was murdered by the SS upon their invasion. Krulikowski became sad, stood in salute before the photograph, apologized to the photograph in the name of the *furher* for the fact that he had been murdered, lowered his hand, and continued to shout, "But you are Jews…!" and the rest of the repertoire. Franz wanted to calm him, and took a flask of whiskey from his pocket. They both began to drink. After each glass Krulikowski saluted, turned to the photograph and offered his respect, then ranted on at us again. He repeated the scene after each glass, until four o'clock in the morning.

Who knows what would have happened if I had not kept appealing to our acquaintance with Franz and he had not tried to quiet Krulikowski. The night was horrible, with snow all around, cut off from our neighbors and from people in general, trapped in the house with two drunken SS-men who threatened to shoot us every few minutes.

It was about that same time that thieves (it was probably neighbors) stole our whole supply of flour, plus the grain, and we had to begin buying bread from the *Judenrat*. The *apparatchik-aide* N.P. said that we were not on his list, and so he could not sell us any bread (200 grams a day for the whole family – 5 people). My wife went every day, literally in tears, to beg him for the 200 grams of bread.

From time to time the Germans organized *aktzias*. In the beginning, the local *Judenrat* concerned itself with the small villages around the town, first reducing the number of Jews there. They determined who would be in a contingent. Ranked first were the ill, the old, those unfit for work and the children. During the forced roundups they also killed people in the street. The streets ran with blood. Younger people were loaded onto trucks to be 'resettled' – what they called the shipping of Jews to the extermination camps. There was no limit to their cynicism. When one of the murderers saw how a daughter, whose mother was being transported, gave her a package for the journey and wept, he told her "Give her gold things and diamonds, they will be useful there", knowing well that the captured Jews were going to an extermination camp. He spitefully mocked the daughter. Naive people did believe this, and gave them valuables, all of which the murderers stole from them along the way.

These constant roundups of Jews, transporting them to extermination camps, opened the Jews' eyes. They began to understand clearly that the 'solution to the Jewish problem' meant complete liquidation. Indeed a few looked for ways to save themselves and their families. Some forged Aryan papers and set off along the roads, but almost none of them survived. Others joined up with 'trustworthy' gentiles who were supposed to provide them with safe hiding places. But many of them fell victim to denouncements, or perished from hunger in hiding because the 'reliable' gentile had not given them any food in the hiding place. The apparatchik-representative of the *Judenrat*, N.P., who doled out 200 grams of bread per family to the unfortunates, himself died of hunger along with his family. The 'reliable' gentile took his money but did not give them any food in the bunker.

The situation this created, the conditions, the striving to save oneself even at the expense of other unfortunates, demoralized and broke down the characters of people who had previously been known as upstanding, solid citizens, good Jews, community workers. They believed that possessions would save them; that drove them to immoral deeds. A rich Jew, a respected man, often called upon to read Torah, formerly a *Gemeide-Ratnik* [city-council member] and *Kultus-Ratnik* [cultural committee member], and now a '*JudenRatnik*' [*Judenrat* member] – saw a woman lying dead in the street during an aktzia, and took her jewelry from her and hid it. Later the dead woman's brother learned about this and demanded his sister's jewelry from him. The respectable Jew first denied it and then gave up the jewelry at the Rabbi's; and 'it was said' that he had only turned in a part of it.

As I already wrote, we were 'resettled' in Zborow. This was a difficult experience for us and especially for my mother-in-law, may she rest in peace. She had lived in Jezierna for more than 20 years, every corner of it held its history for her, everything was dear to her, she remembered the effort it had taken to absorb it all, and now she had to leave it all.

The last days were unbearable. Women with their families, as if in a procession, would walk from house to house, look around the home, view the furniture, evaluating their inheritances. Each of them had already decided where they would live and what they could take. We were standing there and our hearts were breaking; we almost wept. Our sorrow was great and our pain unbearable. There were moments when we paradoxically said that the living were envious of the dead, who had not lived to see this.

Life in Zborow

We were in Zborow until November 20, 1942, until the Jews were confined in the ghetto. We left Zborow before dawn. A deep snow had fallen, and we traveled in a sleigh. We traveled without knowing to where – to martyrdom in

God's name. Our wish was only to run away from there as fast as possible, not to let ourselves be enclosed in the ghetto. It was a dangerous undertaking. Traveling in those times, not knowing where to or to whom, was a suicidal plan. But we were convinced at the time that we were saving ourselves from death.   They had driven the rest of the Jews from the villages together in Zborow, organized them in a ghetto and planned ways to liquidate them quickly. No *aktzias* took place during that time. I had used that time to procure my own papers and also to get some documents for my wife and child. I knew that we had to have 'good' papers now, for if not, we would very quickly fall into the hands of denouncers and '*shmaltzniks'*. We knew that many had been caught with false Aryan papers but no one knew where they had been taken and killed.

The surviving widow of Dr. Litvak and her son Lesia had settled in Lemberg [Lvov]. She was caught and shot and the son was beaten to death on the street by his Ukrainian schoolmates. The Master of Science and pharmacist Spindel and his wife and daughter, who had been living in the Lublin area on Aryan papers, fell into the hands of the Gestapo in April 1944 and were all shot. Polish collaborators had denounced them.

In Zborow I met with my colleague Waraszinski, a former high-school teacher in Złoczów. He introduced me to the Roman Catholic priest, Jan Pawlitzki, from whom I received documents for my wife and child. From now on my wife would be called Maria Konisz and our daughter, Janina Konisz. They both had Catholic birth certificates. Maria Konisz was a little older than Hanya Duhl, but that is how it had to be. On the blank forms that I had from Jezierna, I attached an identification permit with a photograph of my wife with the name Maria Konisz. That, along with the birth certificate, were her new documents. I had to translate my birth certificate into German and have it authorized by a notary. I could not get that done in Zborow because the notary there was a Ukrainian; one could only get it done in Tarnopol with a Polish notary. The priest Pawlitzki sent one of his people to Tarnopol and he delivered it to me. I burned the original.

My wife had a lot of friends in Zborow as she had worked there for two years in a pharmacy. Besides that everyone there knew my father-in-law of blessed memory. Zborow and Jezierna were like a house and a side room. Also, the head of the *Judenrat*, Janek Fuchs, former community activist, was an acquaintance and his wife was even a friend of my wife's. We certainly had 'protektzia'! [special connections] So of course we were given a location near the Fuchs family, in a room in which four other families were quartered, and we were the fifth. For our five souls, we had about six square meters of space. That is what the '*protektzia'* looked like. Fuchs and his wife and one child lived in a nice little house with several rooms and lovely furnishings; we five people, in an area of six square meters. We slept on the floor (at least, not in hell). Our good friend Sanie Auerbach, the contact person [for the Gestapo], lived in his previous apartment, that had fine furniture and everything up to 'hummingbird's milk'. We looked at the contrasts with sadness: Jews walking on the street were deathly pale, starving, tattered and torn, in fear that a murderer could shoot them at any minute, shuddering with every passing German. Once they were wealthy, honorable people – and now? Mrs. Fuchs stands in her apartment ironing the laundry, and probably her husband's shirts, puts them into the chest, prepares a good meal for her husband and daughter with meat, a compote, better than in the pre-war times when everything in the town was normal. Sanie Auerbach's wife stands in her kitchen decorating a big chocolate cake with a swastika in the middle and the initials of the SS-man who heads the Jews' camp in Zborow. He would receive the cake on his birthday from the grateful Zborow Jews. In the town, among all the Jews – sadness, poverty, fear, tragedies, and here a life of luxury: ironing shirts, making a cake for the murderer of the Jews in the camp.

For repairing of the sidewalks, the Germans used the tombstones from the Jewish cemetery. Once they grabbed some Jews, among them the Rabbi, and led them to the cemetery and ordered them to knock down the stones and load them onto wagons. The gentiles were standing and waiting by their wagons. The Ukrainian police gave the order, "Work! Pull out the stones and load them!" Not one Jew moved a muscle. Eventually the Rabbi, may his strength continue, stepped out of the line and went to stand by a tombstone, the stone of the old Rabbi, his grandfather, may he rest in peace. He recited *Kaddish* and *El molle rakhamim* ["God full of mercy" prayer]. The fields and forests echoed with that *"Yisgadal v'yiskadash…"* and when he concluded with the words "and may they rest in peace in their resting-places, and let us say Amen!" he wept and the Jews answered, "Amen". He begged forgiveness from the dead for interrupting their rest, turned around to the Jews and told them to begin the work. While the rabbi was praying, the gentiles knelt and crossed themselves, and the guards stood at attention. They started screaming soon enough and dealing out blows, but the work had already begun. The work went on all day. The tombstones were carted away and the sidewalks of Zborow were repaved with them. The Jews were forbidden to use the sidewalks and the religious of the non-Jews avoided the sidewalks in order not to tread on the tombstones. Rumors went around among the non-Jews that at night, voices and wailing came from the graves where the stones were taken, and passersby felt afraid.

The pharmacists Lucia and Marek Reiss had worked in the apothecary in Zborow for twenty years. Young and old, men and women, Jews and non-Jews, everyone knew them and appreciated them. More than one pauper had his prescription filled for free, sometimes with the addition of a few *groschen* to buy bread for the children. They were treasured by Jews and non-Jews alike. The Germans drove them out of their shop and out of their home, but they did not lose their courage. Lucia kept her spirits up, consoling those victimized. After each *aktzia* she would seek out the affected families, bringing them bread, a little sugar, sharing her last bites of food with them. She would bring reports that redemption was near. The persecuted families believed her, looked to her as one looks to an angel who brings good news. Her words of comfort were repeated from person to person until…until she herself fell into the hands of the murderers.

It was with difficulty that they stuffed her into the heavy truck that was already full of captured Jews. They were all destined for the extermination camp at Belzec. Lucia knew that this would be her last journey. She was seeing for the last time the pharmacy where she had worked for so many years, the little house where she had lived and the people among whom she had lived, sharing in their joys and sorrows. Instinctively, she stood up and shouted at the Gestapo guards in a strong voice, "Murderers! The shame of the twentieth century! For our pain, for our suffering, for our innocent blood spilled, you will receive your due… from our blood, from our bones, will rise an avenger!" Then she turned to her brothers and sisters in the truck and said, "Lift up your heads! Do not be afraid of these murderers, we are dying for the sanctity of God's name!" And when she cried out, "Long live the Jewish people!", a Gestapo-man dealt her such a blow that she fell down dead. She had remained in Zborow, in the town that she loved and where she had spent the best years of her life. Her husband Marek heard that Lucia was already on a truck that would take her to an extermination camp and begged the *Judenrat* to save her, and when he learned that it was already too late he committed suicide. After that aktzia, the couple Lucia and Marek Reiss were kept together in a joint-grave in the Jewish cemetery.

November 1942. Now 17 months have passed since the Germans carried out their murderous work: forced roundups, re-settlements, labor-and-extermination-camps have brought about their results. The number of Jews continued to shrink and the remaining Jews were packed into small, crowded living quarters; so many families in one house, they literally suffocated. That is how they enclosed them in the ghetto. They were forbidden to walk out of the ghetto. It was all a preparation for the final solution, the complete liquidation. In Zborow, as I have already mentioned, the Jews from the surrounding villages had been driven together and in July 1942 the fate of the few surviving Jezierna Jews was bound up with the fate of the Zborow Jews and those of the villages.

* * *

We – myself, my wife and child – left Zborow on November 20, 1942, and began to ramble with our Aryan papers. Our life was not easy then either. Everywhere outside the ghetto, they were searching for Jews; we were always endangered, without one restful moment, by day or by night. We lived in constant fear, frightened of every known and unknown person; anyone could turn us in to the Gestapo. Danger hovered over our every step.

In Jezierna, before the deportation, I used to meet with the poet Sh.Y. Imber. We had made plans, but he did not live till the redemption. Before the war there had been a judge, a Jew named Ziemer, in Buczacz. His secretary was a young Polish woman. He had fled Buczacz in 1940 and settled in Jezierna, where the Germans caught him. His secretary became his wife and fled with him. The *Judenrat* gave him a function, as an assistant and night watchman. His non-Jewish wife kept watch with him in the *Judenrat* office at night, and protected him from every *aktzia*. Dyga called her many times and told her, "Traitor! Leave that lousy *Zyd*, bitch, or you will be killed along with him…" All the threats made no difference; she never left him. She went to the Russian-Catholic priest Bialowons for help, but he chased her away from him. I met them several times in Zborow, and then they disappeared. I learned later that they both survived and were living in Poland.

I survived the Hitler hell as a Karaite, along with my wife Hania Klinger – Maria Konisz – and my daughter Julia – Janina Konisz. We were pursued for more than three years, living in terror, without any rest by day or by night. Every minute was a risk, every minute tense. It was a miracle that we came out of that slaughter alive. During those horrible times that we lived through, we encountered good people (few, unfortunately), for whom the highest goal was to help or rescue a person; they reached out their hands to us in times of trouble and helped. But there were also informers, animals in human clothing, who for a few coins or a bottle of whiskey delivered innocent people to the murderers. Their hands are stained with the blood of the innocent victims.

* * *

That day is a day of wrath,
A day of trouble and distress,
A day of Shoah [catastrophe] and desolation,
A day of darkness and gloominess,
A day of clouds and thick fog.

Prophet Zephaniah, Chapter 1.

[Pages 254-264]

Our Prison Journey
(A Fragment of My Memoirs)
by Menahem Duhl
Translated from Yiddish by Ida Selavan–Schwarcz

Summary of a Family

I survived the Hitler years of hell with Aryan papers, together with my wife and daughter, who was three years old at the time of the outbreak of the Second World War. When I remember the horrible times, I ask myself the question: How did it happen that I and my family survived the massacre, which swallowed up millions of our brother and sisters along with my mother **Batya,** my in–laws, **Augustina** and **Wilhelm Klinger**, my sister **Etie Neuberger** and her husband, children and grandchildren, my sister **Sarah Mann** and her husband and children, my brother **Feibish** with his wife and children and many close and distant relatives? My brother–in–law **Yisrael Mann** died in the Jezierna camp: I was there at the time, and walking past the Jewish camp I saw him. He was standing near the wall and leaning on it. Swollen from hunger, he could not stand on his feet, and suffering, he slowly expired. His eyes were half closed, and he murmured, quietly saying something (perhaps it was his *Vidui* ? [confession]) Suddenly he opened his eyes, eyes full of sadness and tears, cast a glance at me … and it seemed to me that he recognized me and said: "Mendele, save me … write to **Sali** how I died" … Those were his last words. Diga, the chief of the camp, gave him a few lashes with his whip and he fell dead.

I could not fulfill his final wish to write my sister how the last words on his lips were her name and the names of their children, because she was also no longer among the living. She and her daughter were killed in the crematorium in Belzec. Also my sister Etie was killed in Belzec.

Her husband **Avraham** and their children and grandchildren were murdered in the *Aktzias* [anti– Jewish campaigns] and their two sons fell in the struggle against the Nazis. My brother was murdered in the work camp in Barki near Tarnopol and his wife and his two children in the Rudolfmuele [Rudolf Mill –a three story grain mill] in Stanislaw.

As I write these memories, I tremble; pain grips my heart and tears flood the paper.

We Are Arrested

My memories of those horrible times! … a fragment of them:

This happened in Berezhany in 1943. We were living at the time with 'Aryan papers'. The time – between Pesah and Shavuot, on a Friday, about eight in the evening, the landlord's dog started barking. We knew then that there were strangers in the yard. We lived in constant fear, afraid of our own shadows. We used to listen very carefully to who came and to whom. We heard a knock on our door and someone asked: "Does Duhl live here?" Three men came in, two were Poles, former Granat Polizei [Polish police of the general government] and the third one seemed to be a German. As soon as they came in they said, "We have been informed that you are Jews. You are under arrest and you must come with us." I tried to say something, to explain, but they did not want to listen. "You will say everything there, at the Gestapo," they said, and they led us out of the house, locked the door, and took the key with them.

When we were arrested and taken out of the house, our neighbors, the Vaitzik family, made merry. They drank liquor, sang, and laughed. The record–player played dance music and they actually danced. Voices of the drunkards escorted us as we left the yard. That is how the world looked then, the world that Hitler built upon the destruction of our people, of our existence. They led three Jewish souls: a father, a mother, and a small child to jail and perhaps to death, because they were Jews, and there, the informers rejoiced. Yes, we had reached the point where, for the 600 zlotys which they would get from the Germans for denouncing us, they used us as a source for merry–making.

The way to the prison was about one kilometer. The policemen led us 'discretely'. They walked with us in this manner, so that no one would suspect that they were leading prisoners. We walked and kept quiet, but our child held on to her mother's hand tightly. I was sure that this would be our next to the last journey. The last one would be from the jail to the gathering place at the cemetery. That would be the end of our life upon this earth.

But it was fated that we would yet live and survive this hell. As I walked along silently, without hope of surviving prison and moreover, being privileged to live a free life, I sank deep in thought and before my eyes I saw pictures of my life, as if through a kaleidoscope. People were walking along the street, but I saw no one … Here I see my mother, she is carrying little Mendele to Dr. Kitner … Mendele is studying in Leib Yosef's Cheyder. He walks home at night with his lantern in his hand. It is snowing and freezing outside and the children sing: "Good night to you, we have begun walking at night." It is merry and gay … Mendele goes with his father to the Kopitchintzer [Kopychyntsi] Rebbe; Father wants to ask the holy man if he can send Mendel to study in the gymnasium. The holy man lifts up his head, looks into Mendele's little black eyes with his own clever eyes, and says "Yes." He gives Mendele an amulet… Mendele strolls along proudly on the Borshtshev [Borshchiv] sidewalk, with his student cap on his head and a silver stripe on his collar … His brother Fishl, the wage earner of the family, is sick. Before his death he leaves a will: "Mendele should continue his studies." Those were his last words. His friend Dr. Feldshuh, the first Borszczower doctor, stands next to his bed and cries … Father takes his son's death very hard, the pain is great, he studies Mishna and weeps at the loss of the young soul … December 1914. Father is lying on his sick–bed … he dies … Mendele is an orphan … the Russian invasion … they capture men for forced labor … the terrible night of 1917 – the withdrawal of the Cossacks. They beat Jews, plunder their homes … rape Jewish women … the Austrians are back– the redemption, the salvation; the saviour mobilizes and sends into war … Mendele is again studying in the gymnasium … Austria falls apart, Ukraine … Petlyura … Poland …

The pictures come and go quickly: Mendele graduates and enters the university … studies … hard times. It is hard to study without money … the academic house on Therese Street in Lemberg … anti–Semitic excesses … Mendele become a teacher in the gymnasium in Zalishtchik [Zalishchyky] … they look at him, he hears one boy telling another "The professor is a boy from Borshtshev. His name is Duhl"… Horodenka … government gymnasium in Pshemishl [Przemyśl] … Mendele's rank is reduced and he loses his job … again hard times to make a living … antisemitism grows stronger … Mendele stands at the Lemberg Kuratorium [Board of Trustees] before the vice–supervisor Shedewe, who had reduced his rank and who says to him with a smile: "Your name is Mendel, I remember you"… and he really remembered! … After a year without income he goes back to work … back to Pshemishl … Lizhensk [Leżajsk] … Tarnobrzeg …

The pictures disappear and return: the wedding in Jezierna, many people, it is merry … Hanya stands pale under the canopy and shines like the sun, people are pushing, wanting to see the bride in her veil, the congregation wants to see Hanya's bridegroom. I hear someone say "How beautiful Hanya is in her veil"… the rabbi says and I repeat after him "Behold you are consecrated"… Lemberg, in the Salos sanitarium Hanya gave birth to a little daughter … again rejoicing … the grandma and the grandpa are overjoyed … and the father … another time of rejoicing. I receive tenure in the government gymnasium … 1939, the war … we flee from Tarnobrzeg, driven out … we are wanderers … and again in Jezierna … Zolochiv [Zloczow] … troubles and worries … the German–Russian War, the pogrom in Zolochiv … again Jezierna … the father–in–law … my father–in–law is murdered … we run away … wander … Jezierna … Zborow … Kozova … Berezshan [Berezhany] …

Again the pictures end. A cry goes out from my heart: "I have lived an honest and upright life"! Hanya embraces me and says: "Calm yourself Manek, we shall yet be saved!"

The Prison

Now we are standing in front of the gates of the prison. The heavy iron bars of the gate open, we are led in and the gate closes behind us. We are cut off from the outside world, I, my wife, and our seven–year–old child became residents of the Berezhany prison. My first night in the Berezhany prison. I was led into a cell which was partitioned into three compartments, each meant for two prisoners. My wife and daughter were taken to a women's cell. The cells were designated for non–Jews. I met a familiar person in my cell. He had been an official of the sick fund in Berezhany; his name was Batza. He was imprisoned for taking money from the fund. He was a Pole and his wife was Ukrainian, a chauvinist and an anti–Semite. We knew each other from the 'Bata' firm where his wife was a saleslady. He knew that I was a Karaite and he behaved nicely to me. Of the other four prisoners, one was the owner of a Ukrainian accountancy firm in Rohatyn; he had been imprisoned for six weeks, not knowing why. He was a religious man and he went to communion every Sunday. The second man was a Pole, a train mechanic. His wife was German. He was condemned to two years imprisonment for causing a collision between two trains. Thanks to his German wife his punishment was relatively mild. The third was a cobbler, a Ukrainian, charged with robbery and smuggling. The fourth was a fourteen–year–old gentile boy, a Roman Catholic, who used to sneak into the ghetto and steal items from the poor oppressed Jews. He was caught and put in prison. I was the sixth. We were complete, an honorable society. I introduced myself to my 'comrades'. The room–commander assigned me a place on the bunk together with the fourteen–year–old burglar. But he protested that he did not want to sleep with me; it did not suit him. In addition, he behaved rudely. The cobbler, who was in charge of our cell, resented this. He rebuked the boy for his attitude, took his own belongings and moved next to me. So the incident was resolved and I remained in this cell until we were freed. The prison was difficult to get used to. The bedbugs bit, the fleas leaped about, the straw mattress was full of lice, but we had to 'endure'. There was a strict regime: At six o'clock in the evening we had to put our shoes out, in a row and the guard made sure that all the shoes were put outside. We wished him "Good night", and he locked the door. At six o'clock in the morning he opened the door of the cell. We greeted him with "Good morning." Then the room–commander took in the shoes, and the day began. The regime was concerned about the religious life of the prisoners and every Sunday there was a service in the chapel, which was in the courtyard. Many of the prisoners received communion on Sunday. They became religious in prison. My family and I also used to participate in the service, listening intently to the sermon of the priest and his appeal to the prisoners to repent, to believe in God, in Jesus, and his mother Mary. I stood in a corner and looked at my wife and child and they looked at me. This was the only opportunity to see each other at least once a week, even from afar. Tears ran down from my eyes as I looked at them and my neighbors thought that the priest's sermon had touched me.

The 'Karaite'

When I was "quartered" in the cell, the room–commander informed the guard through the window, that there was a new tenant, a Karaite. The guard asked "What is a Karaite? He will go with the others," and he pointed to the cell where the 'others' were imprisoned, meaning Jews. They had been dragged out of bunkers, captured in the forests or in the fields, and brought here to wait for their death.

My cell mates, who had been there for a while, had the privilege of working at various occupations. They would leave in the morning and I would remain there by myself.

In the morning and in the evening the prisoners would pray. No one organized it. It started by itself and became a custom. It was initiated by the train engineer. One could assume that the form of prayer belonged to the daily routine of the prison. All the prisoners participated. The train engineer's experience of the train wreck, the interviews by the Gestapo, his suffering in the hospital, (he had jumped out of the train at the time of the catastrophe and had been wounded)– all of this left an impression on him and he became a religious fanatic. In the morning and evening he would kneel by the window. He would chant the prayers from his prayer book, including the interpretations of the text which were in brackets, from beginning to end. Looking at him, all the prisoners in the cells also knelt and prayed as if ordered to do so. It made a strong impression. The prayers united Poles and Ukrainians, men and women, freethinkers and just plain thieves, bandits, smugglers, and some who did not even know why they were in prison.

The Jews were in a separate cell. They had been caught, and they knew that they were awaiting their deaths. Mournfully, they sat in the cell weeping and waiting for the Gestapo murderer Hermann. Perhaps influenced by the prayers they said their confessions and prayed with fervor to the Master of the Universe, who would decide their fate. They had been handed over into the hands of murderers, and designated for 'martyr's deaths'.

Every day the voices of the chanting and prayers resounded over the courtyard, echoed in the gates of the prison and reached far far... Perhaps the tears which the Jews shed in their cells, the bloody tears of people awaiting death, arrived through the Gates of Tears there … far far away …

Imagine my situation, the situation of a Karaite, who had never seen a Karaite temple, never heard Karaite prayers, did not know their language and customs. Berezhany was not far from Halicz where there was a group of Karaites. But I never visited them. At such a time, when everyone prayed, I also had to pray to 'my God', the 'Karaite God', so that I would not seem to be an 'atheist #8217;. My imagination did not leave me and being sure that no one knew what a Karaite was and how their 'pagan' prayers sounded, I improvised. I raised my hands, and then fell with my face to the ground, to the dirty floor of the prison chamber and 'prayed'. No one heard my words, they did not know in what language I was praying (and perhaps they feared my pagan prayers?) I would frequently call out "Allah, Allah". This they understood. That was how my original improvised prayers, Karaite prayers sounded. My companions observed me. They knew how Jews prayed. And this form of prayer was new to them, unknown. They looked at me with different expressions, even with some respect–they had an 'exotic' cellmate.

In My Wife's Cell

My wife and daughter were in the women's cell. My wife was known there as Maria Kunysz and my daughter as Yanina Kunysz. They also found themselves in respectable society. Their cellmates were even more exalted than mine.

There was a woman who had been caught with Aryan papers and had been in prison for over a year. She was investigated and now awaiting a result. Another woman had been a cook at the home of a Jewish Professor Haas. There was a restaurant owner, a former prostitute, and two other women who were prison simply for theft. The room–commander was the restaurant owner. When she got to know my wife, she told her a story that there had been women there who had prayed and kissed the cross all day long. They had Aryan papers, and every second word they said was "Jesus" and "Holy Mother". They were there for a long time, until finally they were told the results of the investigation:

where they came from, what their real names were, where they had obtained the false papers, and in the end they were shot. Another time she told about a dream that all of those with Aryan papers were taken by the Gestapo. A third day she told another story from her repertoire, in order that my wife should know where she stood and in whose hands.

When they all left the cell, and my wife and our daughter were left alone, she would teach the child and instruct her how to behave. Then the child would curl into her mother's arms and cry, "Mamele, we will live, we must live, Mamele." And the mother heard this with a broken heart, and did not allow even a tear to fall.

Once, the woman who had Aryan papers also stayed behind and poured out her heart to my wife. Her husband had been a water–carrier and before the war they lived in Rzeszow. When the Hitler–soldiers marched in, they left Rzeszow and moved not far from Berezhany with Aryan papers. Her husband was soon captured and she was being investigated.

She had been in prison for a year and always afraid, uncertain what the night or the day would bring. She was frequently taken to the Gestapo where she was abused physically and psychologically. "Why didn't they shoot me along with my husband?" she cried. "Then there would be an end to my suffering."

During an *Aktzia*, the guard (actually a Polish woman) opened the cell door and pointed her out to the Gestapo, saying that she was a Jew. They dragged her out of the cell and took her to the cemetery. When the head of the prison (also a Pole) heard this, he quickly ran to the execution place. She was standing there, naked, waiting her turn. He covered her with his coat and brought her back. She sat in prison a few months, and then they found out where she came from, and what her name was in Rzeszow and how she had gotten her papers, and finally she was shot. She stood at the execution place twice. The greatest proof against her was that she did not know the Catholic liturgy, so she was suspected and arrested.

Another day Professor Haas's cook stayed behind. She explained that she had been a cook for the professor for many years before the war, even before he was widowed. When war broke out, and he was already a widower, he took her to a notary and transferred the property rights to his house and clothing to her in his will. When the riots and *Aktzias* started, she built a hiding place in the house and hid the old professor there, fed him and took care of him. They had a Polish neighbor, a tailor, who notified the Gestapo that a Jew lived in the neighborhood. Hermann, the murderer of Jews, came with two Ukrainian policemen, found the hiding place, dragged out the old man, and shot him there and then, and she was arrested. Thus she had been sitting in jail for a year. She was investigated by the Gestapo all the time. She was given a gynecological examination to check if the old man had not, Heaven forbid, broken the law against mixed racial sexual relationships. She was told that she would be freed soon, but meanwhile she was without hope. With tears, bloody tears, she told about what she had suffered.   (In 1949 I met her in Wroclaw, and she was delighted that we had remained alive).

Two dreams. After we were arrested there was a search in our dwelling. All of our documents were inspected. Everything was in order. There was not one document to show that we were Jews. My wife and daughter had Roman–Catholic identities and I had Karaite documents. Hanya remembered in prison, that she had not burned her papers from before the war, in which was written, 'Hanya Duhl wife of Maximilian, secondary school teacher in Tarnobrzeg.' She had sewn it into a small pillow. Now her name was Maria Kunysz and not Hanya Duhl. She was very worried, because if these papers were found, we would be lost. She could not rest. Finally she fell asleep and dreamed that her mother came to her and said, "Do not worry, the place has not been touched."

(When we were freed, and returned to our dwelling, we found that all of our bed linens had been cut up, everything was in chaos, but the little pillow had not been touched …)

In the morning of the 29th of May, the restaurant worker told my mother of a dream she   had, where an officer of high rank called my wife and spoke to her in a very friendly way. She interpreted the dream to mean that she would be freed from prison.

FREED!

That same day the commander of KRIPO [kriminalpolitze], Captain Kawalski, came. First of all he called me and said that I was free; then he had my wife and child brought in and told them the same thing. With tears in our eyes, in his presence, we embraced and kissed. We were free, we had won our life back.

How did it come about that we were freed? – no one would ask. Therefore I want to respond. Not all the Christians were informers like our neighbors, who probably got drunk and sang and danced when we were arrested. Good people worked to get us out of prison. The first was Dr. Bilinski, the director of the hospital and Chairman of the Polish Aid Committee. The second one was circuit court judge Karol Bogotski, my childhood friend, who put himself in danger but went and testified that he was my friend from the local government school and he knew that I was not a Jew. There were also Poles and Ukrainians who testified in our behalf. A woman neighbor, Aniela Podohovits, the widow of an official and the daughter of our landlady, used to bring us lunch every day. The circuit court judge, Dr. Tortel–Tabinski, from Czortkow, who was then a lawyer in Berezhany, sent us bread and butter every day (which was never delivered to us). All of this made an impression on the prison guard and on our cellmates. They saw that the upper class Polish intelligentsia was interested in us.

***

We survived the Hitler hell. We were homeless and pursued, living in constant fear of acquaintances and strangers, knew no rest, night and day for over three years. We feared everyone; we could be caught and destroyed at any moment. Anyone could hand us over and get a reward.

We survived the massacres through a miracle.

In the course of those three years of oppression and murders, we met good people who stretched out a hand, for whom "Love thy Neighbor" was not an empty phrase. We also met informers, wild animals, whose hands were smeared with the blood of innocent Jewish victims. And even though those times are long over, these experiences left a deep impression upon us. We are not the same as we were before the war. The experiences are deep in our souls and consciousness. They do not allow us to live quietly. Even now, the horrible scenes appear in dreams before my eyes.

Editor's Note: Below is a Release from Prison document issued 27 May 1943 in Berezhany, for Duhl Maximilian, Kunysz Maria, and Yanina Kuny.

This Duhl family, Menachem, his wife Hanya and daughter Yehudit managed to survive the war using false names on their documents, which identified him as a Karaite and the women as Roman Catholic.

[Page 265]

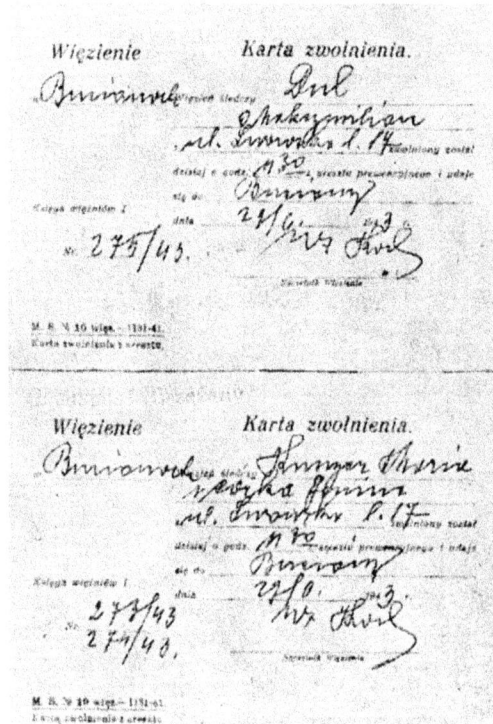

My Private Hell
by Dr. Nachum Kalafer
Translated from Yiddish by Sheldon Clare

I am a Jeziernian, but before the war I lived in Bodzanov. My wife came from Kopyczynce. Our little daughter was barely five years old when the war broke out. When the Germans entered Bodzanov, I experienced for the first time the launching of persecution and *aktions* (assembly and deportation of Jews). And when they expelled the Jews from Bodzanov and made it Judenrein (empty of Jews), my family and I were forced to run away to Kopyczynce where my wife's family lived.

The situation became worse day by day. When I realized that it would be difficult to endure and survive here, for a kilo of gold I received permission from the Gestapo leader to go to Probużna . This town was already Judenrein and only two Jews remained living there: I, a dentist and Dr. Brandwein - a general physician. And by the end of the last liquidation of the ghetto, I had to run away again.

My wife Sala, her sister Gusta, and my little daughter Rita, settled in a place near a 'reliable farmer' where she kept them in a bunker; I alone went into a forest, about 20 kilometers from the place. Every night, I would visit them, going by foot. But this did not last. The peasant neighbors informed on them to the Ukrainian police, who identified them. They were taken to a field and were shot. My daughter was shielded by her mother and was only wounded. At night, when she recovered her wits, she dug herself out from under the dead bodies and began to wander, all bloody.

A good-hearted old peasant of Ukrainian descent took her in and kept her as her own. From time to time I came out of the forest to see the child. After being freed, I rewarded the peasant.

On March 23, 1944, the Soviet army freed us. I began to work as a dentist in a military hospital. When the 'front' withdrew, I was nominated to become a regional examiner; my duty was also to investigate the evidence about the arrested prisoners and to certify that they were able to be transported. Among the arrested people, I found a well-known former Ukrainian policeman. The murderer of my family, the Ukrainian superior police officer, I did not find.

The vicious Nazis murdered my mother Sheyndl, my sister Maltsheh, my brother Yidl, along with my grandfather Sanyeh Rozenfeld, my uncle Natan Rozenfeld with his wife and two of their sons - Natziyeh and Matik.

When the war ended, I went to Poland. As a result of the difficult experience, I am now a sick and broken person.

From my large family, almost no one survived; they were all murdered.

[Page 266]

One Fate Everywhere
by Jaques Katz, Paris
Translated from Hebrew by Simon Godfrey

Rennes, 23.7.1966

My Dear Friends,

On January 5th 1943 I was arrested by the Gestapo as a Jew who was not obeying the Nuremberg laws and was not wearing the shameful symbol. They held me in the central prison in the city of Marne. After 15 days I was transferred to Compiegne [internment and deportation] camp and in mid–February, as part of a full transport, I arrived in Auschwitz–Birkenau.

As a student in the University of Cannes, I had studied advanced mathematics, analytical mechanics and electronics; I declared myself to be an electrical engineer and thus I was saved.

In September, after a 'selection', I was transferred to a concentration camp in Warsaw, which was established in the area of the Ghetto. We were in the hands of thugs from the Majdanek concentration camp which, because of the advance of the Russian army, was relocated there. The conditions were seven times worse than in Auschwitz.

In August, 1944 the Poles of Warsaw rebelled. The fighters surrounded the camp in which there were about 300 people and we were released. They all dispersed, but I joined the rebel–army under the command of General Bor Komorowski as a volunteer engineer. In the meanwhile the Russians arrived on the other bank of the Vistula but refrained from taking part in the fighting; the Germans, as was their nature, increased their attacks and began blowing up building after building. It was real hell and almost like the inferno of Stalingrad.

In my view, as there was no hope of help or escape, I obtained for myself some civilian clothes and approached the first German officer I encountered. I succeeded in convincing him, in his own language, that I was not a Polish fighter but a French worker who had left his country and volunteered to come here in order to help in the effort towards the coming victory of the Third Reich.

Never–the–less, the officer was suspicious and to be on the safe side he sent me to the Gross–Rosen concentration camp in Silesia and from there I was sent to the Mauthausen concentration camp.

Using an assumed Aryan name I was sent, together with a group of prisoners, to work as forced laborers in Vienna. In April 1945, with the Russians approaching, we were ordered back to Mauthhausen. For a month we wandered without rest and were fed from the corpses of horses left behind by the Hungarians.

On the 5th of May 1945 the Mauthhausen concentration camp was liberated by the American army and on May 22nd 1945 I returned to my wife, to my children and to freedom. Unfortunately I never had the opportunity during the whole time to meet even one Jew from Jezierna, Tarnopol or Lvov.

Jaques Katz, Paris.

Footnote:
Before us, in brief, is the powerful history of someone born in Jezierna who, after completing high school, moved to France to continue his studies. When the Nazis entered the town where he lived he was arrested by the Gestapo and went through seven hell–fires in internment and extermination camps. He took part in the battles when the Poles of Warsaw rebelled and finally was freed and able to return to his family who remained in France.

Until the end of his life he worked as the principal of a vocational school and passed away a short time ago. M.D.

Editor's Note: Article was received in a letter sent by Jaques Katz to Professor Menahem Duhl

[Page 268]

Wandering in Foreign Places
by Lipa Fischer
Translated from Yiddish by Tina Lunson

Twice I left Jezierna and twice succeeded in returning; the second time I came back to a shtetl without Jews…

With the outbreak of the German–Polish War in 1939 Jezierna organized a fire brigade of Poles, Ukrainians and Jews; all had served in the military, and I among them; we were all assigned to that brigade. Besides putting out fires, we also served at night, because various elements roamed around among the villages of Poland at that time. We had to protect the rear zone while the army fought far away at the front. But soon there was a panic. The army had been beaten and its remnants were being withdrawn to the east. People started to evacuate, and Moshe Byk and I also decided to leave Jezierna to get closer to the border between Poland and Russia. I tried to convince some others – for example Dr. Litvak and Avraham Chaim Paket (Tsirel Menye, as we called him) – but they would not be talked into it. During that time, when I was packing my things, my sister burned the newspapers and books with anti–fascist and anti–Hitler content, and cried while doing it.

It was *erev Rosh–Hashana* [eve of the New–Year]. But few people thought about the holy day. We thought about the great danger that lay in wait for Jews. Suddenly Mechil Fuchs came in shouting "Let's save the children!". His horse and wagon were prepared and he proposed that we drive with him to Podvolochisk (Pidvolochysk). We climbed up, sat in the wagon and drove off. We were six people altogether. We drove through Zborow and Hluboczek; we traveled through the fields because it would have been impossible to use the main road (*kaiserstrasse*). We arrived in Podvolochisk right after the prayer services. There were a lot of refugees there already. The locals invited us to lunch and we later also spent the night with them. Just a few days ago we also had refugees in our town, and now we were refugees here.

In Jezierna, a woman spent the night with us; she and her husband had fled from western Poland. Along their way an airplane shot at them; the husband was killed; she buried him in a field outside of Zloczow and she went on alone. She arrived in Jezierna at night, exhausted and broken. I gave her my bed. And now we were the refugees. We spent two nights with an old woman, whose attitude toward us was very motherly. On the second day it rained and it seemed that there was thunder and lightning during the night, but in the morning we realized that it was an exchange of fire between the Polish and Soviet soldiers. Injured soldiers were walking around, and lying on stretchers were severely wounded Polish soldiers. A Polish airplane was circling in the air, which was the only airplane that we saw during the war. A few days later we learned that Stalin had made a pact with Hitler and divided the former Poland: the Soviets took up to the San and Germany took the rest. We were happy that we could return home to Jezierna.

The Red Army began its invasion. Jews went out freely and without apprehension into the streets; we were also happy. The soldiers passing through smiled at us and we started to think of the fastest way to get back to Jezierna. A huge military force marched in, everything motorized, big tanks, heavy artillery. Moshe Byk and I went to the Podvolochisk train station. There were train cars that had been shot up and bombed. Women and children had been evacuated in those cars; the German air–pirates had shot them during their journey. The scene made a horrible impression on us.

Meanwhile they had opened the shops in town; the merchants started selling their goods and there was no lack of customers… they were mostly people from the other side of the border. On the way to our guest house we saw arrestees being led away. Moshe and I tried to analyze the political situation while we were walking. I had the seal of the Jezierna *Histadrut–Poalei–Zion* in my pocket. I threw the seal away.

On the second day Fuchs harnessed his horses and we were on our way back. Along the way – about 25 kilometers from Tarnopol – I got off the wagon and continued on foot. It seemed to us that it would be more comfortable that way; it was certainly more fun. Military people were marching, cars were driving, we saw a lot of people. Here and there we did hear shooting and it seemed that they were shooting right over my head; it was a few remaining Polish artillery men shooting and the Soviet soldiers were answering. Further along the way there were murdered Polish policemen lying on the road; Polish prisoners and also arrested civilians were being led awa

I walked along that way for a few kilometers until I finally got tired. When I spied a Red Cross horse and wagon approaching, I went to them and asked if I could ride with them to Jezierna. They questioned me in detail; I showed them my documents, I proved my identity but in the end they did not allow me to travel with them. I did not have any alternative and so continued on by foot. Later a small wagon came along. I asked the soldier and he let me climb aboard; he was a Jew and we spoke Yiddish along the way. He told me to take off my watch and hide it; a watch is a danger, he said. I traveled with him as far as Tarnopol. There I already felt like I was home. Tarnopol was already Soviet. Armed militia were walking around in the streets, dressed in civilian clothes with red bands on their sleeves; most of them were Jews. The Polish church on Dominikan Place was damaged; people said that it was from there that they shot at the Soviet soldiers. Some houses had been destroyed too, destroyed together with the residents. A lot of policemen had been dragged out of their apartments and shot without a trial.

* * *

I set out toward Jezierna on foot. It was already afternoon. But then I rode – a soldier took me to Jezierna. When I arrived home it was already dark. At home they already knew that I was on my way because the military hospital that I had met along the way and not allowed me to come with them, had already arrived in Jezierna, taken up quarters in our house and told [the family] that I was on the way. We greeted one another like old friends.

In Jezierna too a militia had been organized and the commander was an Ukrainian nationalist by the name of Terentshuk. Their headquarters was in Dudye Blaustein's house, where the Polish police station had been. The next day I met with Moshe Byk, Dr. Litwak, and Avraham Chaim Paket and we decided to turn to the military commandant to discuss with him various problems regarding the Jewish population. Among other things we wanted to insert a few Jewish lads into the militia. The commandant agreed and I was among those lads, with Schmuel Bien; Munye Steiger, Yekil's son, Naftali Charap, Nuchim Yekil's son. We served in the shtetl day and night. There were attacks on Jews. In the village of Połowce, a local peasant killed a Jew and his wife in the presence of their children and buried them at the entrance of their home. The murderer was sentenced by the Soviet courts.

I only belonged to the militia for a few days. I soon got work in the post office.

* * *

That was a hard time for my father and for other Jews in his position. He was considered to be in the category of rich peasants (*kulaks*) and they squeezed the life out of this particular group. My heart was sore. For example, my father, who was an ordinary laboring Jew, who had spent his whole life working hard in the field as a land laborer, connected to agriculture – had now become an exploiter, a parasite!?

One Friday night when he had arranged to go to prayer services, he was called to the community offices. Two party–members were sitting there and he could smell the odor of whiskey from both of them. They took a lot of money from my father, shouting and demanding. My dad was not shocked, but the fear was that he would be shipped off to Siberia, as that was something that they could do. They had already sent a lot of Jezierna men to Siberia. I had seen what they had done to the Polish colonists; it was a terrible scene. They woke them in the middle of the night, dragged them out of bed, told them to pack a few things, and led them away. Along with them they took an old smith and his family. Their entire possessions consisted of two hectares of soil, a cow and a few hens. He left behind all of this and in his old age, with his children and grandchildren went to Siberia.

I was the only one of my whole family making a livelihood. Our cousin Faivel Ohrbach was living with us at the time. He came from Sasow, and was a teacher in the Jezierna school; he helped us out a little too and so our family maintained itself. When the Germans arrived, Faivel went back to Sasow, where he fell into German hands in a camp; at the liquidation of the camp he and some friends mounted a rebellion and a few of them fled into the forest and survived there. I located him again in 1958, in America.

In Jezierna things got worse and worse. I left my post and began work in Hluboczek and later in Tarnopol. During the last period before the outbreak of the Soviet–German war, I was wandering around without work.

* * *

The war broke out; the Germans bombarded the large cities, but the small towns did not get any rest either. The Soviets mobilized the youth. The retreat began. For two days before the arrival of the Germans in Jezierna I was with my papa, mama and sister, but I decided to leave Jezierna and evacuate. I was not successful in influencing my friends; they did not want to leave. The Germans had already bombed Jezierna and I was still in the town. It was not easy to abandon my home and to travel, as panic ruled along the roads; the German airplanes bombed the roads, the streets and the rail lines. I was fortunate to leave with a Jew from Zborow who was living on our farm – I cannot recall his name – he was a a manager in the bazaar. He packed his bags and I set off with him. We traveled according to my plan. It was already September. We went through Zborow, Hluboczek, avoiding the main streets, and came into Tarnopol through a back alley. From Tarnopol we traveled to Podvolochisk. The second day in the morning we were already at the old border. Our documents were checked there and we were allowed to travel on. During the journey I went by foot some of the time because it was hard on the horses. In Volochysk [Woloczyska] the owner of the wagon told me to take my pack and go ahead on foot, and he himself took off at a gallop.

The road to Proskurov was not an easy one, but along the way some soldiers took me along in their car, and after that a peasant gave me a ride. These transports were shot at by German airplanes. The terror was great. This is how I slept that whole night. Wearily, I lay under a hut in a *kolkhoz*[collective farm] and fell asleep. I got up when it was still dark but all around there was loud noise, explosions and fires. I quickly got to my feet and went with everyone else – military and civilians were mixed together, militia men, NKVD agents – everyone on foot. The military people did not want to take anyone with them; there was no trust; we were suspicious of one another because there were spies everywhere and diverse characters. Everyone was greatly afraid.

I trudged on until Proskurov, where I succeeded in getting on a truck to Kiev. From there to Dniepropietrovsk I traveled on a ship over the Dnieper [River]. Our little ship was camouflaged and when German airplanes approached, we stayed by the shoreline. We suffered from lack of food. It is certainly pleasant to take a boat on the Dnieper, but not as we were traveling then. And so I arrived in Dniepropietrovsk, a large industrial city with big, beautiful buildings, huge business centers; but all that was not for me; I had to flee further. I spent the night in the train station; there were dead and wounded; thousands of refugees were waiting, each wanting to move on as quickly as possible. It was pouring rain; people were stuffed into open cars, waiting to travel on. I managed to get into a car that was already closed, and traveling like that, arrived in Kuban, in the North Caucasus, Krasnodorskiy area. From there we were transferred to the Krylovskaya station. Here, along with other refugees, I got off and stayed.

* * *

For the first time after such a long haul, since leaving my home, I took off my clothes and washed myself. There were *kolkhozn* here and they divided us among them. I was assigned to *kolkhoz* "Ukraina". All the refugees were assembled in an enclosed area, and the *kolkhoznikes* [collective farmers] came and chose workers. I was given to a Cossack who was a brigadier. There were a small number of Cossacks in that *kolkhoz*, most of whom were "*inaradnie*", which was a low caste in the Tsar's time. They worked for the Cossacks who were privileged. I was a field worker, and for my labor received food, a little grain and a little money. I worked there for one month.

The Germans were coming a little closer. Rostov was already in their hands, and I debated moving further along. Things were getting darker; the trains arrived overloaded with the wounded and refugees.

In the *kolkhoz* people prepared for partisan warfare. I got permission to travel further on; I forfeited my earnings and set out. The train was full of refugees, mostly Jews. We traveled deep into the Caucasus Region. The first large train station that we stopped at was Armavir, about 75 kilometers from Krilovskaia. All the walls were plastered with posters with slogans: "The enemy will be destroyed, the victory is ours"; "The Hitler–beast will be crushed in his lair".

The train took us further through the Caucasus settlements, and although I was in a difficult situation, I forgot about it all and looked at the Caucasus landscape, simply letting my mind wander; I was so moved by its beauty. We traveled for a couple of days. It was hard to get food and especially bread. We traveled without paying.

I arrived in Derbent, a town in Dagestan, South Caucasus. The food industry was well–developed there, and there were a lot of canning factories. Jews were living there too. There was a synagogue and on the Sabbath I went to pray. From there I went to the fortress town Makhachkala on the Caspian Sea. The town was full of refugees. I succeeded in catching a ship and traveled to Krasnovodsk, middle Asia. From there the way was open to Turkestan and Uzbekistan. Trains were leaving one after another, all full of refugees going to Tashkent. The way led to Turkmenistan, whose capital Ashgabat was located not far from the Persian border, about 18 kilometers. The train stopped for about an hour. I met a large group of Polish Jews in the station, and I decided to stay there.

* * *

The place for refugees there was at Karl Marx Street number 7. The NKVD had agents there who supposedly smuggled people over the border into Persia, for which the agents took money and then turned the people over to the NKVD. So I fell for that, along with a certain Azriel Diner from Trembowla. We were arrested and stood before a military–court.

This is how my arrest in Ashgabat took place: This was a town where every newly–arrived person was followed by agents who proposed taking people over the border illegally into Persia. The agents were Turkmen. Such provocateurs approached me several times, proposing to take me over the border, but I refused. Then, one time, I received an order to leave Ashgabat within 24 hours. Now when such a provocateur approached me proposing to sneak me over the border for a few hundred rubles, Azriel and I went for it. They took us, and when we were already outside the city, in a field, NKVD agents were waiting for us, opened fire on us and shouted "Hands up!" Our guide had suddenly vanished, and we were arrested. The commandant of the NKVD group was Meir Shefer; he began his conversation with us in Yiddish. He said, "Stupid Jewish bastards, you wanted to go to the Wailing Wall, now we have to shoot you."

The NKVD building was located in the center of the city, not far from the theater. When one went past the building, one would think that it was a charitable institution. Terrible tragedies took place in that house. No one went free from that place. He was either shot or sent to a forced–labor camp in Siberia. The interrogation lasted about a month, day and night with just short intermissions. When I was sleeping they woke me up and questioned me further. After they finished the investigation they brought us before a military court. I defended myself. The trial lasted for three days and we received the verdict. Azriel Diner from Trembowla was sentenced to death and I 'only' ten years of hard labor in a camp in Siberia. They sent me to the South Urals. Before that, I sat for three months under arrest in Ashkhabad.

On the 15th of February 1942 I arrived in Turinsk, and was left there; it was a large camp and the inmates did hard labor with a 12–hour work day. I arrived there sick, swollen and covered with carbuncles, so they did not send me to hard labor for a couple of months. When I felt a little better, they sent me to work. The work was beyond my strength. I got sick again and was considered an invalid. From that time on I began to work as a barber – it was much easier for me. I was employed in that line of work until 1957.

In 1943 I was transferred to Verkhnaya Tavda; there I finished my ten years of prison (labor camp). When I was freed, I settled there for another six years, working until March 1957, when I traveled back to Poland.

[Pages 277-288]

Return to Jezierna
(Continued)
by Lipa Fischer
Translated from Hebrew by Avril Hilewicz

A Letter from Home

In 1951, when the camp gates and the Soviet prisons in Siberia, where I had spent ten years of my life suffering from physical and mental torment, were thrown open, I was already aware of the fate of the Jezierna Jews. Long before, in 1944 I had written to my family back home in the hope that someone was still alive, but to my sorrow, received an answer only from Dozia Blaustein, Ben-Zion Blaustein's daughter; from her I had learned the whole terrible truth of the extermination of our town's Jews. Upon my release, I again tried to make contact with people I knew in Jezierna and sent a number of letters to farmers with whom I was acquainted. When none of them replied, I almost gave in to despair. However, after a while and to my great surprise, I received a letter from Azriel Pollak, the town's only remaining Jew.

I wrote to Mikhail Leskof and his wife Yekatarina, the only Ukrainians in our small town who had helped the Jews during the Nazi occupation; they had hidden Rosa Blaustein and her daughter, Dozia (Devorah). Otherwise, they would not still have been alive. It was his wife who had given Azriel my address, immediately after which he wrote to me. My joy knew no bounds in far-off Siberia – a letter from Jezierna! And written by a Jew, one of the last Jews, at a time when I had lost any hope of getting any sort of news from there.

* * *

It was a wintry day in 1951. It was freezing cold, and because of my fatigue at the end of the long work-days, I forgot about everything and everybody, even my past life had been erased from my memory. Following the difficult years in the camps, behind three barricades, I thanked God for letting me move about freely again. So, I finished my work and returned to the *obsizitia* (the workers' living quarters), where I lived in one room with two other Russians. The elder of the two, Nikolai Radionowitch Baranov, was a Muscovite; his friend, Sascha the hunchback, was a local man. The younger one was more easy-going. We became friendly and there was an atmosphere of understanding and tolerance in our room. Every day we would have a little something to drink, sometimes tree-sap alcohol, sometimes eau de cologne. Due to our friendly relationship, I couldn't refuse them and even shared a little of my hard liquor with them. Since it was so freezing cold, I walked quickly and when I arrived home it was dark outside. My room mates were waiting for me and when I opened the door, Saschka told me that I had received a letter from my 'homeland'. The letter had been placed on my little cupboard. I scrutinized it. Polkov was written instead of Pollak as the sender, instead of Azriel – Adolf and instead of Schmuel – Sigmont. But I immediately understood that it was Azriel Pollak who had sent me the letter. I was so grateful to him. I read and reread the letter, tears running down my face – after being cut off for ten years, I was once again in touch with my town!

After a number of months of corresponding with him I decided to visit Jezierna. I made the necessary travel arrangements. It was not an easy journey. Six days one way. I was living in the Urals in Verkhnyaya Tura, in the Sverdlovsk District, so-called after the name of the river Verkhnyaya Tura, which divided the city into two. The river is about 150 meters wide, and small boats were used to traverse it from one bank to the other. The river is hundreds of kilometers long. Despite being able to accommodate only relatively small ships, it is a very important waterway, serving both the state commerce and citizens, who want to reach the Tundra settlements in the far north. Trees used to be transported on rafts along this waterway. The river was rich in fish, in addition to providing the residents with water. There was also a local train station, the last stop in the north, the only line, connecting the city to the main city of Sverdlovsk. There was one train a day to Sverdlovsk which then returned to Verkhnyaya Tura.

I learned what had happened in Jezierna during Hitler's regime from Azriel Pollak's letter. His son, Pavel, a Polish soldier, was killed in the battle with the Germans for control of Warsaw. His daughter, Regina, served in the Red Army. His wife and three other daughters died in the Zborow Ghetto.

On My Way to Jezierna!

His letters increased my sense of longing and pain at one and the same time. My decision to reach Jezierna was unswerving. I went to my manager Ivan Adriavitch Botorin, a Russian, who had always been very sympathetic towards me, and asked for time off. This Russian had fought the Nazis and after the war had worked in a plywood plant – Funir Kombinat - as the supply department manager. Upon my release in 1951, I contacted him. He gave me work till I left for Poland in 1957. Now he authorized my vacation and even added an extra ten days since the journey itself required 12 days. After years of not having traveled on a train, I would be traveling this time from the Urals as far as my home town, Jezierna.

The train sped through the Ural forests, fields and mountains. A weird sensation took hold of me: here I was, traveling to my home town, where I had left my mother, father, sister, relatives and most of my friends and acquaintances. Now, the town was no more, even its graves no longer existed. I would only be able to see the place where they had all taken their last steps driven forward by the Nazi murderers and their Ukrainian collaborators.

Although I set off with a heavy heart I felt that I was once again in touch with the real world. I am able to travel freely! The route to Sverdelovsk, which ran through various villages, towns and settlements, was interesting except for the *kolkhoz* collective farms which appeared very backward from the outside.

I had to change trains for Moscow in Sverdelovsk. Even changing trains wasn't that easy. I had to re-confirm my ticket and there were not many seats available. As soon as all this had been organized I had to get in line. Half an hour before the train was due to leave the station there was a long, winding line. Everyone wanted to get on the train as quickly as possible; myself included. I was about to begin a three-day journey as far as Moscow where I would once again have to go through the same process as before, in order to get a seat on the train for Tarnopol. At long last I managed to get my seat on the train. I paid for bedding, which the conductress brought me. Tired out from all the aggravation, I fell asleep. The train took me westwards. I sensed that my dream of seeing my town of Jezierna was about to come true. New hope began pulsating through my veins.

However, I felt as though my liberty was still restricted … aspects of camp life were deeply etched in my mind, even though I was able to move around freely. When I woke up from my first sleep, it was already dark outside and so was unable to observe the scenery. I lay down again and thoughts which replayed like a movie reminded me that, 11 years previously, I had been transported under heavy guard to the place I was now leaving. I remembered my friends who were with me at the time, some of whom were no longer alive. They did not have the strength to endure the harsh conditions or the humiliations meted out at the NKVD 'Labor-Education Camps'. I, myself, could hardly believe that I had been through all that and now was traveling via Moscow to Jezierna as a free man. I could not even imagine that it was possible to live through ten such years, as I had done. Some sort of super-power kept me going and strengthened me, encouraged me and gave me the ability to endure and overcome everything. I had hoped that, when the war ended, I would be released, but I was wrong. The war had ended but I still remained in the camp. It took six years for those gates to open up before me!

All these harrowing thoughts went through my mind during the night. The sun broke through and my thoughts disappeared. Leaning against the window pane I could see the scenery changing. The train only stopped at the larger stations or industrial depots. On the third day of the journey we returned the bedding to the conductress, as there had been an announcement that we were approaching Moscow. On arrival, we stopped at a station called White Russia. There I was informed that the train for Tarnopol would be leaving from the Kiev station which was quite a long way off. I went there on the subway reaching the station fairly quickly. I confirmed my ticket once again and received a seat on the train. All these arrangements were also not easy. I had waited for a day and a half, so when I saw my seat in the cabin my joy knew no bounds. Once again, a conductress brought me bedding and again I made up my bed and fell asleep feeling good, as the train sped along, taking me to Jezierna.

* * *

Traces of war could still be seen west of Moscow; pockmarked fields full of shells, ruined houses, signs of intense and persistent battles; barbed-wire fencing was still discernible and large train stations were left in ruins. At times we got close to the Ukrainian border where there were a great many signs of the war. During the day I looked at the passing landscape, at night I rested. My anticipation of seeing Podolia, on the Polish-Russian border, was especially great since, after 11 years of wandering, I would soon be close to my home town…

I recalled fleeing Jezierna 11 years previously and reaching Podwoloczyska with other refugees. The Nazis were, by then, shelling Jezierna and causing casualties. I remembered parting from my mother, father and sister as well as my father's blessing for my journey. Could it be that, thanks to them, I was lucky to have remained alive? But, they are no longer with us. Now I am on my way to where? To whom?...

As we neared that area, my sorrow surfaced. I am traveling over a land drenched with so much blood of innocent Jews ... and all of a sudden, the train reached Proskurov. I was here during the transport in July 1941. At that time, the roads were full of soldiers and civilians. There were many recruits from the towns and villages all over Galicia. It was here that I came across people from Jezierna. It was safer at that time to walk since the train stations and their lines were the enemy's bombing targets; those on foot were able to hide in the undergrowth of the fields.

I shall always remember how the Nazi Messerschmitts bombed the Russian airport near Tarnopol. The bullets whistled over our heads; what danger we were in! On the way to Proskurov, while sitting and longing for a short respite, I suddenly heard my name being called out. It was the voice of the doctor who had worked at the hospital in Jezierna; he was now traveling in a Red Cross convoy as a military doctor. We shook hands warmly and talked about how miserable we were. I placed my bundle on his cart and continued walking next to it. I followed the convoy like this for a few kilometers, then we each went our own way.

This is how I met Josef Blasser, who was a soldier. I managed to get on a truck which took me quite a long way. Then I continued on foot again. The closer we got to Proskorow the harder it was to make our way along the road which was blocked with cars, horses, carts and people on foot. I found Munya Zamojre, David Feiering and others in amongst the soldiers. My meeting with Simcha Katz was especially friendly. He had a few black rusks in his side-pack. This was all a soldier was given for his journey. There was no time to cook for themselves, they were continually retreating. Simcha gave me some of his meager rusks, parted warmly from me and we each went our own way.

All this had taken place when I fled Jezierna. Suddenly, I woke up from my daydreaming and could make out the suburbs of Podwoloczyska, where the train was now approaching. Here, I saw quite a different picture. Where once there had been houses there were now empty plots, and those huts which were still standing had fallen into disrepair. I heaved a deep sigh and was overcome with tears...

The train started off again - this time for Tarnopol. Through the window I could see the desolated villages; those murderers had even cut down the trees! I arrived in Tarnopol over an hour later. I looked around and could not believe my eyes. Was this reality? The train station had been completely destroyed. Farmers' wives were wandering around wearing *kopeks* (padded jackets), leg-warmers and overshoes. Everyone stared at me as if to say: Who are you? Where have you come from?

* * *

I arranged my ticket for Jezierna and went off to see the town. It was hard to recognize the streets of Tarnopol: some of them had completely disappeared and you had no way of knowing which way to turn. I no longer saw familiar faces. The Jewish Quarter which was once the center of the hustle and bustle of Jewish life, the roads which used to be full of people, had all turned into heaps of rubble! I sat on one heap and cried my heart out: the city, in which about twenty thousand Jews had lived, was now *Judenrein (*cleansed of Jews). And I, Lipa Fischer, the Jezierner, had come from freezing Siberia after ten years of arduous camp-life, in order to sit on the ruins of Tarnopol and cry over its monstrous destruction...

As I slowly made my way through the rubble I met a Jew who told me that about thirty families were now left in Tarnopol. He said that there had been more immediately after the war. A monument in memory of those murdered had been erected in the cemetery, but the following day it was found overturned and destroyed... It was repaired and put up again only to find it destroyed the following day. And this is why there is no memorial monument for the victims of Tarnopol. The Soviet authorities stood by and did nothing, allowing the criminals to move around freely. Miskovici Street had been partially restored and taking pride of place in front of the church was a statue of Bohdan Khmelnytsky, the great Cossack 'revolutionary', toward whom we, the Jews, hold 'hypersensitive' emotions, for his name is etched in blood in the annals of our history.

When I got back to the station, the train was about to leave for Jezierna. As I went to get on the train and find my seat, I heard a number of anti-Semitic cries shouted in my direction by Ukrainian *Komsomol* (Soviet youth organization) members. I got on the train and couldn't forgive myself for not having reacted on the spot. Everything seemed different as I made my way towards the town after getting off the train. I felt like a stranger. The familiar farm and its yard seemed to be closer to the train station. It's large garden filled with fruit trees had disappeared, totally decimated.

It was now ten in the morning. Trampling through the mud I reached Zabramska Street looking for Azriel Pollack's address. He was living in Hirsch Laufer's house. He was more than happy to see me. His apartment was in a bad state. No words can describe the poverty and paucity I saw there. He lived in one room with his Christian wife and seven children. He kept a goat in the other room. The walls were covered with icons. There was no bread to be had. Since Jezierna was considered a *kolkhoz* (collective village) it had to produce its own bread. There were no commercial bakeries there. That single goat kept the family alive. They used to make milk soup with rolls made from unrefined flour.

About Sights of the Destruction and Insights on Them

The most important thing was meeting the non-Jews whom I had known, in order to learn about what had happened to the town during the Nazi occupation. I decided to walk through the town's lanes and alleys in case I found old neighbors to speak to. First of all, I went in the direction of my father's house. The village committee had seized his house and in its place had erected a monument to Taras Shevchenko. I stood still and imagined that I could see my mother and father in their house. I felt dizzy and everything nearly went black … at the same time a farmer I knew passed by and could clearly see how distressed I was. He looked at me and said: "Aren't you pleased that there is a monument here in honor of Shevchenko? Would you have preferred a monument to some rabbi or other?"

I didn't answer him. This was the first *Shalom Aleichem* (greeting) I had had in my town, from a gentile acquaintance. The first Ukrainian to give me a friendly welcome was Fedko Yawrovski from Hazarodka. After bringing up all that had happened here during that period, we all sat and wept. We talked about it for hours and hours. He took out a bottle of home-made liquor and we drank a toast. The atmosphere was depressing. They made a point of saying that the Germans had also killed non-Jews. When it got dark, I had to go back to Pollack. If I had had to make my way back alone, through the forsaken and desolated huts belonging to Jews, I would not have been able to leave; luckily, one of the men accompanied me back. On the way, he continued to tell me how the Germans had mercilessly and mindlessly killed (he meant not only Jews). The remaining Jewish huts appeared abandoned and desolate. The whole area shrieked sadness, and I imagined I could hear crying …

The next day, I went out with Pollack to wander around the town. Instead of the large synagogue there were mounds of rubble. Instead of the houses – empty plots. Everyone I met said how sorry they were. Each one recounted how the local Jews had been annihilated. Walking, we found ourselves at the cemetery. Not a single headstone was left standing. Here and there we could see slabs of the destroyed headstones. I felt better standing among these slabs than I had felt with the town's non-Jews … the last Jews to be slaughtered had been burned alive here. We stood and said *Kaddish* [prayer for the dead] …

This was in September 1952. I am unable to relate everything that the local people told me. I tried to find out the fate of my father Leib, my mother Rachel, and my sister Reisel. I asked my gentile neighbors, who had felt 'at home' in our house. I went to one of them, who was always coming and going, at our house. She invited us to a meal, served wine and told us that, on one occasion, my father had come running to ask her to hide him in her house. She had not allowed him in, not even into her barn. That whole night he stayed out in the cold. By the time morning came, she took pity on him, let him into the barn to "warm up" a little and even gave him a slice of bread. This is how she described the great 'kindness' she had extended to my father, may he rest in peace. We were so disturbed by what she told us that we did not partake of the meal and drink which she had gone to such pains to serve us, and left her 'friendly' house.

* * *

At this point, I will try to present some details that I heard from local non-Jews: In 1957, when I was already in Poland (Wroclaw), I met Stefa Czerda, a Polish lady from Jezierna who had been a teacher. She told me about the anti-Jewish committee that the Germans had established after entering the town. The committee, composed of the Ukrainian "intelligentsia", was headed by Antoniakova (the wife of Antoniak, former principal of the school) and her daughter, who all excelled in their blood-thirsty anti-semitism. They demanded of the Germans, so she told me, to let them to make Jezierna *Judenrein*. The priest was also a member of the committee. Only Pryhoda, the Ukrainian teacher, refrained from joining. According to what Stefka told me, this is what happened: after the Germans had entered Jezierna, they issued a decree ordering every Jew of the town to gather together at the synagogue. The plan was to ignite the synagogue together with all the Jews who were inside. The Jews assembled there but the plan was never carried out because of the commotion started by the gentiles, who came from the nearby streets shouting: "The Jews are butchering people", and demanded to take their revenge. Apparently, she said, this ploy was a Russian army offensive. The Germans left the town in confusion and the Jews returned to their homes. A short time later, the Germans returned and whoever fell into their hands became a victim. The first was Dr. Chune Litwak, a forward-looking man and a sharp businessman; the Ukrainians had informed on him. The murderers stabbed him with knives and smashed his head in with axes. When he said that he was a doctor, they replied that they didn't need doctors and continued to torture him until he drew his last breath. On that very same day, about 200 Jews were killed and buried in a mass grave in the center of the town.

The head of the Jews' camp was Richard Dyga. The most vicious murders were attributed to him. Many people told me about the commander of the *Ordnungsdienst* (Jewish police), called Schenkelbach. The Russians had expelled his parents from Tarnopol and they had moved to Jezierna. His daughter-in-law lived in the town. He and his daughter-in-law had the 'privilege' of being killed by Dyga himself. From what I heard, he was an honest, refined and educated person. Practically everybody, without exception, talked about the cruelty of this murderer, Dyga. While I was in Poland (1957), the town's mayor, Kubelski the dentist, told me that Dyga had been like one of the family [in Schenkelbach's home], in spite of his atrocities. He didn't forget to point out that Dyga was not a welcome guest in his house. It was clear that coercion had been used. He received him cordially *under duress*, had a friendly drink with him *under duress*, played cards with him *under duress*. He had hidden Azriel Pollack's Jewish wife and three daughters in his house but, being scared of Dyga, he made them leave while *under duress,* after which they were all slaughtered.

* * *

While roaming the town I met the young Sovitch. The Jews of Jezierna knew him well. His father was the town's *Shabbas Goy* [a gentile who performs work forbidden to a Jew on the Sabbath]. After the Sabbath Eve prayers he would extinguish the candles in the synagogue; it was to him that they used to sell the *hametz* (leavened food) before Passover; on *Yom Kippur* (Day of Atonement), he would make sure that the memorial candles did not drip from the heat. His son used these words to tell me: "The *Nimkim* (which is what he called the Germans) damn them, forced my father to transport the Jews they had killed to the cemetery. Three days and three nights my father, the *Shabbas Goy*, poured boiling tar over them to burn them to ashes. Those *Nimkim* should be burned themselves! My father returned home utterly exhausted, with the terrible odor of burnt bodies!" This had taken place during the final extermination of the Jews of Jezierna, who were interned in two different camps, one for men and one for women. On the day of extermination, the local non-Jews led by the Ukrainian priest, Dudik, came to watch the extermination of the town's Jews. This time, Stefka Czerda (Wroclaw 1957) told me, those poor people knew what was in store for them and tried to resist. They decided not to leave the camp in Dom Polski, which they turned into a stronghold. Dyga ordered hand grenades to be thrown into the camp. A fire broke out. The Nazis put the fire out and forcibly dragged out the Jews who were wearing only their underwear. Two Ukrainian policemen stood at the entrance and each Jew who passed between them sustained hammer blows to their heads. With their dying breaths they were thrown onto the trucks and taken to the cemetery to be burned. Both Sovitch and others confirmed this. The extermination of the women's camp was different. The women were put on carts as if they were to be taken to Zborow. Dr. Wilhelm Tenenbaum was with them. He had worked as a doctor in Jezierna for many years. The town's gentiles gathered to gleefully watch how the last remaining Jews were to be removed from the town. The carts purposely moved slowly along the alleyways so that the non-Jews could fully satiate themselves with the sight. Dr. Tenenbaum sat on one of the carts. He doffed his hat and said goodbye to his patients. He had continued treating his patients right up to the very last day. He was also Dyga's doctor, for which Dyga had promised to let him live. The carts started off in the direction of the cemetery. Now everyone knew where they were being taken, knew that this would be their last journey. The carts came to a halt at the cemetery. The women were arranged in a line, naked. Flammable material was poured over them and they were burned. When Tenenbaum came to say goodbye to those left, Dyga suddenly shouted: "Damned Jew, run!" Tenenbaum started running and the sadistic murderer shot him in the back. This is how Dyga kept his promise to his doctor. Jezierna was officially pronounced *Judenrein*. Dyga had fulfilled his duty. * * * One of the last families to be murdered in the town was that of Moshe Bergstein. As a tailor, he had sewn whatever Dyga needed and so was permitted to live covertly in a house belonging to a Ukrainian in Deluga Street. After the final extermination the local Ukrainian police commander had met him and asked who had given him permission to be there. Bergstein reminded him that it was Dyga. The commander went and informed on him and Dyga, himself, shot him, his wife and child inside the house. That was his reward for all those years of working for Dyga.

I knew that the Leskof family had hidden Rosa Blaustein and her daughter, Dozia. I went to visit them. His wife, Yekatarina and daughter worked in the *kolkhoz*. She complained that she didn't have the strength to work and so didn't have anything to live on. She also told me how she had hidden the two women. What she had done seemed heroic and self-sacrificial. It is only fitting that Mikhail and Yekatarina Leskof's loyalty to the Jews of Jezierna should be recorded in our Memorial Book, thereby adding them to the list of Righteous Among Nations. Shmuel Scharer also pleaded to be saved. His maid, Aniella Kutna, hid him. When the residents of Jezierna were moved to Zborow, because of the battles taking place in the vicinity, Aniella had planned to move him in a trunk in order to save him. However, a few days before they planned to flee, a gentile from Jezierna informed on him to the Gestapo and he was shot.

How My Family Was Killed

My father, Leib, survived the first pogroms and lived with his family until 1942. During the large round-up of the Jews, when hundreds of Jews were grabbed, including my father, in order to ship them to the Belzec extermination camp, my mother Rachel and my sister Reisel dashed out of the house and confronted the murderer, to get him to leave them alone, during which time my father escaped. The murderer shot at him and when he was about 200 meters from our house, he collapsed. My mother and sister were sent to Belzec. The blood of my good and upstanding father was absorbed into the soil of a park in Deluga Street. I was shown the spot where my father had fallen and I had the privilege of saying *Kaddish* for him there.

The Germans paid money for each Jew handed over to them. Dyga would give a bottle of liquor. Solovka Lobachevski who was to 'inherit' Yukel Czaczkes' tavern, was outstanding at finding and kidnapping Jews and was rewarded with the bottles of liquor promised to him by Dyga. Lobachevski was a *Banderowicz* (member of the Ukrainian Fascist Organization).

Other Incidents

Two boys, Bertchi Heliczer's youngest son and Lander's son ran away and managed to stay in hiding for some time. A Ukrainian called Wolozin, the son of the mechanic at Fischer's flour mill, informed on them. Wolozin also belonged to the Banderowiczes, who would terrorize people, especially the Poles, for a while after the entry of the Russians. Michel Fibover and others were hung dangling on the barbed wire. The Soviets killed this gang including Wolozin. One of the Nazis' loyal helpers was the carpenter Trenczuk, the son-in-law of Nicsz the cobbler. He was sentenced to 25 years in a Siberian camp. Many were Ukrainian fascists, who had actively participated in the liquidation round-ups of the Jews of Jezierna. Even today, they move around freely in various countries, including Russia. It is our greatest hope that the long arm of justice will reach them wherever they are, so that their punishment can be meted out. Among other incidents of 'good' non-Jews informing on and handing over Jews to the Gestapo, is the story I was told about the Moschzisker family. Moschzisker was David Blaustein's son-in-law. He was a rich Jew who lived in Lwow. At the time, they had moved to Jezierna, where they remained even after the entry of the Germans. Dr. Moschzisker worked at the Polyclinic in Jezierna and his family was hidden by a 'safe' gentile. This cost him a great deal of money. Every day he received messages from his family via a non-Jewish acquaintance. One day his contact brought him the news that the 'safe' gentile had betrayed his family (his father and mother, his wife and child) to the Gestapo and they had been murdered. Shocked and broken by this tragedy, the young Dr. Moschzisker committed suicide by cutting his wrists.

Poznakowski's Garden

In one of Azriel Pollack's letters he wrote that when I came to Jezierna, we would go to Zborow to meet Motel Hornstein, so that we could, perhaps, encircle the fence in Poznakowski's garden where 12,000 Jews murdered by the Nazis were buried. After I had been in Jezierna for a couple of days, we decided to go to Zborow and meet Hornstein. He was the manager of the *kolkhoz* and was working when we arrived. His Russian wife, Madia Ivanovna, welcomed us. In the meantime, we walked around Zborow. Seven years had passed since the terrible events of the war, but the whole city looked as if it was just taking place; the scene was the same as in other places in the area; the large synagogue still stood in one piece and the Hebrew lettering on it had not been erased. It was being used by the Administration. Hornstein came home in the late evening; he was tired and did not have time. Therefore, Azriel and I decided to go off on our own the next morning. Poznakowski's garden was about one kilometer from Zborow going towards Zloczow.

After every round-up the Nazi murderers were in the habit of bringing the Jews naked to a pit and gunning them down with machine guns. Many would fall injured but not yet dead into the pit. Without checking to see if anyone was still alive, soil was shoveled over them. As we neared the grave, we noticed a green strip of grass. This was the grave. Animals grazed here. The smell of both animal and human droppings (the shepherds relieved themselves there) was noticeable from afar. We stood on the large grave, ashamed and in awe of the sanctity of the place. Here lay 12,000 Jews murdered by the Nazis! All around there were headstones of various 'heroes', but the grave of thousands of victims was neglected and desecrated, not even fenced in. It didn't make any difference that they had been persecuted and murdered by the Nazi murderers, haters of Socialism and progress... Was this not a crime perpetrated by the authorities? I wanted to appeal to the town hall of Zborow but I was afraid that they would exile me again for another ten years in the place I had come from. Mordechai Marder was also buried in this grave. It is said that he could have saved himself, but he would not leave his wife and so was killed together with her.

We both stood there and said *Kaddish*. Our hearts were like stone and we couldn't even shed a single tear. Heartbroken and mute we returned to Zborow.

We returned to Jezierna. The whole time Azriel would sigh and mumble: "My wife and three glowing daughters! And my son, my son, you fell in the battle for Warsaw!" ...

* * *

The next day we traveled to Lwow, where Josef Blasser, the step-son of Schwartz the barber lived. He told us that his step-father, Jehoshua Schwartz, had resisted the S.S. when they came to take him, and they had shot him on the spot. He also said that the Ukrainians had requested that Dr. Tenenbaum be saved, since he had been an officer in the

Ukrainian army in 1919, when Ukraine was an independent state, but he did not want to [accept]. He had believed in Dyga's promise…

While in Lwow, we also learned that a synagogue was still standing and we decided to go there. It was *Rosh Hashanah* (Jewish New Year). After 12 years I was once again standing in a synagogue full of worshipers. The mood of the holy day prevailed here. I stood and looked in wonder, was this reality or was I dreaming? Jews with beards and *peyote* (side-curls), a prayer-leader, and the prayers – as in the good, old days … in the remaining Jewish synagogue which stood in Krakow Square. There were three dates written on the walls, the dates of the last three round-ups in which the Nazis exterminated the Jews of Lwow. There were a few hundred *Torah* scrolls which had been returned by the local farmers.

I spent the religious holidays in Lwow with Blasser, immediately after which I returned to the Urals. I continued to return to Jezierna every year between 1952-1957 to visit my parents' graves at the ruined cemetery and say *Kaddish* and to meet up again with local people and to hear once again the stories of the horrors which had taken place during the war. I went to my town Jezierna six times, and during all those years nothing changed, only the shadows of those murdered and the echoes of the horrors kept me company and would not leave me wherever I went there. Indeed, nothing should be forgotten, everything should be remembered and retold forever.

Editor's Note: Lipa Fischer's 2-part memoir was written in Yiddish. This second part was translated into Hebrew by the Jezierna poet Shlomo Shenhod. Only the Hebrew version is printed in the book.

[Page 289]

S. Y. Imber in Jezierna under the Nazis
by Dozia (Dora) Blaustein, New York
Translated from Yiddish by Pamela Russ

Dora Blaustein, daughter of Czina Blaustein, lives in America today. She lived through the persecutions and the hells of Hitler in Jezierna thanks to a Ukrainian man, Michael Leskof, and his wife who hid her during that time. Here she tells of one of the episodes of those terrible times: the life and murder of the poet Shmuel Yakov Imber at the hands of the Nazis, and tells of the influence that he had on the Jezierna youth at that time.

The Editorial Committee

Shmuel Yakov Imber is considered to be a Jezierner even though he was born in Zloczow. He spent his youth in the town and was married in Jezierna to the eldest daughter of the pharmacist Mintz. She was also a pharmacist. From time to time, they would come to visit their parents in the town. When he was in Jezierna, one could see him strolling through the streets. He would meet with friendly people, with activists in the *Ichud Gordonia* organization, and have discussions about their work and the evolution of their youth organizations. He would go to the local organizations and inform himself about what the youth was reading and what sort of literature interested them. He was pleased that in such a small town the youth was interested in the most recent literature. The librarian Etke Pulwer would show him books. He would have discussions with Lipa Fisher and Moishe Bik and then they would accompany him to his lodgings. As they walked, they would ask him about his own position in the areas of literature and journalism, about his articles in the Jewish newspapers, and his struggle with Hitlerism and antisemitism in Poland. He invited them in, gave each of them a copy of his book "*Asy Czystej Rasy*" (Pure Race Aces), and a copy for the library. He made a tremendous impression. They cherished the book, but along with everything else, the book was destroyed. The Germans invaded Jezierna. Difficult times began, persecutions, roundups. Imber would hide during these roundups, as did the other Jews. Aside from that, he and his wife were affected by the murder of his father-in-law, the pharmacist Mintz, and his mother-in-law's suicide. The pharmacy continued to be run by Imber's wife. Even while hiding in his bunker, Imber wrote about these events, and even though he knew that the Germans were looking for him, in his secretly written articles he gave us courage. Reading his writings, we believed that our suffering was not in vain and that the victims had not died in vain either. Imber also fell into murderous hands. They prepared a horrific death for him. They were able to kill the man, but the poet Imber they could not destroy. That which he created will remain forever, just as the light that he gave us during those dark days, that shone like the sun.

[Page 290]

Dora the Nurse
by Menachem Duhl
Translated from Yiddish by Ida Selavan–Schwarcz

Dora Mantel, who survived Hitler's hell, told many stories about her experiences, but from my conversations with her I saw that she still had a lot to tell, and each time she adds new material to her stories. In Zborow, Dora put on a white coat and became a nurse in the ghetto. The children used to call her "Mrs. Dora". When we write about the *Judenrat* (Jewish Council), *Ordnungs Dienst*, (storm–troopers), *Lager–Verbindungsmanner*,(camp –intelligence agents), fighters in the ghetto and the partisans, we should also tell how Dora helped the sick, neglected, and unfortunate Jews in the ghetto and helped relieve their terrible suffering. The Tzifris family lived in a tiny dark room – husband and wife and a few children. He had been a cobbler, but now lay paralyzed. His wife lay with a high fever; the neglected children ran around dirty, naked, and hungry. Desolation and need reigned in the tiny room. Dora happened to come in; the children cried and begged for food, the mother looked at her children and wept bitterly and the father gazed open–eyed at the ceiling as if help would come from above. Dora rolled up her sleeves, washed the father and the children, brought them some food and medicine for the mother. She visited them every day. The Rebbetzin. She was a refugee from western Galicia who came to Zborow. Her husband, the Rabbi, died on the way, and their children were murdered in the '*aktions*' [campaigns to murder Jews]. She lay alone on the floor of a little shed, her head full of lice, her whole body full of sores. Where she lay there was a fetid odor like a corpse repository. She lay there all alone. Whoever opened the door immediately ran away. Her hair was greyish–white, her face pale, but she had a majestic appearance. She prayed with her prayer book in hand all day long. Forgotten by God and man, she lay there. Dora came to visit her. She went in and the old woman raised her head, looked at her closely and began to cry. "Who are you, my dear daughter?" she asked. She had not seen a soul for a whole week. Dora washed her, brought her medicine, changed her clothing. The old woman would bless her and tell her that for these good deeds Dora would merit life. Her ancestors, rabbis and virtuous men, would bring her case to the Master of the Universe and ask that she live and be well. She repeated this prayer every day. A week later, during an *aktion*, the old Rebbetzin was murdered. "I can still see her to this day, the old Rebbetzin who prayed for my welfare, and I hear her weak voice, her prophecy that I would remain alive", says Dora. "Every year, on the date of the last *aktion*, I light a memorial candle for the old woman's soul. She blessed me, that I should live, and I was indeed saved from the murderers,"

Dora continues. In the Zborow ghetto, there was a "hospital" for epidemic illnesses (typhus and cholera), in the synagogue. The Torah scrolls, the lecterns, tables and benches had been removed. On the floor, on a bit of straw, lay the sick men, women, and children, one next to the other, like herring in a vat, half naked, with high fever. Every day the Burial Society would drag out the dead bodies, and their places were taken by new victims. It was horrible to see. Lice bit them, fleas leaped over them, bed bugs crept all over, and the helpless sick people lay there. The only Jewish doctor would come in once a day and Nurse Dora a few times a day. She was well known. When she entered, the sick people would stretch out their hands and ask for help. She had a comforting word for everyone and tried to help everyone, but what could she do? Hundreds of people expired in the dirt and desolation, in the fetid odor, with the smell of dead bodies. The conditions created by the epidemics liquidated a sizable number of the Jews in the ghetto. Dora also told how the camp commander killed 19 Jews who had committed a terrible crime – they had brought food into the ghetto, and she, the 20th person on the list, miraculously remained alive. She believed that the old Rebbetzin, with her rabbinical and virtuous forefathers, had been intermediaries for her survival.

[Pages 293-303]

A Chronicle of Watches and a Photograph
by Menachem Duhl
Translated from Yiddish by Ida Selavan–Schwarcz

It was a Tammuz [July] day, 1941. Almost a week had passed since the German-Russian war had broken out. The large Soviet army was awaiting withdrawal. The hospitals were full of wounded. Schools were converted into hospitals. On the streets of cities and towns lay the broken body parts of dead Russian soldiers. You could even see men still burning like torches. Wherever the Russians were retreating and the German SS groups were advancing, the whole roadway was smeared with the blood of Jews. In every city and *shtetl,* the Germans snatched Jews off the street, took them to a collection center and shot them. Yes, blood and tears accompanied the entry of the Germans into our cities and towns. Everywhere - pogroms and slaughter. I, along with my wife and daughter had survived the first pogrom in Zloczow. The dreadful news of the murders and what was going on went from city to city, from town to town, from mouth to mouth. The news spread everywhere, until it reached Jezierna. Fear fell upon the Jews, and when the Germans entered Jezierna, they all began to tremble. The atmosphere became restless. On the hillside near Kozowik's property, a large, deep pit had been dug. No one knew what it was needed for... The men began to hide wherever they could. The S.S. with their murderous faces and hand grenades were running around like wild beasts, kidnapping Jews on the street and leading them away. It started a panic. In his home on the estate, Wilhelm Klinger was very concerned. The news of the Zloczow pogrom had already reached Jezierna. He was very worried about our fates, the fate of his daughter, his son-in-law and the child – whether we were saved, did we have anything to eat? He was especially anxious about the fate of his granddaughter Julia. He loved her passionately. He thought he heard her cry, she wanted to eat, and we had nothing to give her... His wife Zayne, my mother-in-law, asked him to hide, but he rejected her advice, saying: "I know the Germans well, we went hand in hand with them in the war against the Russians and the Italians in 1914-1917; this is the people of Goethe and Schiller. They are soldiers, and soldiers do not murder, they are not thugs. I was also a soldier." He believed in the foundations of culture and humanity. And then two SS men entered the house, took him out of his home and told him to go with them. He went quietly. It did not even occur to him that he was being led to be killed... He saw no one in front of him, not even the pit. With a shout, one of the murderers ordered him to stand still. He stopped automatically. He still did not believe that this was the minute before his death. He still believed in the culture of the people of Goethe and Schiller- a bond that binds together the fighters at the front (combatants). Then the shot came to the base of his head and a kick from behind, and he fell into the large, wide pit. Faith in culture and humanity and in the alliance of fighters went down with him to the grave. That is how he was murdered, Wilhelm Klinger, a Jew of Jezierna, who believed wholeheartedly in humanity and culture, who committed all his life to doing good deeds for Jews and Gentiles. Indeed, both Jews and Gentiles mourned his death. His pocket-watch fell into the pit together with him. It was an Omega watch made of silver, bought at the Jubilee Exhibition of 1900. The watch was received as a gift from his grandfather when he joined the army. It came with a blessing- To be protected from all evil and all bad trouble. Indeed, he always kept the watch as if it was an amulet from a rabbi, even taking it with him when he fought the Russians in bloody battles in the Carpathians, when thousands were killed or wounded. He was lightly wounded and taken to a hospital, and he kept the watch with him. Also on the bloody front in Italy, by the Piave River and Isonzo - the watch was with him.

Austria fell. The soldiers scattered to their homes and the watch was well hidden, because there were bandits on the roads who took everything, even peoples' clothes. He returned home safely, to his wife and children. Even when he walked among the *Petlura* people, who controlled the Ukraine, he hid the watch and guarded it well. And, as stated above, even then, when the murderers shot him and threw him into the mass-grave, the watch was with him. It stopped ticking in the common grave, along with the heart of its owner. A few days later, when they exhumed and transferred the holy martyrs to the Jewish cemetery, where they were all laid together in a common grave, in a grave of brothers. My mother-in-law, A'H [may she rest in peace], received the watch - the protector/guardian - which was taken from the grave. In this round-about way, the watch returned to the family, except that the one for whom thewatch was a talisman, he did not return; he remained in the grave.

***

I will now stray from the main topic for another event, which is connected to it.

I have already mentioned that during the first pogrom we lived in Zloczow. We lived in a hiding place and our daughter became ill with appendicitis. My wife Hanya took her to a doctor in the hospital. The doctors there were all cordial. Their opinion was that it was too late to operate on her. You can understand our pain. The doctors were interested in our fate and asked how we had survived the pogrom. Our neighbor Dr. Ambas, who had also survived the pogrom and was still afraid to go out, stealthily entered our hiding place and treated the child. A few days later, the girl fell asleep, and so did we. We slept for a long time. The first one to wake up was Hanya, with a scream, and she shouted: "My father, my father is not alive! They killed him!!" In her sleep she dreamed that her father was standing before her, without saying a word. "My father is not alive! My father is not alive!" she cried, as tears flowed from her eyes. Then we learned that it was true. The Nazi murderers had murdered him. Our child also stirred from sleep. Her condition had improved and gradually she recovered. A few days later my mother-in-law, may she rest in peace, sent a wagon for us, We left Zloczow and moved to Jezierna. Approximately two weeks after the pogrom we arrived in Jezierna. A few days after our arrival, as I was cutting wood in the yard, I suddenly heard footsteps of heavy boots on the stairs leading to our house and I heard talking in German. They were two German soldiers, a sergeant and a private. I immediately went into the house and they came after me. I went out through the window and they approached my wife and daughter, who had remained at home: "Where is the Jew who was in the yard?" They began to terrorize, shouting and shooting everywhere. The child began to cry out loud. For nearly two hours the shouting continued. Meanwhile, I ran to the army headquarters and reported what was happening. My intervention was successful. A junior officer returned with me, calmed the thugs and drove them away. I could not believe he would get them out so quickly. During the episode and terror, the German sergeant saw the watch. He liked it and he took it. He put two marks on the table and said: "Here, Jews, money for the clock. We do not take without paying.

The junior officer who saved us was named Heinz Lege who came from Hamelin, on the Weiser River. For almost two weeks he dropped in to see us every evening, to protect and support us, because we lived on the outskirts of the town. A few days later I told him that the two thugs had taken the watch that was a special souvenir for us; that we had received it, salvaged from the extermination pit. He groaned and said, "The sergeant has gone already; Why didn't you tell me that before?" The fate of the watch was to be different. One evening, a few days later, Lege came to our house as usual, sat down, talked a little, and suddenly pulled out the watch, put it on the table and said: "Here is your clock". We sat there, stunned to see it; we thanked him and returned the two marks. The watch was in our hands again.

After the war, when we were already in Israel without his address, I wrote to Heinz Lege of Hamelin, and… he received the letter and immediately answered it. Here are a few sentences from his letter:

"Hamelin on Weiser. 4th January 1960. Dear Duhl Family! I am highly delighted to hear from you after almost 18 years, since I was released from the army, a long time, and unfortunately a sad time. You began your life in Haifa, Israel. When I read the first lines of your letter, there arose in my memory the events of our first meeting in Jezierna near Tarnopol. You arrived one afternoon, bathed in sweat and requested our commander's protection for your family. I happened to be there and was able to take part; I rose and strapped on my weapon to go with you. I accompanied you quickly, dear Mr. Duhl, to your house, which was high on a hill, accessible via stone steps. We got there at a crucial time. As you have already written, there were two German soldiers, one of them a sergeant in the army and the other a private in the railway service, who attacked your wife and tore her clothes and were abusing her, like pigs rioting in your home. When I ordered them to leave and threatened them with my gun, the two louts became frightened and left your house. I stayed with you for a short time and we talked. I promised to visit you in the future, because I saw that your neighbors also caused you trouble because of your possessions. I felt it was my duty to protect you in your time of need. … Also, I knew that if the incident came to the attention of my department staff, I would be heavily punished. Luckily, the event was not reported, as I also helped other Jews, because the murder and inhuman procedures went sharply against my conscience and my acceptance. I saw it as my duty to retrieve and return to you the watch that was robbed from you, that remained as a precious memento after the death of your father. Can you tell me about the assistant pharmacist in Jezierna (he meant Mrs. Imber, the pharmacist Mintz's daughter), who took care of my troops when we were sick. Is she still alive...? Are there other people from your town who survived the Nazi terror? As you may remember, we were six brothers, all soldiers, and my only sister who married a half-Jewish man. This brother-in-law, together with his mother, brothers and sisters were sent to a K.Tz.-Lager [labor camp] and were murdered there. My brother-in-law Robert Kalf, who with his mother landed in the Theresienstadt camp, was released at the last minute by the Americans. But his mother died there. The rest of the brothers and sister were taken to other camps. Of we six brothers, three fell in combat, and that's all because of that damn war... I hope and wish that there will be no more wars and all our peoples will live in friendship and tranquility." After Lege received my letter, the [Hameln newspaper] Deister-und-Weserzeitung, issue 113/4, published an article on the 6th of January 1960 headlined "An Airmail Letter from Haifa", with Lege's story about how he helped us survive during the war in 1941 and what he did for us. In his second letter of 11 March 1960, Lege wrote: "I repeat my question about whether you are settled well in Haifa. I hope so and I wish you well, and that you are in good health and managing well,….and that you forget all the troubles and worries, and that the people of Israel will reach an understanding with the Arabs. It was in the newspapers and on the radio, that here in Germany there are again problems of antisemitism, of attacks and break-ins of private houses and synagogues, but don't be concerned. Never again will there be another Hitler-style state in Germany. This you can believe - every Jew here will be respected." Now I quote a few sample lines from Lege's letter: "We hope that you have forgotten all the troubles and horrors from there, but can we completely forget all this? It left a mark on our whole lives. The memories remain and will never be forgotten. I know that 25 years later, I can still see the screaming faces of the murderers. I see them even today in my dreams. Hess's S.S. assassins and their assistants come to me often in my dreams; the Aktzias [deportations]; Jews are snatched from the street; I run away…. they grab me… take me to the assembly point… the mass grave is full of dead bodies… Standing there is a long line of naked men, women and children…soon …soon… I join the line… I become frightened. It was a dream. How is it possible to forget all this?"

**

It was June 1942. Isidore Steinberg, an engineer from Borshchiv was brought to the Jezierna work-camp, and he said that he wanted to see me. The Judenrat approved the meeting. He told me how he happened to land in this camp. He took out a pocket-watch and asked me to hide it, because he was afraid the camp officials would take it away from him, but he could not let that happen. For him the watch was a keepsake like an amulet. He had received it in 1914 when he was an officer in the Austrian army, before being sent into the fighting. When he lay in the trenches, while the bullets whistled around him and people were being killed and wounded, he kept the watch close to his body and survived. He was captured by the Russians and taken to Siberia with many other captive Austrian soldiers. Summer and winter, through mountains and valleys, in forests and fields, past roads, villages, towns they tramped. They went on foot, clothes torn, with rags tied on their feet, always hungry, but the watch was well guarded by him. He believed that he would return alive and well to his wife and child. The revolution broke out in Russia, the prisoners were released and he began to travel again... home to his wife and child, to Borshchiv. Again he walked through fields and forests, highways and Polish pathways, through cities and towns. Often he had to hide, until finally he reached home. He survived the invasion of the Petlura gangs, the western Ukrainians. He married off his daughter, he had a grandson, and now he fell into the labor camp, and who knows what will happen to him here? He would probably end up like all the Jews in the camp. He asked me to keep his watch, and after his death to send it to his family. I took it from him, but returned it before our deportation from Jezierna.   The Judenrat, in the hope that they would receive considerable compensation for Steinberg, gave him a respectable position- he became an employee of the Judenrat, and a personal servant of Obmann [representative] Lander. After the war, we met at Gliwice (Upper Silesia). His wife had redeemed him from the camp, a Polish family hid them, and he and his wife remained alive. But their daughter, husband and grandson were killed by the Nazi German murderers; and the ache for their children and grandson they carried with them forever. In America, where they had finally settled, they testified against the commander of the Jezierna camp, Richard Dyga. A few years ago he died there, leaving behind him the watch and his wife, who then immigrated to Israel and lives in an old age home in Netanya . She keeps the watch with honor, A timepiece that could tell us much about the experiences of the life, suffering and death of it's owner.

***

And now, more about the fate of the photograph.

I studied mathematics at the University of Lemberg and beginning in September 1923 I was a high-school teacher, one year in Zaleszczyki and 5 years in Horodenka. These were the first years of working in my profession. I lived with the students and their parents, sharing their concerns and joys. The towns were close to my heart and years later, when I met a former student or acquaintance from those towns, I was as happy as someone who met an old friend after many years. When I began teaching in Horodenka, the children were ages 10, 12, and 15. During the 4 years that I taught them, they grew physically and developed emotionally. From young boys and girls, they matured into adults with world views and wide horizons. Many of them continued to study, completed high school and spread to the four corners of the earth. Many of them found themselves in Israel holding valuable positions and becoming useful citizens. The little children of those days became fathers and mothers and perhaps even grandparents. They have worries, but also pleasure and pride from their children and perhaps even grandchildren. In the year 1929, the first class in Horodenka graduated. In the window of Stefanowitsch's bookstore hung a composite photograph of all the eighth grade school teachers and the graduates of the first year 1929; the first such picture ever published. For a whole week there were parents, relatives and friends of the students, and even ordinary Jews and non-Jews going specially to view the poster. "Look" - said one boy to another, pointing to the picture -"The one in the Slavic shirt is Imek, and that one with the stiff collar and tie is Sala". The second boy replied: "And there in the middle is Moshke (Minna). Our picture next year will be nicer", said the seventh year student. 1943, fourteen years later, in Brzezany. The Jews – those who were still alive, were taken to the ghettos or labor camps; epidemics, Aktions, hunger and torture swallowed up victims every day, and others who had Aryan papers lived in fear that they might be caught. We lived on Aryan papers during that time. No one was left alive from our family. After a hard winter came spring. The sun began to warm, nature came to life, people went out to breathe fresh air and warm themselves. Except for those few Jews who lived in bunkers, buried underground, or imprisoned in ghettos. In Brzezany (Berezhany), in a two-storey house of the Ukrainian Cooperative (Sayoz), in the Statistics Department, worked a clerk named Maximillian Duhl, a Karaite. His supervisor, Magister Paslawski, was pleased with his work. The three managers of the cooperative knew that Duhl was working well. They were interested in him and wanted to discover his secret. They knew that he was a high school mathematics teacher and wanted to know if he was indeed a Karaite, or, God forbid, a Jew. The supervisor, Magister P., would say different things every time. Once he told Duhl that his own wife was a teacher and came from Horodenka. Then he related that she remembered a teacher from there, who had the same name as me. Some time later he told me about a German a "Captain" in Brzezany, who was a Polak, Dr.Grobin. He was in charge of the region, supervised several departments, played a large role in administration until it was discovered that he was an imposter, "just some Jew", named Dr. Rubin. He ran away.

It was clear that these were proactive attempts. While he was talking, he would look at me carefully to see what impression the stories had on me. Almost every day he would tell me about various incidents that occurred during the Aktions. During those times my skin was covered in goosebumps, while there were shot Jewish martyrs lying in the street and Jewish blood was being spilled like water. I did not even listen or comprehend what he was telling me. My heart ached. My head was with my wife and my child. Had something God forbid happened to them? Will I find them when I return home? In this atmosphere I worked.

In Horodenka during this time, there was a Jewish teacher named David Baumgarten who taught Latin. He was originally from Berezhany. He also appeared in the newspaper picture from 1929. A few days after the Great Aktion the manager came to work happy and in a good mood and told me that he had changed his residence. He had been given a new single-family house with a garden and a yard. The previous tenant of the house was a Jew, a court secretary named Baumgarten. He and his family were liquidated in the last Aktion and my manager received his house. Baumgarten had two sons, he continued to tell me, and one of them was a teacher at the high school in Horodenka. In this dwelling the manager had found a 'Directors' Report of the Polish Horodenka Gymnasium', and in there he found that one teacher was named 'Duhl'. "But", he added, "you are called Maximilian, and the other one was called Mendel. You are a Karaite and he is a 'Yid', you were a mathematics teacher and he taught Jewish religion." In addition, he found a copy of the composite photograph [from the first graduation year]. "But the teacher of religion in the picture does not look like you", he said. 14 years after publication, the picture fell into antisemitic hands and was liable to serve as proof against me.

The war ended. I, my wife and daughter were saved, but the composite picture of the graduates of the first year, 1929, from the Polish high school in Horodenka remained with Magister Paslawski, in Brzezany, in the town where David Baumgarten lies in a mass grave.

[Page 304]

Memorial plaque for Jezierna. Holocaust Cellar Museum on Mt. Zion, Jerusalem

In Eternal Memory
of the Martyrs of the Community of
JEZIERNA
(near Tarnopol)
and surrounding area, may God avenge their blood,
who were annihilated by the Germans
and their collaborators, cursed be they,
during the years of the Holocaust
5701 – 5704, 1941–1944
Memorial Day 7 Tammuz
May their souls be bound in the bonds of life
Their memory is perpetuated by the Association of Jezierna Descendants in Israel and the
Diaspora

Yizkor Memorial Prayer

May God remember the souls of our brothers and sisters of Israel, victims of the Holocaust and its heroes and heroines, six hundred tens of thousands souls of Israel, put to death, slaughtered, strangled, buried alive, and the holy communities destroyed in sanctification of the Holy Name. May God remember their sacrificial binding, together with the sacrificial binding of the other holy ones of Israel and the heroes from days of yore and may their souls be bound in eternal life. They were beloved and pleasant in their lives and in their deaths were not parted; may they be joined together in peace in their resting–place and let us say, Amen.

* * *

We remember with reverence:

The bravery of our brothers and sisters who offered up their souls for their people in   holiness and purity;

The saga of the heroism of those besieged in the ghettos and the fighters who rose up and kindled the fire of rebellion saving the honor of their people;

The heroic and constant struggle of the common masses of the People of Israel for their human identity and their Jewish culture;

The righteous among the nations who endangered their lives to rescue Jews.

[Page 305]

About The Life of the Jezierna Jews in America
Compiled by Lipa Fischer
Translated by Dorothy Wolfthal, New York

As told by Chava Fuchs–Feuering

The first World War brought political, demographic and cultural changes. For Jews in the shetls of Galicia life became confining, and younger people began to emigrate to America. Also Jezierna's Jews, those who had family in America, began to make contact with them and emigrate.

Life was hard for the immigrants. Many had to change their professions and adjust to the ways of big cities, etc. By that time the 'Chevra Bnei Shloymeh' (society named for Reb Shloymeleh, of blessed memory) already existed and was of great help to the new immigrants.

It is important to mention several people who were active at that time:

Itzy'aleh–Yitzchak Fuchs was financial officer of the American–Jewish Congress and was befriended by Stephen Wise.

Mrs. Rosa L. Lipman was President of the Jezierna Women's Society, which worked on an equal basis with the 'Bnei Shloma Society'.

The following are the names of those who raised money and gave aid for Passover for the Jezierna Jews: **Itzy'aleh Fuchs, Esther Feuering, Simcha Feuering, Yitzchok Lechowitz.**

As told by Nuchem (Nathan) Eidel

The 'Chevra Bnei Solomon' [legal name of the society] developed extensive activities in economic, religious and social areas. They had a "sick fund", their own "sanctified ground" [cemetery] at 'Mount Zion' and 'Mount Hebron'. Among those active I remember: **Ben Teichholtz, Yitzchok Shonhaut**, son of Reb Nahum, **Itzyeh Lechowitz, Mrs.Rosa Lipman.**

As told by Joseph Charap

I left Jezierna in 1922, but the shetl with its streets, little houses, shops and marketplace still remain before my eyes. In America I received great help from 'Bnei Shloymeh'. I live in New York and am employed as a salesman. My closest [relatives] in the shtetl were killed by the Nazi murderers.

As told by Moshe Fuch

I left Jezierna in 1937. On my arrival in New York I was introduced by a friend to 'Bnei Shloymeh'. At that time it was a flourishing organization, with many members and a nice location. They also had their own doctor. There were also Torah scrolls; one could *daven* [pray] there, especially during the holidays. That was where we would meet Jezierna "*mishpocha*" [kinfolk]. It was joyful; people would sing and dance.

In recent years, conditions have changed. As things are now – one generation goes and the next generation comes – the elders are fading away and the young people distance themselves. Some are also distant from Jewish tradition. They move to further neighborhoods and work in different professions, mostly in intellectual professions and sciences. 'Business' is no longer an ambition for the young.

The economic situation of the older Jezierna people is as follows: Some are established in government posts or private firms. Among Jezierna Jews there are hardly any 'big business' people; independent merchants are also few. The few large companies are being liquidated because their owners are no longer able to manage them. Thus, gradually, the young generation moves on.

The young generation seeks after knowledge and their elders encourage them. They attend universities, acquire free professions, and become doctors, engineers, teachers, economists and simply scholars. I would like to mention some of them:

Nachum Fuchs' grandchildren are engineers, doctors and lawyers;

Itzy'a Zilberberg's are intellectuals;

David Blaustein's grandchild is a famous children's doctor;

Motel Fischer's grandchild is a lecturer on atomic–physics in an advanced school for atomic research;

Moishe Lachman's granddaughter is a student of humanities and will remain at the college to do advanced research;

Berl Feiering's grandchild is a college professor. I have only listed a few.

Note by MD: For other items about A.M. Fuchs, see Pages 27, 63 and 305

As told by Esther Feiering

Jezierna Jews in the American Army in both World Wars. In all armies that waged war from 1914 to 1918, Jews participated. **Benjamin Feiering**, an American citizen (a Jezierner) was an American soldier and fought in France. His brother, **Simcha Feiering**, an Austrian citizen, fought in the Austrian Army against France. Hence, Benjamin Feiering fought against Simcha Feiering – brother against brother. This was not the only case.

In World War II, 1939–1945, Jezierna Jews fought in the American Army against Japan and against the Nazis. I will mention just a few: **Yossi Fuchs**, an American soldier fought against Japan – became a prisoner of war. He suffered for four years, longing to return home.

In Europe, fighting against the Nazis: **Chuna Fuchs, Anschel Lachman, Motel Herzog**, and others. They fought face–to–face against the Nazi murderers, taking revenge for the Jewish Martyrs. They had the privilege of freeing the Jewish survivors of the death camps.

In America as told by Joseph Fuchs

By the time I came to America almost all immigrants, especially those from Galicia including Jezierna Jews, lived in an established neighborhood. The Jezierna Society, which provided material help to all, was also there. As time went on, black people began to move into the Jewish neighborhood. Co–existence was not always ideal – many white people, including Jewish people, Jezierna Jews among them, moved away to other areas, far from the populated centers. This disrupted the ongoing work of the Society and weakened its effectiveness. Fewer and fewer people came to the meetings and work became harder for the secretary, **Joseph Zilberberg**, of blessed memory. The current secretary also struggles with these difficulties and is not able to bring the Society to its previous state. Only the cemetery remains and when a Jezierner dies he receives a Jewish burial.

I myself am also a member of 'B'nai Brith'. I am also active on a higher level within the organization. As a fighter in World War II, I am also a member of the Jewish War Veterans Organization of the United States.

At the outbreak of the war against Germany and Japan I was mobilized and sent to the Japanese front from 1941 until the end of the war. I lived through very hard times. Barely three years had passed since I left Jezierna. I still breathed Jezierna air. Before my eyes I saw the house where we lived, my family, my friends with whom I was born and raised. And then the dreadful times began: Japan, allied with Nazi Germany, attacked the United States.

And I – a Jezierna Jew and an American soldier in the Far East, at war with Japan. Could our ancestors have imagined such a thing could happen?

I was stationed in the Philippines. On December 7th, 1941, the Japanese attacked our base. We were in a battle that lasted until April 8th, 1942 – that is, fully four months!

Severe attacks from the east, west, north and south. We were in big trouble – without food, without ammunition – But we were determined to fight. Daily casualties were almost 80%. But the survivors, I among them, did not surrender. Our battles and our heroic struggles are recorded under the names "Bataan" and "Corregidor" – names of the half–island Bataan and the island of Corregidor in the [South–West] Pacific Ocean. In those battles I was taken prisoner of Japan.

The treatment of war prisoners in Japan was inhuman: hard physical labor, little food – suffering hunger. Many prisoners soon died. Everyone needs to have a little luck. Taken prisoner along with me was a Doctor Bilsky who worked at his calling here as well. Thanks to him I remained in the camp as a tailor. I was put into the sewing workshop as a sewing assistant. The chief tailor was a Texan. He taught me how to work on the sewing machine and that's how I came to remain a tailor by trade.

When American planes began to bomb us, it was decided to move us to a camp in Japan. While we were being transferred I fell off the truck and hurt myself badly, and they moved me to a local hospital. The ships that were carrying the prisoners were bombed by the Americans – Japan had not marked these ships to indicate that they were carrying prisoners – and of the two thousand, only seventy survived.

When I recovered from my injuries they transferred me to a camp on a Japanese island where conditions were awful. The Japanese guards were demoralized, basically because of American air bombing. American planes would fly freely. They would drop letters, medicine and even food for us. We never got newspapers. But we began to notice that the guards were starting to act friendly toward us, and were often talking amongst themselves.

From the parachutes that fell I sewed together an American flag, and when we were freed, we marched under that flag. The flag is now in the American War Museum.

I was rescued, stayed alive and received a commendation from the American government.

Coordinated, Transcribed & Edited by Zeneth Eidell, New York

YAD VASHEM

(MEMORIAL)

Note: The list of martyrs on pages 156 – 169 (original book pages 312 – 318) is a transliteration of names from the original book. The page numbers refer to the original book page numbers.

[Pages 312-318]

List of the Martyrs

Memorial Book of Jezierna

Transliterated by Vivian Singer
Edited by Ann Harris

Family name(s)	First name(s)	Sex	Marital status	Maiden name	Father's name	Mother's name	Name of spouse	Residence	Additional family members	Remarks	Page
EIDEL	Shalom	M						Jezierna	and his family		312
APTER	Meir	M						Jezierna	and his family		312
AST	Yaakov	M						Jezierna	and his family		312
OLEXENTER	Arush							Jezierna			312
ALTMAN	Frume	F						Jezierna			312
ALTMAN	Moshe	M						Jezierna	and his family		312
IMBER	Dr. Shmuel Yaakov	M						Jezierna	and his family	Writer	312
ORDREICH	Moshe	M						Jezierna	and his family		312
ALTMAN	Moshe	M						Dovzhanka	and his family	In Jezierna, Ukraine during war	312
ADLER	Avraham	M						Jezierna	and his family	In Krosno, Poland during war	312
BIEN	Meir	M						Jezierna	and his family		312
BIEN	Moshe	M						Jezierna	and his family		312
BIEN	Zelig	M						Jezierna	and his family		312
BIEN	Yechiel	M						Jezierna	and his family		312
BIEN	Shmuel	M						Jezierna			312
BYK	Yaakov	M			Leyzer			Jezierna	and his family		312
BYK	Binia	M			Leyzer			Jezierna	and his family		312
BERGER	Azriel	M						Jezierna	and his family		312
BLEICH	Leib	M						Jezierna	and his family		312
BRAUN	Nota	M						Jezierna	and his family		312
GLASS	Shlomo	M						Jezierna	and his family		312
GLASS	Avraham	M						Jezierna			312
GOTTFRIED	Eli	M						Jezierna	& his family		312
		Sex						Residence		Remarks	Page

Family name(s)	First name(s)	Marital status	Maiden name	Father's name	Mother's name	Name of spouse		Additional family members		
GOLDBERG	Yaakov	M	Married				Itte	Jezierna	and his family		312
GOLDBERG	Itte	F	Married				Yaakov	Jezierna	and her family		312
GLAZER	Meir	M						Jezierna	and his family	caretaker	312
GINSBERG	Avraham	M						Jezierna		Son-in-law of Wolf Fisher	312
GOTTFRIED	Mordechai	M	Married		Eliyahu		Malka	Syrovary	and his family	Ukraine during war	
GOTTFRIED	Malka	F	Married				Mordechai	Jezierna			312
GOTTFRIED	Binia	M			Yosef			Jezierna			312
GOTTFRIED	Mordechai	M			Aharon			Jezierna			312
GOLDBERG	Zissel	F						Jezierna			312
GLASS	Arush Aharon	M						Jezierna			312
GLASS	Mania	F						Jezierna			312
GLEIT	Meir	M						Jezierna			312
GLEIT	Yisrael	M						Jezierna			312
GLEIT		F						Jezierna		Several sisters	312
GOTTFRIED	Maltche	F			Yosef			Jezierna			312
GOTTFRIED	Yoel	M			Eli			Jezierna			312
DIAMANT	Mendel	M						Jezierna	and his family		312
DANZER	Yaakov	M						Jezierna	and his family		312
BRAUN	Yaakov	M						Jezierna	and his family		312
BERNSTEIN	Berel	M						Jezierna	and his family		312
BERNSTEIN	Dr. Nissan	M						Jezierna	and his family	Doctor	312
BERNSTEIN	Moshe	M						Jezierna	and his family		312
BERNSTEIN	Micha'el	M						Jezierna			312
BARAN	Shevach	M						Jezierna			312
BLAUSTEIN	Ben-Tzion	M						Jezierna	and his family		312
BLAUSTEIN	Munia	M						Jezierna			312
BLAUSTEIN	Munia	M						Jezierna	and his family		312
BYK	Mottel	M						Jezierna	and her family		312
BYK	Naftali	M						Jezierna	and his family		312
BYK	Yaakov	M						Jezierna	& his family		312
BYK	Mattel	M			Binia			Jezierna	& his family		312
BYK	Moshe	M			Binia			Jezierna			312

Family name(s)	First name(s)	Sex	Marital status	Maiden name	Father's name	Mother's name	Name of spouse	Residence	Additional family members	Remarks	Page
BLAUSTEIN	Aharon	M						Jezierna			312
BLEICH	Shalom	M						Jezierna	and his family		313
BILER	Shimon	M						Jezierna	and his family		313
BRAUN	Mordechai Hersh	M						Jezierna	and his family		313
BRAUN	Beri	M						Jezierna	and his family		313
BLASSER	Moshe Munia	M						Jezierna			313
BLASSER	Aharon Tonia	M						Jezierna		Tonia - misspelling in Hebrew?	313
BLASSER	Devora	M						Jezierna	and her family		313
BLATT	Shlomo	M						Jezierna		Father-in-law of Meir Zamoyre	313
BLATT	Mania	F						Jezierna			313
BARAN	Isser	M						Jezierna			313
BLAUSTEIN	David	M						Jezierna			313
BARAN	Ita	F						Jezierna	and her family		313
BYK	Breina	F						Jezierna	and her family		313
BLAUSTEIN	Yaakov	M						Jezierna	and his family		313
BARAN	Roza	F						Jezierna			313
BYK	Yosef	M						Jezierna	and his family		313
BARAN	Hersh	M						Jezierna			313
BLEICH	Aharon	M						Jezierna			313
GOTTFRIED	Yosef	M	Married		Aharon		Figa?	Jezierna	and his family		313
GOTTFRIED	Figa?	F	Married				Yosef	Jezierna	and her family		313
GOTTFRIED	Yaakov	M						Jezierna	and his family		313
GOTTFRIED	Vilka							Jezierna			313
GOTTFRIED	Mottel	M						Jezierna			313
DANZER	Avraham	M						Jezierna	and his family		313
DANZIGER		M						Jezierna	and his family		313
DANZER	Yaakov	M						Jezierna			313
HAZELNUSS	Mania	F						Jezierna	and her mother		313
HECHT	Mordechai	M						Jezierna			313
HALPERIN	Yitzchak	M						Jezierna	and his family		313
HIRSHHORN	Aharon	M						Jezierna	& his family		313

Family name(s)	First name(s)	Sex	Marital status	Maiden name	Father's name	Mother's name	Name of spouse	Residence	Additional family members	Remarks	Page
HIRSHHORN	Avraham	M						Jezierna			313
HIRSHHORN	Rivka	F						Jezierna			313
HIRSHHORN	Nota	M						Jezierna	and his family		313
HEILREICH		M						Jezierna			313
HALICZER	Berzia	M						Jezierna	and his family		313
HALICZER	Rakele							Jezierna			313
HOCHBERG	Avraham	M						Jezierna			313
HIRSHHORN	Leizer	M						Jezierna	and his family		313
HIRSHHORN	Mattia	M			Lazar			Jezierna	and his family		313
HALICZER	Moshe	M			Yosef			Jezierna	and his family		313
HALICZER	Yosef	M			Moshe			Jezierna			313
HALICZER	Chaim	M			Moshe			Jezierna			313
HALICZER	Moshe	M			Shimon			Jezierna			313
HOCH	Yechezkel	M						Jezierna	and his family		313
HOCH	Yisrael	M						Jezierna	and his family		313
HIRSHHORN	Mattia	M						Jezierna	and his family		313
HALPERIN	Chaya	F						Jezierna			313
HOFFENBERG	Shmuel	M						Jezierna	and his family	Son-in-law? of Chaya Gitl	313
HOCHBERG	Moshe	M						Jezierna	and his family		313
HIRSHHORN	Shalom	M						Jezierna	and his family		313
HERZOG	Avraham	M	Married				Roza	Jezierna	and his sons/children		313
HERZOG	Roza	F	Married				Avraham	Jezierna	and her sons/children		313
WILNER	Shlomo	M						Jezierna	and his family		313
WILNER	Reuven	M						Jezierna	and his family		313
WILNER	Pinchas Piner	M						Jezierna			313
WILNER	Meir	M						Jezierna			314
WILNER	Soshe	M						Jezierna			314
WINTER	Yisrael	M						Jezierna	and his family		314
WINTER	Munia	M						Jezierna	and his family		314
WIESELTHIER	Moshe	M						Jezierna	and his family		314
WIESELTHIER	Zische	M						Jezierna	and his family		314

Family name(s)	First name(s)	Sex	Marital status	Maiden name	Father's name	Mother's name	Name of spouse	Residence	Additional family members	Remarks	Page
WARHAFTIG	Moshe	M						Jezierna	and his family		314
WASSERMAN	Yitzchak	M						Jezierna			314
WASSERMAN	Bila	F						Jezierna			314
ZANDBERG	Chana	F						Jezierna	and her family		314
ZAMOJRE	Meir	M						Jezierna	and his family		314
ZAMOJRE	Yaakov	M						Jezierna	and his family		314
ZILPA	Yosef	M						Jezierna			314
ZILBERBERG	Meir	M						Jezierna	and his family		314
ZAMOJRE	Chana	F						Jezierna			314
ZAMOJRE	Avraham	M						Jezierna	and his family	Written in parentheses "Wolf Fisher". Meaning not clear.	314
ZAMOJRE	Yisrael	M			Avraham			Jezierna			314
ZAMOJRE	Eida	F						Jezierna			314
ZEIDMAN	Naftali	M						Jezierna	and his family		314
ZAMOJRE	Marcus Mordechai	M						Jezierna			314
ZILBERBERG	Kreine	F						Jezierna			314
SALTZ								Jezierna	and his family		314
ZILBERBERG	Atziv?	M						Jezierna			314
CHARTENER	Sara	F						Jezierna			314
CHARAP	Nachum	M						Jezierna	and his family		314
CHARAP	Naftali	M			Nachum			Jezierna	and his family		314
CHARAP	Shalom	M						Jezierna	and his family		314
TENENBAUM	Dr. Wilhelm	M						Jezierna	and his family	Doctor	314
TURKEL	Gershon	M						Jezierna	and his family		314
TURKEL	Natan	M						Jezierna	and his family		314
TURKEL	Melech	M						Jezierna	and his family	Son-in-law of Chaya Gitl	314
KATZ CHARAP	Naftali	M			Shalom			Jezierna	and his family		314
CHARAP	Simcha	M						Jezierna	and his family		314
CHARAP	Berish	M						Jezierna	and his family		314

Family name(s)	First name(s)	Sex	Marital status	Maiden name	Father's name	Mother's name	Name of spouse	Residence	Additional family members	Remarks	Page
CHARAP	Avraham	M						Jezierna	and his family		314
CHARAP	Yosef	M						Jezierna			314
CHARAP	Chava	F						Jezierna			314
JAFFE	Shalom	M						Jezierna	and his family		314
JAFFE	Yosef	M						Jezierna	and his family		314
JAFFE	Sheva	F						Jezierna			314
JAFFE	Malka	F						Jezierna			314
JAFFE	Nachum	M						Jezierna			314
KATZ	Hersh	M						Jezierna			314
KATZ	Yaakov	M						Jezierna	and his family		314
KATZ	Matia							Jezierna	and his family		314
KATZ	Hersh	M						Jezierna	and his family		314
KATZ	Abba	M				Miriam		Jezierna	and his family		314
KATZ	Sommer							Jezierna	and his family		314
KATZ	Hersh	M						Jezierna	and his family		314
KATZ	Eidel	M						Jezierna	and his family		314
KATZ	Shimon	M						Jezierna			314
KATZ	Simcha	M						Jezierna			314
KATZ	Yaakov	M						Jezierna	and his family	In Krosno, Poland during war	314
KATZ	Klara	F						Jezierna			314
KATZ	Andel	F			Somer?			Jezierna			314
LANDER								Jezierna	and his family		315
LITVAK	Dr. Channa	M						Jezierna	and his family	Doctor	315
LITVAK	Alyss	M			Chane?			Jezierna			315
LAUFER	Hersh	M						Jezierna	and his family		315
LAUFER	Vilka							Jezierna			315
LAKHER	Yechezkel	M						Jezierna	and his family	In Krosno, Poland during war	315
LEITNER	Zev	M						Jezierna			315
LEITNER	Babale							Jezierna			315
LEITNER	Batia	F						Jezierna			315
LACHMAN	Shalom	M						Jezierna			315
LACHMAN	Malka	F						Jezierna			315
LACHMAN	Rachel	F						Jezierna			315
LACHMAN	Feige	F						Jezierna			315

Family name(s)	First name(s)	Sex	Marital status	Maiden name	Father's name	Mother's name	Name of spouse	Residence	Additional family members	Remarks	Page
LACHMAN	Natan	M			Shalom			Jezierna			315
LACHMAN	Leitzi	F			Shalom			Jezierna			315
MANTEL	Chaya Gittel	F						Jezierna	and her family		315
MANTEL	Mattia							Jezierna	and his family		315
MANTEL	Yaakov	M						Jezierna			315
MOSHCHISKER	Zalman	M						Jezierna	and his family		315
MOSHCHISKER	Dr. Yosef	M						Jezierna	and his family	Doctor	315
MARDER	Mordechai	M	Married				Roza	Jezierna			315
MARDER	Roza	F	Married				Mordechai	Jezierna			315
MINTZ	Ludwig	M						Jezierna	and her family	Pharmacist	315
MARGOLIES								Jezierna	and family		315
MIGDAN	Moshe	M						Dovzhanka	and his family	In Jezierna, Ukraine during war	315
NARMAN								Jezierna			315
SIGAL	Leib	M						Jezierna			315
SIGAL	Lana	F						Jezierna			315
SIGAL	Ben-Tzion	M						Jezierna	and his family		315
SOKOLSKI								Jezierna	and his family		315
FUCHS	Berish	M						Jezierna	and his family		315
FUCHS	Shmuel	M						Jezierna	and his family		315
FUCHS	Nachum	M						Jezierna	and his family		315
FUCHS	Leibish	M						Jezierna	and his family		315
FUCHS	Yosef	M						Jezierna			315
FUCHS	Micha'el	M						Jezierna			315
FUCHS	Avraham	M			Ayzik?			Jezierna			315
FUCHS	Gittel	F						Jezierna			315
FUCHS	Kressel?							Jezierna			315
FUCHS	Shula							Jezierna	and family		315
FUCHS	Losha							Jezierna			315
FUCHS	Abba	M						Jezierna	and his family		315
FUCHS	Mirel	M						Jezierna			315
FUCHS	Viktor	M			David			Jezierna	and his family		315
FUCHS	Yosef	M			Eydl?			Jezierna	and his family		315
FUCHS	Sania							Jezierna	and family		315
FUCHS	Zische	F						Jezierna			315

Family name(s)	First name(s)	Sex	Marital status	Maiden name	Father's name	Mother's name	Name of spouse	Residence	Additional family members	Remarks	Page
FUCHS	Shlomo	M						Jezierna	and his family		315
FUCHS	Yitzchak	M			Pinchas			Jezierna	and his family		315
FUCHS	Shmulik	M			Yitzchak			Jezierna			315
FUCHS	Matta	M			David			Jezierna	and his family		315
FUCHS	Monyek	M			Matta			Jezierna	and his family		315
FUCHS	Leib	M			Avigdor			Jezierna	and his family		315
FUCHS	Micha'el	M			David			Jezierna	and his family		315
FUCHS	Baruch	M						Jezierna	and his family		315
FUCHS	Moshe	M						Jezierna	and his family		315
FUCHS	Gittel	F			Baruch			Jezierna			315
PERLMUTTER	Zische	M						Jezierna	and his family		316
PERLMUTTER	Mendel	M						Jezierna	and his family		316
FALK	Feige	F						Jezierna	and her family		316
FALK	Eidel	M						Jezierna	and his family		316
FRIEDFELD								Dovzhanka		In Jezierna, Ukraine during war	316
PUNDYK	Moshe	M						Dovzhanka		In Jezierna, Ukraine during war	316
FREILICH	Hersh	M						Jezierna	and his family		316
FREILICH	Yaakov	M						Jezierna	and his family		316
FINK	Avraham	M						Jezierna	and his family	Son-in-law of ??	316
FUCHS	Henia	F					Shlomo	Jezierna			316
FUCHS	Chaya	F					David	Jezierna			316
FUCHS	Salka	F			Matye			Jezierna			316
FUCHS	Moshe Gedalia	M						Jezierna	and his family		316
FUCHS	Yitzchak	M						Jezierna	and his family		316
FUCHS	Hersh	M			Chayim			Jezierna	and his family		316
FUCHS	Sania							Jezierna	and his family		316
FUCHS	Bonia	M			Chaim			Jezierna	and his family		316

Family name(s)	First name(s)	Sex	Marital status	Maiden name	Father's name	Mother's name	Name of spouse	Residence	Additional family members	Remarks	Page
FUCHS	Hersh	M						Zboriv	and his family	In Jezierna, Ukraine during war	316
FUCHS	Yaakov	M						Zboriv	and his family	In Jezierna, Ukraine during war	316
FISHER	Leib	M						Jezierna			316
FISHER	Rachel	F						Jezierna			316
FISHER	Reizel	F						Jezierna			316
FISHER	Mendel	M						Jezierna	and his family		316
FISHER	Chaim	M			Mendel			Jezierna	and his family		316
FISHER	Reuven	M			Mendel			Jezierna	and his family		316
FISHER	Moshe	M			Mendel			Jezierna	and his family		316
FISHER	Nunia				Mendel			Jezierna	and his family		316
FISHER	Tzila	F			Mendel			Jezierna			316
FISHER	Shalom	M			Wolf			Jezierna	and his family		316
FISHER	Leibish	M			Wolf			Jezierna	and his family		316
FISHER	Mottel	M			Wolf			Jezierna	and his family		316
FISHER	Yosef	M			Wolf			Jezierna	and his family		316
FISHER	Rivka	F						Jezierna	and her family		316
FISHER	Shalom	M			Moshe			Jezierna	and his family		316
FISHER	Chaim	M			Moshe			Jezierna			316
FRANKEL	Chaim	M						Jezierna	and his family		316
PACKET	Avraham	M						Jezierna	and his family		316
PACKET	Nunia	M						Jezierna	and his family		316
FISHER	Yosef	M			Avigdor			Jezierna			316
FISHER	Moshe	M			Avigdor			Jezierna			316
FISHER	Malka	F			Avigdor			Jezierna			316
FEUERSTEIN	Henich	M						Jezierna	and his family		316
FINK	Pinchas	M						Jezierna	and his family		316
FINK	Sara	F						Jezierna			316
FINK	Tzipa	F						Jezierna			316
PACKET	Nashke?							Jezierna	and family		316
PACKET	Yitzchak	M						Jezierna	& his family		316

Family name(s)	First name(s)	Sex	Marital status	Maiden name	Father's name	Mother's name	Name of spouse	Residence	Additional family members	Remarks	Page
PACKET								Jezierna	and his family		316
PACKET	David	M						Jezierna	and his family		316
PACKET	Yitzchak	M						Jezierna	and his family		316
PULVER	Yaakov	M						Jezierna	and his family		316
PULVER	Heshia	M						Jezierna			316
PULVER	Atila	F						Jezierna			316
PULVER	Rozia	F						Jezierna			316
PACKET	Nota	M			Moshe			Jezierna	and his family		316
PACKET	Munia	M						Jezierna	and his family		316
PACKET	Fenia	M						Jezierna	and his family		316
PACKET	Roza	F			Fenia			Jezierna			316
PACKET	Yaakov	M			Fenia			Jezierna			316
FEURING	Yisrael	M						Jezierna	and his family		316
FEURING	Yosef	M						Jezierna	and his family		316
FEURING	Shlomo	M						Jezierna	and his family		316
PACKET	Eli Baruch	M						Jezierna	and his family		316
PACKET	Avraham Chaim	M						Jezierna			316
FISHER	Wulf	M						Jezierna			316
FUCHS	Vilka							Jezierna			316
FLAMM	Yehoshua	M						Jezierna			316
FEUERSTEIN	Henoch	M						Jezierna			316
FEUERSTEIN	Rivka	F						Jezierna			316
FEUERSTEIN	David	M						Jezierna			316
FEUERSTEIN	Monyek	M						Jezierna			316
FEUERSTEIN	Avraham	M						Jezierna			317
FEUERSTEIN	Shlomo	M						Jezierna			317
FREILICH	Zalman Yosef	M						Jezierna			317
FUCHS	Itzia	M			Avigdor			Jezierna			317
FUCHS	Avigdor	M			Itzia			Jezierna			317
FUCHS	Shimon	M			Avigdor			Jezierna			317
CZACZKES	Mattel/Mottel	M						Jezierna	and family		317
CZACZKES	Yokel	M						Jezierna	and his family		317
CZACZKES	Dozia							Jezierna	and family		317
CZACZKES	Avraham	M						Jezierna	and his family		317
CZACZKES	Munia	M						Jezierna	& his family		317

Family name(s)	First name(s)	Sex	Marital status	Maiden name	Father's name	Mother's name	Name of spouse	Residence	Additional family members	Remarks	Page
CHATENBERG	Chaim	M						Jezierna	and his family		317
CZACZKES	Shimon	M						Jezierna	and his family		317
CZACZKES	Henich	M			Shimon			Jezierna	and his family		317
CZACZKES	Itzia	M			Shimon			Jezierna	and his family		317
CZACZKES	David	M			Shimon			Jezierna	and his family		317
CZACZKES	Tinia							Jezierna			317
CZACZKES	Zissel	F						Jezierna			317
CZACZKES	Adia							Jezierna			317
CZACZKES	Henich							Jezierna			317
CZACZKES	Elke	F						Jezierna			317
CZACZKES	Zische							Jezierna			317
KALMAN	Moshe	M						Jezierna	and his family		317
KALMAN	Yosef	M						Jezierna	and his family		317
KALMAN	Chana	F	Married					Jezierna			317
KALMAN		M	Married				Chana	Jezierna			317
KALAFER	Sheindel	F						Jezierna			317
KALAFER	Maltsche							Jezierna			317
KALAFER	Eidel	M						Jezierna			317
KASSER	Hersh Lozer	M			·			Jezierna	and his family		317
KAMINKER	Zacharia	M						Jezierna	and his family		317
KURTZER	Eira	M						Jezierna	and his family		317
KURTZER	Binyamin	M						Jezierna			317
KURZROCK	Avraham	M			Moshe			Jezierna	and his family		317
KORN	Shmuel	M						Jezierna	and his family		317
KURZROCK	Shlmon	M						Jezierna	and his family		317
KURZROCK	Avraham	M			Shimon			Jezierna			317
KASSER	Avraham	M						Jezierna	and his family		317
KASSER	Fischel	M						Jezierna			317
KURZROCK	Reizel	F			Mordechai			Jezierna			317
KURZROCK	Chana	F			Mordechai			Jezierna			317
KURZROCK	Moshe	M						Jezierna	and his family		317
KURZROCK	Avraham	M			Mordechai			Jezierna	and his family		317
KURZROCK	Asher	M			Gershon			Jezierna	and his family		317

Family name(s)	First name(s)	Sex	Marital status	Maiden name	Father's name	Mother's name	Name of spouse	Residence	Additional family members	Remarks	Page
KLEIN	Berel	M						Jezierna		Son-in-law of Lazer Shtayger	317
KLEIN	Rachel	F						Jezierna			317
KLINGER	Wilhelm	M	Married					Jezierna			317
KLINGER		F	Married				Wilhelm	Jezierna			317
KASSER	Chaim	M						Jezierna			317
KAMINER								Jezierna			317
KASTNER								Jezierna	and his family		317
ROZENFELD	Batia	F						Jezierna			317
ROZENFELD	Berel	M						Jezierna			317
ROZENFELD	Isaac	M						Jezierna	and his family		317
ROZENFELD	Mattia	M						Jezierna	and his family		317
ROZENFELD	Reiza							Jezierna			317
ROZENFELD	Natan	M						Jezierna	and his family		317
ROZENFELD	Natzia							Jezierna			317
ROZENFELD	Sania	F						Jezierna	and her family		317
REIS	Shmuel Moshe	M						Jezierna			318
REIS	Henia	F						Jezierna			318
ROZENFELD	Moshe	M			Avraham			Jezierna	and his family		318
ROZENFELD	Yehuda Hersh	M						Jezierna	and his family		318
ROZEN	Yaakov	M						Jezierna	and his family		318
ROZEN	Avraham	M						Jezierna			318
ROZEN	Avraham	M						Jezierna	and his family		318
RAPPAPORT	Efraim	M						Nesterovtsy	and his family	In Jezierna, Ukraine during war	318
RAPPAPORT	David	M						Nesterovtsy	and his family	In Jezierna, Ukraine during war	318
REIS	Yosef	M						Jezierna	and his family		318
RAPPAPORT	Moshe	M						Jezierna	and his family		318
ROZENFELD	Yitzchak	M						Jezierna	and his family		318
ROZENFELD	Velvel	M						Jezierna			318
RAPPAPORT	Hersh	M						Malashkovtse		In Jezierna, Ukraine during war	318
ROZENFELD	Baruch	M						Jezierna			318

Memorial Book of Jezierna

Family name(s)	First name(s)	Sex	Marital status	Maiden name	Father's name	Mother's name	Name of spouse	Residence	Additional family members	Remarks	Page
SCHLITA	Rabbi Lipa	M	Married					Jezierna	and his daughters		318
SCHLITA		F	Married				Lipa	Jezierna	and her daughters		318
SCHLITA	Gitela	F						Jezierna			318
SPINDEL	Yitzchak	M						Jezierna	and his family		318
SCHERER	Shlomo	M						Jezierna	and his family		318
SCHERER	Shmuel	M						Jezierna	and his family		318
SCHARF	Yechel	M						Jezierna	and his family		318
SCHAPIRA	Brana	M						Jezierna			318
SCHAPIRA	Binia	F		Shapira	Brana			Jezierna			318
SCHAPIRA	Ester	F				Binia		Jezierna			318
STEIGER	Henzel							Jezierna	and family		318
SCHWARTZ	Yehoshua	M						Jezierna	and his family		318
STOCKHAMMER	Hersh Leib	M						Jezierna	and his family		318
SCHWEIGER	Shlomo	M						Jezierna	and his family		318
SCHWEIGER	Magister Maltsche							Jezierna			318
STEIGER	Chaim	M						Jezierna	and his family		318
SCHERER	Zalman	M						Jezierna			318
SCHAMM	Isaac	M						Jezierna	and his family		318
SCHAMM	Yaakov	M						Jezierna	and his family		318
SPINDEL	David	M						Jezierna	and his family		318
SPINDEL	Magister Mottel	M						Jezierna	and his family		318
SPINDEL	Buma	M						Jezierna	and his family		318
SCHEINHAUT	Shimon	M						Jezierna	and his family		318
SCHEINHAUT	Shmuel David	M						Jezierna	and his family		318
SCHEINHAUT	Sender	M						Jezierna			318
SCHEINHAUT	Nachum	M						Jezierna			318
SCHEINHAUT	Chaim	M							and his family	In Jezierna, Ukraine during war	318
SCHEINHAUT	Yaakov	M						Jezierna			318
SCHOR	Yosef	M			Chaim			Jezierna	and his family		318

Family name(s)	First name(s)	Sex	Marital status	Maiden name	Father's name	Mother's name	Name of spouse	Residence	Additional family members	Remarks	Page
STEIGER	Lozer	M						Jezierna	and his family		318
SCHOR	Nachum	M						Jezierna	and his family		318
SHAPIRA	Moshe	M						Syrovary		In Jezierna, Ukraine during war	318
SHAPIRA	Perel	F						Plotycha		In Jezierna, Ukraine during war	318
SHAPIRA	Malka	F						Plotycha		In Jezierna, Ukraine during war	318
SHAPIRA	Bela	F						Plotycha		In Jezierna, Ukraine during war	318
SCHWARTZ	Peretz	M						Jezierna			318
SCHORMAN	Moshe Shemesh	M						Jezierna	and his family		318
SCHOR	Yitzchak	M						Jezierna		Brother of Nachum	318

Edited by Ann Harris

Prepared by Lippa Fischer
Completed by Pesach Altman, Azriel Zmora, Yitzhak Charap. Shimon Kritz

[Page 319]

Personal Family Memorials
Assembled by M.D.
Translated by Ann Gleich Harris

For Those Close to Our Hearts
Who Were Destroyed at the Hands of the Evil-Doers
To Immortalize Them Forever We Perpetuate Their Names

Our beloved sister, Feige Altman and her husband Wilka,
Our brother, Moshe Altman, who perished in the Shoah.
May they be remembered forever

REMEMBERED BY:

Pesach Altman
Michael Altman
Shmuel Altman

Haifa

[Page 320]

Their Souls Are in Heaven
Our Parents:
Esther Malka Charap Barer
Hersch Barer

OUR FATHER, Hersch Barer, one of the respected men of the town, brilliant scholar, educated in Torah, literature and general knowledge, an honest man who observed the commandments, a man of faith and devoted to tradition, who always walked the path of truth and honesty, a good heart, dedicated to family, pursued justice, accepted by all people, admired by all who knew him, he was active in public service.

OUR MOTHER, Esther Malka, a modest woman, gave charity to the poor, preserved and was faithful to tradition

May their memory be preserved FOREVER

THEIR CHILDREN: Leah Barer Korngold
Reisel Barer
Haifa, Tel Aviv

[Page 321]

In Eternal Memory of my parents, **Esther and Wolf Fischer**, who died in Jezierna. My father Wolf was a communal activist, head of the community for many years, a charitable man, he helped the poor and needy in various ways. He used to distribute potatoes at Pesach and wood in the winter. He was a learned man.

My mother Esther was a house wife who helped needy women . She went to pray every Sabbath, kept kosher and preserved the traditions of our forefathers.

From the 7 siblings, I am the only one that remained among the living after the time of destruction. Four brothers and their families and two sisters and their families were murdered.

IN ETERNAL MEMORY OF THEM:
Leibish Fischer and his family
Josef Fischer and his family
Scholom Fischer and his family
Mottel Fischer and his family
Josef Kelman, my brother-in-law and his family
My sister, Chana, and her husband Avraham Zamojre
and their son, Yisraelik
My brother, Scholom Fischer

They will never be forgotten!
REMEMBERED BY: Regina Fischer Ginzburg,
Tel Aviv

[Page 322]

Epitaph to remember our beloved parents, who were murdered in the Shoah.
Sara Fuchs, daughter of Esther and Gerschon Turkel
Leib Fuchs, son of Yosef and Jocheved
To remember forever our brother
Jakov Fuchs, son of Leib and Sara Fuchs
Who went through the Circles of Hell of the Shoah.
He survived and died of a heart attack at only age 59.

May Their Memory Be Blessed

REMEMBERED BY:

Their daughters and his sisters
Deborah Gilad—Elisheva Fuchs Yaffe
Hadera

[Page 323]

TO REMEMBER FOREVER

Our Parents: Eliahu Gottfried—Sarel Gottfried
Our sister: Devora Gottfried Fuchs
Our brother-in-law: Avraham Fuchs

Our father was a respected man, who adhered to the mitzvot, honest, pursued justice, philanthropic, a dedicated Zionist, a man with a good heart, devoted to his family.

May Their Memory Be Blessed

REMEMBERED BY:

Deborah Zmora Gottfried—Shlomo Gottfried
Hadera

[Page 324]

IN COMMEMORATION

Our Parents

Meier Zamojre
Ettel Feuring Zamojre

Our Sisters and Brothers

Ida Tyncie and her husband Jakob Zamojre And their
children
Azriel (Dzionek) and Ronia
Mina and her husband Shloma Blatt

We are heart-broken over them, murdered at the hands of
the evil ones.

May they be remembered forever

REMEMBERED BY:

Devora Zamojre Gottfried
Azriel Zamojre
Chaim Zamojre

Hadera, Haifa

[Page 325]

TO THE ETERNAL MEMORY OF
OUR LOVED AND DEAR ONES
Parents and Siblings
My mother, Miriam Eidel
My father, Sholom Eidel
My sister Leitzi and her husband Yechiel Bein
My sister Esther and her family
My brother Buni, who died as a hero in the First World
War in 1916
HONOR TO THEIR MEMORY
"May their souls be bound up in the bonds of eternal
life"
REMEMBERED BY:
Nathan Eidel and his family
United States
YYYYYYY

ETERNAL REMEMBRANCE
My grandfather David Blaustein
My grandmother Taube
My mother Shoshana (Roza)
My father Ben-Zion Blaustein
My brother Moishe
Their souls are in Gan Eden (Paradise)
REMEMBERED BY:
Dozia (Devora) Blaustein Izower
United States

[Page 326]

HEAVENLY SOULS
In Memory of Our Beloved Parents
My father David Blaustein
My mother Taube
My brother Ben-Zion Blaustein
And his wife Shoshana Lechowicz
And their son Moshe
May they be remembered forever

REMEMBERED BY:
Regina Blaustein Schwalb
Tel Aviv

HEAVENLY SOULS
In Memory of my beloved sister and family
Shoshana (Roza) Blaustein Moschisker
her husband, Shlomo Moschisker
their son, Dr. Yosef Moschisker, physician, and his son Moshe
Charlotta Blaustein and her sons Ben-Zion and David
Freida Blaustein Karp
Her Husband Asio Karp
their daughter Tosia
Johasia Blaustein Nussbaum
Her husband Bronek Nussbaum
Their daughter Tosia and son David
May they be remembered forever
Regina Blaustein Schwalb
Tel Aviv

[Page 327]

A Memorial To Our Friend—Beloved and Honorable Son of Jezierna

Joseph Zilberberg, Son of Jacob
Died in New York, USA.
For many years he was the secretary of the Jezierna Society in the United States
"Sons of Solomon." A man of Torah and general knowledge, dedicated to
tradition, walked in a righteous path, adhered to the commandments, honest and
well regarded by all his friends, participated in public life, helped the needy,
good-hearted. His house was always open to his friends and acquaintances.
He was a devoted Zionist.
May he be remembered forever

REMEMBERED BY:
The Organizing Committee of Jezierna Descendants in Israel
Pesach Altman, Menachem Duhl, Yitzchak Charap, Azriel Zmora, Chana
Yardeni, Devora and Shlomo Gottfried, Shimon Kritz, Yakov Segal, Lipa
Fisher

TO THE ETERNAL MEMORY OF OUR LOVED AND DEAR ONES
Our Parents and Sisters
My mother BLUMA CHARAP
My father AVRAHAM CHARAP
My sister PUPE and her husband JAKOB BYK
and their children
My sister RACHEL and her husband
Their memories will be honored!
Their names will be inscribed forever
They will never be forgotten

REMEMBERED BY:
JOSEPH CHARAP
United States

[Page 328]

Our hearts ache for these, who were murdered by villains

CHAIM ZOTTENBERG

My Grandfather. He was an honest, decent man, a scholar, intelligent. He dealt with community matters not for the sake of any award, a Zionist. He kept the complex mitzvot as well as the easy. All his life was devoted to helping others. He had discussions with the non-religious in order to show them that Jewish law is the truth so that they would do complete repentance. He was a moderate person, devoted and faithful to tradition, never spoke badly about anyone or gossiped, all his life. He was a moderate person. He followed the path of truth and honesty. One could say about him that he was a Tzaddik. He educated his two daughters in the ways of justice and honesty: my mother Rivke and my Aunt Miriam.

my mother RIVKE

was a woman of kosher ways, a good heart, smart and intelligent. She was devoted to me with all her heart as the love of a mother for her son.

Aunt MIRIAM and Uncle YAKOV AST, of blessed memory,
and their two daughters SHIFRA and ESTHER
My Aunt Miriam was always ready to help others
"May their souls be bound up in the bonds of eternal life"

REMEMBERED BY:

Yehoshua Glickman, Givatayim

MEMORIAL CANDLE for THOSE MURDERED in the SHOAH
In eternal memory of our dear grandfather, aunt, and unforgettable sister and their families,
who were destroyed by the Nazi murderers and their accomplices, may they be damned.
Our Grandfather AZRIEL SCHWAB
Our aunt BASCHA and her husband BEREL ROSENFELD-BLEICH
Our sister FRUMA and her husband SIMCHA
and daughter MALKA
Our sister MANYA and her husband YITZCHOK
and children MONEK and FEIGELE
Our sister PEREL and her daughter FEIGELE
May their holy souls rest in Gan Eden - May God Avenge Them!

REMEMBERED BY:

Their Sister Sima and her husband Shlomo
and the Warhaftig (Amitai) Family, Affula

[Page 329]

**IN MEMORY OF OUR BELOVED
PARENTS
AND SISTER**

Our beloved mother REISEL
KATZ
Our beloved father YUDEL KATZ
Our beloved sister SLOVA KATZ

**Their memory will never depart
from us**

REMEMBERED BY:

CHANA KATZ RICHMAN
MAX RICHMAN

Canada

TO REMEMBER FOREVER

HUSBAND and FATHER
YOSEF KASPI (Zilberman)

He was born in Jezierna and emigrated to Israel in 1936. He made his contribution to building the country. When we walked in the streets of Haifa, especially on Mt. Carmel, he used to find and proudly point out the fences that he had built by hand--hands of an artist. He was a member of the Haganah, a senior clerk in the Ministry of Finance. He devoted himself and his heart and soul to his work because he worked for his beloved homeland.

May he be remembered forever

REMEMBERED BY:
ALIZA, his widdow,
NURIT his daughter

Haifa

[Page 330]

**Our hearts ache for these,
who were murdered by villains.**

Heavenly Souls

OUR BELOVED PARENTS

ERNESTINA ROZENSTOCK KLINGER
WILHELM (Zev) KLINGER

Cousin

SELKA CHARTINER

Murdered by the Nazis , may they be damned,
and their accomplices in the Shoah.

May Their Memory Be Blessed

REMEMBERED BY:

ANNA KLINGER DUHL
granddaughter Dr. YEHUDIT KLINGER
SCHARF
MENACHEM DUHL

Haifa

✡ ✡ ✡ ✡ ✡ ✡

**IN MEMORY OF MY FAMILY WHO WERE MURDERED IN THE SHOAH
BELOVED:**

SALA DRESSLER KALAFER my wife
JANETTA KALAFER my mother
AMALIA KALAFER my sister
YEHUDA KALAFER my brother
SANIE ROSENFELD my grandfather
Uncles, Aunts , and Their Families
NATAN ROSENFELD, MATEL ROSENFELD
NATZIO ROSENFELD, MOSHE ROSENFELD
NATAN ROSENFELD cousin

Their names will be engraved forever

REMEMBERED BY: DR. NORBERT KALAFER, Germa

[Page 331]

TO REMEMBER FOREVER

HUSBAND and FATHER
MOSHE (Munie) STEIGER
"Cut down in his youth"
It is hard to get used to the idea that Moshe is no longer with us. All his life, he tried to help the sick and comfort the suffering. He was born in Jezierna and completed high school in Tarnopol. He studied medicine in Italy and continued in Lvov, but never completed his studies. When World War II started, he joined the army and fought the Nazis. After the war, he returned to Poland, but he couldn't bring himself to stay in a country where millions of Jews were killed. He emigrated to Israel and started to work in Rambam Hospital in 1951. He was a member of the workers' committee. He worked with devotion.

May his memory be preserved forever!

His memory will never depart from us

REMEMBERED BY:

BRONIA his widow
DORON-CHAIM his son
Haifa

~~~~~~~~~~~~

[Page 332]

A Monument for Eternal Memory

HEAVENLY SOUL
My Husband, dearest of all people, beloved Father, beloved Grandfather
MOSCHE son of Schimon HELICZER
He was a notable member of the town; a member of the local council; a member of the Jewish community
council; chairman of the wholesale traders group. He was a man of faith; dedicated and loyal to tradition;
honest, and cherished by everyone who knew him; kind-hearted and dedicated to his family; popular, educated,
an active Zionist and philanthropist. His home was open to his friends and for helping the needy.

My heart aches for these, who were murdered by villains.
IN MEMORY OF MY BELOVED PARENTS AND SISTER WHO WERE MURDERED IN THE SHOAH
RACHEL SCHEFS FISCHER my Mother
LEIB FISCHER, son of YECHIEL my Father
REISEL, daughter of Leib and Rachel Fischer my Sister
A Memorial to Their Memory. Their Memory Shall Never Depart from Me.
"May their souls be bound up in the bonds of eternal life"

REMEMBERED BY:

Lipa FISCHER
Bat Yam

His memory will never depart from us

REMEMBERED BY:

Sophie Heliczer Anderman.
Tzila Heliczer Zimer
Zelig Anderman, Jan Zimer,

Michael Anderman

Ashkelon.

TO REMEMBER FOREVER

LUCIA FUCHS, daughter of Nusia and Shauli

Murdered in the Shoah in Zborow

May her memory be holy

REMEMBERED BY:

The Committee of Jezierna Descendants

Haifa

[Page 333]

**In eternal memory of my dearest and beloved
father-mother, uncle, grandfather, grandmother and relatives.**

Uncle Moshe Kurzrok
Grandmother Feige Kurzrok
Grandfather Josef Schecter
and grandmother Henia Gottfried
Schecter
My sister Chana Kurzrok
My mother Reizel Kurzrok
My father Schimon Kurzrok
My brother Avraham-Chaim
and his family
My grandfather Josef Schecter
My grandmother Henia Gottfried
Schecter
My grandmother's brother
Nachman Gottfried
My brother Henik
My sister Chana
My Uncle Mosche Kurzrok
My grandmother Feige Kurzrok
My sister Leah

AND THEIR FAMILIES

[Page 334]

Their Memory Is Honored

Their names shall be engraved
forever.
Their memory will never depart from
us.

REMEMBERED BY:

DAVID KURZROK and family

His wife and daughter

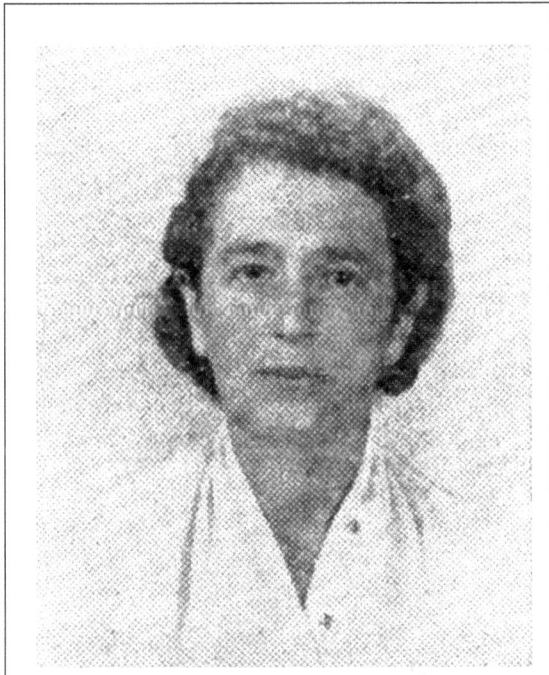

In Eternal Memory
of my wife

SONIA FUCHS

Killed in an accident in Hadar Josef
(Israel). May her soul rest in Gan Eden

REMEMBERED BY:

A. M. FUCHS

[Page 335]

AVRAHAM ROZA, *of blessed memory*
BRACHA ROZA, *of blessed memory*

Our hearts ache for these, who were wiped out
by the villainous Nazi murderers and their accomplices, may they be damned.
In eternal memory of my dear father
Avraham Roza
Who was killed by the Nazi murderers during the First Aktion, July 2, 1941
together with Mr. Mintz the pharmacist, Mr. Klinger the estate manager, and others.
They were reburied with Jewish traditional rites, in a mass grave in the Jezierna
cemetery.
My father was religious and refined Jew, a scholar, a Chasid of Huisatyn. His
students, who received from him the basics of Torah wisdom, of Jewish tradition and
love for the people and the land of Israel are dispersed in various countries and in
Israel.

MY BELOVED MOTHER BRACHA SCHEINHAUT ROZA
Died the 5th of Tammuz 1940
She was a good, pious woman. Bound to the Yiddish traditions of our
forefathers, always gave charity and helped the needy; fulfilled the commandments of
helping poor brides, visiting the sick, and loving the Creator.
Her memory will never depart from us! May her memory be blessed.

REMEMBERED BY HER SON
Zvi Roza
Kiryat Chaim

[Page 336]

IN MEMORY OF DR. CHUNE LITWAK

Born in Zborow, near Jezierna. Graduated medical school in Krakow. He was active in the Zionist movement. In 1933, he was elected to the national committee. Perished in the Shoah with his wife and child.

May their memory be blessed.

REMEMBERED BY:

Lipa FISCHER

TO REMEMBER FOREVER

CHAVA, our mother, Sara Marder Charap, wife and sister-in-law
Our brothers in the Charap Family: Hersch, Lippe, Jakob and their families and Aharon

REMEMBERED BY:

Chaya Harap Houber, *Ramat Gan* and Yitzchak Harap, *Haifa*

May this be an eternal memorial to Lucia.

[Page 337]

School chums, Nov.,1937. Courtesy of Dozia (Dora) Blaustein. Left to right, Unknown, Lusia Fuchs, Dozia Blaustein, Unknown. Fuchs wrote the Polish poem printed at the end of the book. Blaustein survived the Holocaust. She smuggled the poem from the Ghetto and brought it to be printed. [Photo not in original book]

In the Realm of the Judenrat
by Lusia Fuchs, Jezierna
Translated from the Polish by Dobrochna Fire

Zborów, ghetto, February 1943

In the Jewish section of Zborów,
On the main street in the center of town,
Stands a rather large two–story building
That is neither very old nor very new.
You know this building well, my friends,
And curse the owner either aloud or in secret.
You have no need of my explanations.
He is insensitive to groans or pain.
A curved staircase leads up to the residence
Of his excellency, the director of the Judenrat,
The one who rules over us imperiously
And reigns in the town by the grace of 'The Boss.'
He is our representative everywhere,
With no sympathy for poverty or misery.
He plágues us, skins us alive, seeking
Valuables and tributes as presents for 'The Boss.'
We have to think: the Master of lightening
Looks in silence at this den of wolves.

Is it possible that the heavens are protecting him
And shielding him from our curses?!
Our *Duce*.[1] We are his to own,
For he, anointed by The Boss himself,
Was told, "*Die Juden sind deine
Und du Judenaeltester bist meiner.*"[2]
If someone should ask,
"Where is this leader's retinue?"
His question would be just. I will describe
Each one in great detail, to be sure.
This famed institution
Extracts from us a contribution,
And it is called the JUDENRAT,
Much 'beloved' by us.
The Judenrat, but above all its members,
Can be compared to a nest of parasites.
Like parasites, which live at another's expense,
They build their nest on the affliction of others.
There are thirteen of them, you know.
Against each one be on your guard.
Obmann's role suits him so well.[3]
He is energetic and makes a great impression.
One can see from His Excellency *Obmann*'s words
That he has had a sip of intelligence.
Truly worthy of his position,
He forges ahead, though the road is slippery.
When he leaves the Judenrat building
And walks down the street, head held high,
He is followed by everyone's gazes
And by a flock of … wishes.
We invariably all wish him the same
Each day of our suffering.
But he remains unaffected
And continues to reign over our town.
He is respected by both great and small,
As he maintains excellent order in the town.
He fulfills his duties in a praiseworthy way
Sprouting up even where he is not needed.
He gets along well with the Nazi authorities.
When he is summoned to the Gestapo, his heart does not pound.
But this is not sorcery; we would all be this brave,
For he certainly brings them valuable gifts.
When he walks down the street with them,
They appear to be equals. But this is an illusion.
He has the demeanor, the chutzpah, even his enemy would admit,
Not everyone would be capable of the same.
It took such effort, conniving, deception, and toil
For the people of Zborów to be free of roundups.
Aktions would take place first in the towns
Around Zborów, as long as they existed.
He himself arranged their order. I'll tell you in secret
That his own life and that of his family were at stake;
If only dust remained of the people of Zborów,
Whom would he represent?
His greatest flaw,
Something no man can control,

Is that he suffers from itchy hands,
And is subject to hellish torment.
Only then is he relieved, does he revel, does he live,
When he can bash in the face of a Jew or Jewess.
Something that every Jewish passerby must fear,
Obmann calms down when he has given them a beating.
He gets the greatest satisfaction from the action
Of re–doing a woman's face.
His greatest turn–on is when
The victim of a face bashing is a woman.
He is not ashamed of this,
He may even see it as an asset.
Everyone has to blow off steam somehow,
And he blows off steam by bashing in a face!
Have you seen him, good people,
When on a Wednesday or Sunday,
He would chase about like a lunatic,
Yelling and swinging his horsewhip every which way,
Onto heads or backs, women, children.
"Gather it up," he would scream. "Gather up the trash!"
He wants to show his supervising Nazi
That the town is clean, to impress his Boss.
All in all, this ruling creep,
This beating *Obmann*, this caricature,
Was apparently sent by God himself
In service to the Gestapo, our enemy.
I have devoted enough space to you, *Obmann*.
While I write in despair, you are having an ample breakfast,
A good dinner, and a tasty supper–
While others starve; but you are right.
After him, I must say with pathos, goes
Hersch Shapira, with his long nose;
Not wanting to make him angry
I'll add that he is *Obmann*'s deputy.
A puffy face, blood–shot eyes–you can see
He is no stranger to drink. And for those
Who want to know more, no joke,
He is a lover of 'art', a passionate card player.
Whoever knows how he lived before the war
Also knows that he was a machinist.
Don't look so surprised–
He did his sitting[4] where there were machines.
He should be congratulated
For his clever machination,
For he hangs around at the Ungler Company
With the vigor of quicksilver.
You all know about this well,
Although we don't want to spread it about.
It is also generally known that he and *Obmann*
Get along like cats and dogs.
There is nothing I wish to write about Schwab;
He is always around, interfering, controlling.
In spite of it all, he is really no wit,
He may huff and puff but is truly a nothing.
The camp *Hauptverbindungsmann*[5]
Is tall, handsome, even quite terrific.

God bestowed strength of arms on him.
Who would not complain about that?
And what are you so proud of, Sanie dear?
That the camp inmate fasts and starves while you eat cream!?
That at the camp, you are second–in–line after The Boss?
That you have such self–important confederates?[6]
Not much space on my paper
Will I grant to you, Pilsner.
I know you peer into the kitchen to see
If someone has stolen something from there.
I proclaim, may it be known for all time,
That you have money, secret funds, that you can use.
We can't complain about Rosenberg;
We can only wish more were like him.
You know him–he sells goods in his store;
He's in charge of provisioning, I believe.
He is polite, but is this politeness inborn,
Or are we seeing his fiancé's influence?
Perhaps she, Miss Mania, was the one who extorted
This politeness from him as the price of her 'love'?
Leibaleh Kronisch, the housing clerk,
Has an important function. Ever the official,
He is in great demand. This petty little man is
Forever sullen, never smiling.
People pursue him, quite a few waking him
From his after–dinner nap.
Here is someone with bundles in the yard,
Surrounded by children; he can't take any more.
It's too wet and leaky for one, too dry for the other.
This one is prevented from cooking his offal.
Yet another is cramped, squeezed like a sardine;
He insists on being moved to another place.
This one complains of the darkness, like being buried alive.
His wish is that God grant this to you, Kronisch.
Another complains his neighbors have lice
Not only have them but share them as well.
One has a burst pipe in his kitchen,
While a hole in another's kitchen is smoking.
Arguing here and thrashing there,
This one is threatened with expulsion for theft.
Everyone comes to him. Everyone sincerely wishes that you,
Leibaleh, were in their place, not only now but eternally.
The health clerk is the lawyer Bund,
Yet how can anyone here be *gesund*?[7]
His most secret desire is
To go where the money is.
He has been collecting *Kopfsteuer*[8]
Without fail, from the beginning.
You all know the tall old gent, on daily duty at the secretariat.
He gives out prescriptions to the sick, as you know.
He will give out a prescription even though
The patient is already dead and gone.
Listen up, our dear medic, why do you not take
One of your own prescriptions?
You will be doubled over in pain
And running to the t … every minute.

The Judenrat's cashier is in charge of rations.
An old fellow, in glasses, named Rubinstein I believe.
He is not from Zborów; he favors his own people,
And they are the prime recipients of rations.
With his cap tilted a bit over his eyes,
Here comes the head of our post office.
Do you know whom you have the pleasure
To meet? That's our David Herman.
His hat may be tilted over his eyes,
But he never fails to eye a young girl.
Because he likes such things,
He will never retreat from a young lass.
He still knows how to make eyes at someone,
And although an old fellow, he understands
That the best thing in the world is …
Well, we all know what that is.
He never parts from his briefcase,
Since it gives him official standing.
He hired a female assistant so he himself
Does not have to spend time in his office–it is much
Better for him. Our Marder from Jezierna
Is a placid, quiet, passive man.
He feels like a foreigner among them;
These gambling boys don't understand him.
He does not have Schwab's chutzpa
Or the hand or the mug of some other ruffian.
He has to listen to them, to want what they want,
In order to keep this wretched armband.[9]
The one who should be judged among all others
Is the one who managed to set himself up
As seeming to be a straw widower;
Such men are usually called 'hustlers'.
He left his wife and daughter in the Jezierna camp,
Yet he himself came to Zborów. Here he plays
The bachelor. He won't let a girl cross the street
Without giving her a pinch where it's convenient.
He fondles them, and the girls flock to him
To get information, if needs be,
They cozy up to him to his face
But make fun of him behind his back.
They call him old man. He believes they love him,
But they know how to play him for a fool.
Nunio Paket is this Don Juan's name,
He who plays the bachelor with the girls.
I have finished describing you all.
Enough–I want to rest.
As much as I could and I knew,
I wrote it all down about all of you.
But this is not yet all.
I get the chills when I recall.
If I had wanted, just for fun,
To describe your dealings,
Your shindigs, drunken carousals, parties, the excitement!
Those daily celebrations, hoots, bravados,
Your shouts and head–bashing,
All this decadent life of yours,

There would not be enough room. In all this hoopla,
You've forgotten what is our destiny–
As well as yours. You've forgotten that there is no option;
None of us will avoid our fate–annihilation.
Although you may consider yourselves to be better,
The Gestapo will murder both you and us.
Don't look too far, just look in front of you,
For before you know it, we will be together in heaven.
I may have here used too many words.
These are, after all, our representatives.
When the heart is breaking of despair and pain,
Despair dictates, and the hand records.

Footnotes:

1. *Duce* (Ital.) = leader.
2. *Die Juden sind deine und du Judenaeltester bist meiner* (Ger.) = The Jews are yours, and you, Jewish elder, are mine.
3. *Obmann* = representative [Ger.]. Yanek Fuchs was appointed as *Obmann* of the Zborów ghetto.
4. This is a play on words in Polish: *siedzieć* literally means 'to sit', but it can also mean 'to spend time in jail'.
5. *Hauptverbildungsmann* (Ger.) = chief liaison. The position was held by Sanie Auerbach (see next stanza).
6. *Szwagier* ('brother–in–law') can also refer to men who share the role of lover to the same woman.
7. *Gesund* (Ger.) = healthy.
8. *Kopfsteuer* (Ger.) = head tax.
9. Even though all Jews were required to wear identifying armbands, Judenrat members had special privileges.

[Page 343]

About the Poem by Lusia Fuchs
by Menachem Duhl
Translated by Maya Avis

These lines were written by Lusia Fuchs, daughter of Shaul Fuchs and Nusia (nee Heliczer), in the Zborow ghetto. This young child was also one of the forcefully removed Jews of Jezierna.

She was 15 years old when she wrote these lines. Through the eyes of a child she witnessed the events around her, the demolition and the daily reality which, taken all together, brought her to understand the tragedy of her people, who were sentenced for eradication.   She also saw those few Jews who, at the expense of the persecution and misery of others, were able to live good lives. This wounded her young soul even more. Her wish was that the Jews from the Jezierna that once was, who remained among the living, would know how those days had been; that the whole world would know how the Jews had lived, how they were persecuted and destroyed in the ghetto. These very lines are the voice of one of our martyrs that calls out to us from the grave: DO NOT FORGET!

Dozia Blaustien, who was saved by a miracle, entrusted us with this poem for publication and we are fulfilling the composer's last wish by printing it in Polish, the language in which it was written.

Perhaps, while reading these lines, not just one will shed a tear, and will recall the author. This will be her compensation.

Editor's Note:

'Lusia's friend, Dozia Blaustien, smuggled the poem out of the ghetto and preserved it for this publication.'

Selected Original Verses in Polish from the Poem by Lusia Fuchs

W Zborowie, w żydowskiej dzielnicy,
W centrum miasteczka, przy głównej ulicy,
Stoi dość duży dom piętrowy,
Niezbyt stary, ale też nie nowy.

Na Rosenberga narzekać nie możemy,
Oby wszyscy tacy byli - chcemy,
Znacie go, on towary w sklepie sprzedaje,
Szefem aprowizacji jest mnie się zdaje.

Lepiej. Człek spokojny, cichy, bierny,
Jest nasz Marder z Jezierny.
Czuje się wśród nich obcy,
Nie rozumieją go ci karciani chłopcy.

[Pages 344-348]

Documents
Compiled by M.D.
Translated by Doron Friedman

We wrote about the efforts to bring to trial Richard Dyga, commander of the camp in Jezierna, the murderer, who killed thousands of Jews with his own hands. In this section we present letters and documents regarding that matter.

Document 1

YAD VASHEM _ Remembrance Authority of Holocaust Martyrs and Heroes
19th of Kislev, 5720
Dec 20th 1959
To Mr. Mendel Duhl
Haifa,
82 Hagiborim St.
Dear Sir,
Under Discussion: War Criminal Richard Dyga

The prosecution in the town Waldshut, Germany contacted us with a request to assist them in finding witnesses – survivors of Jezierna Camp near Tarnopol, who can testify regarding the activities of the war criminal, commander of the camp Richard Dyga.

We have been told by our friend N. Blumenthal that you would be able to assist in the mitzvah of bringing the wicked to justice.

We would be grateful if you could provide names of people who have knowledge of the aforementioned criminal.

Sincerely,
(signature)
Dr.Y. Kermish
Director of the Archives

Document 2

Translated from German by Shoshana Rappeport

Staatsanwaltschaft
bei dem Landgericht
Waldshut
Der Oberstaatsanwalt

1 Js 9655/59.

Waldshut, den 5. Februar 1960.

Durch Luftpost!

Herrn

Bachmann Blumenthal,

T e l - A v i v /Israel
Ben-St. Kai Str.2

Betr.: Ermittlungsverfahren gegen
Richard Dyga aus Königshütte,
wegen mehrfachen Mordes.

Sehr geehrter Herr Blumenthal!

Durch Herrn Landgerichtsrat Naumann als Untersuchungs-
richter beim Landgericht Giessen erhalte ich die Mitteilung, daß Sie evtl. in einem hier anhängigen Ermittlungsverfahren als Zeuge Auskunft geben können.

Ich führe ein Ermittlungsverfahren gegen den früheren
Lagerleiter des Zwangsarbeiterlagers Jezierna b.Tarno-
pol Richard Dyga, der aus Oberschlesien stammt.
Falls Sie irgendwelche Kenntnisse haben oder Unter-
lagen besitzen, wäre ich Ihnen dankbar, wenn Sie mir
eine entsprechende Mitteilung machen würden. Sollten
Ihnen Zeugen bekannt sein, bitte ich um Mitteilung
der in Betracht kommenden Anschriften.

Mit vorzüglicher Hochachtung!

(Decker).

Waldshut, the 5th of February 1960

State Prosecutor at
the District Court of
Waldshut
The Attorney General
Waldshut
Bismarckstr. 23
1 Js 8658/59

By Air Mail

Mr.
Nachmann Blumenthal,
Tel Aviv /Israel
Ben Zakai St. 2

Re: Proceedings against
Richard Dyga from Königshütte,
for multiple murders.

Dear Mr. Blumenthal,

I have received notification from Magistrate Naumann, the investigative judge at the Giessen district court, that you may be able to give information as a witness in an investigation currently proceeding here.

I am conducting an investigation against the former camp commander of the forced–labor camp Jezierna in the Tarnopol district, Richard Dyga, who comes from upper Silesia.

If you have any knowledge or are in possession of any documentation I would be grateful if you would communicate this information. Should witnesses be known to you I request notification concerning the possible addresses.

Respectfully,
(signature)
Dr. Angelberger

Document 3

Translated from German by Shoshana Rappeport

3.1.1960

To the
State Prosecutor
at the Waldshut District Court
Attorney General
to Dr. Angelberger
Bismarckstr. 23
Waldshut, Germany

Dear Dr. Angelberger,

We hereby confirm the receipt of your esteemed letter dated 2.12.1959, file number 1 Js 8658/59, regarding Richard DYGA, former director of the central work camp Jezierna in the Tarnopol district.

Due to our connections we were able to locate the addresses of the following witnesses to the crimes of the above named:

1. Mendel Dol
   Hagiborim Str. 82
   Haifa, Israel
2. Anna Dol
   Hagiborim Str. 82
   Haifa, Israel
3. Henia Heliczer c/o Mgr. Zelig Anderman
   Afridar, Pharmacy
   Aschkelon, Israel
4. Zila Zaimer, nee Heliczer
   address can be obtained from her sister Henia (No. 3)
5. Engineer I. Steinberg
   5116 Hamilton St.
   O'ky, Brooklyn 19,
   New-York, USA
6. Max Richman
   184 College Str.
   Toronto, Canada

Furthermore it is known to us that the witness Pepi Scharer and her two daughters are located in Australia; their addresses we will ascertain in the near future, together with those of the important witnesses Zainer (a judge by occupation) and Michal Rajski (Engel), who both live in Poland. Mr. Rajski is presently visiting Israel and we hope to be able to contact him.

In our archive there is a short description of living conditions in the ZAL [central–labor–camp] – Jezierna and about the murder of thousands of Jews during the period of its existence. This was written in Polish by Dr. Liblich for the Stuttgart branch of the Jewish Historical Commission in Munich, which functioned in 1946–48.

In the memorial book "Czortkow", published by Kohen Israel, Tel Aviv, 1956, the war–criminal Richard DYGA is named, in the memories of Mendel Dol (see No. 1)

Testimony is accepted by the Central Court of Justice in Jerusalem via the Israeli Mission in Cologne or by direct contact with the Central Court of Justice in Israel, Jerusalem, Russian Compound. Regarding your willingness to send us additional documentation, this is desirable for furthering the matter; accordingly, we would also like a photograph of DYGA. We will immediately send you further documentation should such reach us. For this purpose it would be necessary for you to keep us informed about the developments of the investigation.

With great respect,
(signature)
Dr. J. Kermisz
Director of Archives

Copy: Mr. Attorney General Schüle

Document 4

Translated from German by Shoshana Rappeport **and** Ayelet Ophir

Jerusalem, 14.2.1960

To the State Prosecutor
at the Waldshut District Court
to Dr. Angelberger
Attorney General
    <u>Registered Post</u>

<u>Waldshut</u>
Bismarckstr. 23
Dear Dr. Angelberger,
Regarding: <u>War criminal Richard DYGA</u>
    We confirm with thanks the receipt of your valued letter of 27.1.1960 with the enclosed photographs of war criminal Richard DYGA. We also thank you for the information about the confrontation of DYGAS by Mr. Simon Wiesenthal, engineer.
    We are endeavoring to find further incriminating evidence against DYGA and will forward such to you without delay.
    With regard to witnesses who presently live in Poland whose addresses we gave you in our letter of 24.1.1960, we would like to add that it is possible to make contact either directly or through the Jewish Historical Institute, A1. Gen. Swierczewskiego 79 Warszawa/Poland.
Copies:
Simon Wiesenthal, Eng.
<u>Linz</u>   Respectfully,
M.Dol, Haifa   (signature)Dr. J. Kermisz
                         Archive Director

Document 5

Translated from German by Shoshana Rappeport

Jerusalem, the 25th of March 1960

To the State Prosecutor
AIR MAIL– REGISTERED

at the Waldshut District Court
to Attorney General
Dr. Angelberger
Bismarckstrasse 23.
Waldshut, Germany
Regarding: War Criminal Richard DYGA
Dear Dr. Angelberger,
    In continuation of our letters from 3.1.1960 and 14.2.1960
we would like to inform you that besides the persons named in
those letters we have been able to locate the following witnesses:
1. Frida Herszfeld
   9, Huntley Rd.
   Melbourne, Australia
2. Pepi Scharer
   c/o Herzfeld
   as above
3. Bronia Feuer– Toraki
   c/o Herszfeld
   as above
4. Mrs. Doris Ozover O'Farril
   630 dtos. Vibra
   Havana, Cuba
    In regard to the last witness named, we would like
to mention that DYGA murdered her father.

            Respectfully,
            (signature)
            Dr. J. Kermisz
            Archive Director

  Copy: Attorney General Schüle
  Central Office of the State Judicial Administration
  Schorndorfer Str. 28, Ludwigsburg/Germany
Mr. Simon Wiesenthal, Engineer
Raimundstrasse 39/III
L i n z, Austria

Document 6

Translated from Polish by Professor Tomasz Rutkowski

227/94

Concentration camp (lager) in Jezierna was created in February 1942 solely as a labor camp (arbeitslager) for male–Jews, which was later converted to an extermination camp (vernichtungslager). Initially, a labor office (arbeitsamt) sent prisoners and then the Gestapo.

A type of work – building roads. Working and living conditions were unbearable. The camp was guarded by Ukrainian police posts – surrounded by a high fence with barbed wire. The sanitation – below any criticism. Long time there was no infirmary and sick people were lying together on a single bunk with healthy, and even after death they lay for a few days. High mortality from typhus. Often they died from exhaustion and the blows they received from the executioners.

Local people, Ukrainian, helped camp executioners. And [they died from] cases of denunciation, accidents, because of elimination from the concentration camp, which were on the daily agenda. Often there happened also murders of Jews, asking for a piece of bread, which were committed by peasants from the same village. When someone of the prisoners (lagerinsas) managed to escape, they would hang in public ten innocents, to terrorize.

For minor offenses [prisoners] were shot, beaten and often hanged publicly. In the concentration camp they killed about 20 thousand Jews either from starvation, disease and execution.

lania.– [slaughtered like deer]

The concentration camp was burned down in August of year 1943.

Dr. Liblich
Histor. Kommiss.
Stuttgart
/ J. Eiger /

Document 7

Luftpost !
Justizbehörden
in
Fra Waldshut

DEUTSCHE
BUNDESPOST
080

Dwora Lempert

Staatsanwaltschaft
bei dem Landgericht
Waldshut
Fernruf 336, 337, 673

Bordaustr.18

N e s - C y j o n a /Israel

- - - - - - - - -

חנה ריכמאן פון דער הײם כ"ץ
נעס ציון טראנספ.

26. 1. 1960

געערטער הער דול.

אײער בריװ האבן מיר באקומען און מיט פרײער זים גע־
לײענס. דער מערדער פון אונדזערע טײערסטע, וואס זענען
אומגעבראכט געווארן דורך אם דעם באנדים, לעבט נאך! ס'איז
שוין 17 יאר צוועק און דער שרעקליכער מערדער דרײס זיך
נאך ארום פרײ אויף דער וועלט. וואס מאר א וועלט איז דס?
איר שרײבס מיר וועגן עדות אפגעבן, זווראי וועל זיך גײן
זײן אן עדות, איך וועל זיך דערמאנען אלץ וואס ער האט
געטאן. שרײבט מיר וווהין איך דארף גײן. מיר וועלן
רא ארײנגעבן אין די צײטונגען, אפשר געפינט זיך אזעלכער
רא אין קאנאדא, וואס איז אויך געווען אין יעזיערנער לאגער.
דארם זענען געווען יירן פון א סך שטעט און שטעטלעך.
איך גערענק ווי דער מערדער רינג, דער שע׳ פון דעם
לאגער שלעג שלאגן און הרגענען יירן אויף דער גאס.
מיט גריסן אײך און אײער פאמיליע
חנה און סאקס ריכמאן

****
Translated from Yiddish / Hebrew by Sari and Daniel Avis
Devora Lempert was invited to submit testimony in the trial against war criminal Richard DYGA.

Judicial Authorities
in
Waldshut
Mrs. Dwora Lempert

State Prosecutor
at the District Court of
Waldshut.
Tel. 336, 337, 673

Nordaustr. 18
Nes Cyjona
Israel

****

Hannah Reichman, born Katz, now in Toronto
26. 1.1960

Dear Mr Duhl,

We received your letter and read it with sadness. The murderer, who killed our loved ones, is still alive!

17 years have already passed and this terrible murderer is still walking free in the world. What kind of a world is this?

You write to me about giving testimony. Of course I will testify. I will remember everything he did. Write to me as to where I should go. We will publish it here in the newspapers. Maybe here in Canada there is someone else who was in the Jezierna camp. There were Jews there from many cities and towns.

I remember how the murderer Dyga, the camp chief, beat and killed Jews in the street.

We wish you and your family well,
Hannah and Max Reichmann

Document 8

Translated from Polish by Dorota Poteralska

Isadore Steinberg, engineer, who spent approximately 5 months in the Jezierna camp and survived, gave testimony at the German Embassy in the USA

I. Steinberg
5116 Ft. Hamilton Pkwy.
Brooklyn 19, N.Y.
Mr. Maximilian Dul
Brooklyn, 18 /XI / 1960
Dear Mr Dul !
I took care of the Dyga matter immediately after receiving your letter, in which you informed me about Dyga being arrested.

At the same time my lawyer got to know about it and took care of the case personally, which he knew well from my testimony in the Wiedergutmachtung [reparations] case. I know that, being a man of law, he knew how to present it well.

A few weeks ago I received a letter of summons from the German embassy for 22 November, to give my testimony in the case. The fore-mentioned lawyer offered to accompany me to the embassy.

When am there I will certainly say that in addition to shooting and tying up Jewish people, he let them freeze, leaving them outside in the winter naked. One of them was the father–in–law of the pharmacist from Jezierna.

[Page 349-352, 353]

Testimony given to Yad Vashem by Dora Blaustein

My name is Dozia Blaustein and I am one of the few survivors from my hometown, Jezierna.

I am the daughter of Ben-Zion Blaustein and Rosa Lechowitz. The names Blaustein-Lechowitz were well known in Jezierna, therefore there is no need for further explanation. We were 2 children, an older brother Moishe, named Munio, and myself.

Before the days of the second war, Jezierna had a beautiful and intellectual community, in which my parents as well as my brother played a great part.

With the outbreak of the second war, and the Nazi occupation, the Jews of Jezierna shared the destiny of the other Jews of Poland. On a rainy Friday, a few days after the occupation, the Nazis did what they called "Ein Accia", and a great percentage of the male population were shot and buried, half dead and half alive, at the outskirts of the town. In that particular massacre my father and brother survived. Since that day life became a constant fear, and survival a struggle.

Shortly after the massacre, the Nazis ordered the formation of a Judenrat (a Jewish committee, composed mostly of Jews) Their first law was that every Jew must wear a 10 inch wide arm-band with a blue Star of David. And on our windows there had to be posted a 10 inch Star of David.

We all had to do forced labor, and as young as I was, I was assigned to the fields to cut the crops. Shortly after, the Nazis formed the first labor camp in Jezierna, and the first to be thrown into the camp were the male youth, among them my brother Munio. At the time of the founding of the camp in Jezierna, the remaining Jewish families from Jezierna and other neighboring towns were sent to a ghetto in the city of

Zborow. Unfortunately, Munio never passed the barbed wire, except when working and in July of 1943 the camp was 'liquidated'. Among those few hundred Jews my brother Munio, age 20, met his death.

Life in the Ghetto and the living conditions are well known to all of us today. My parents and I shared a 3-room apartment, with four more families. From day to day hunger became more acute and the sanitary conditions worsened. This led to an outbreak of typhoid. People were dying daily by the dozen, but G-d was good to us and we escaped the epidemic. Once in a while, the people of the ghetto had to pay a contribution toward The Party. In a short time all of the gold, silver, furs, and any valuables were all collected and given to the Nazis.

While in the ghetto we were all assigned to forced labor. Some of us went to build roads, others to factories, and still others went to sew clothing for the Nazi soldiers. I was assigned, with another group of girls, to do the laundry and work in the gardens of the Gestapo headquarters. A pass was issued to us, and every morning we used to leave the ghetto for work and return at night. The work wasn't hard, but we were slapped without reason -- but for being a Jew. The worst punishment we received from the Nazi officers was their harsh and sadistic statements about the Jews. Often they would give us their camouflage raincoats to be washed; these raincoats were splattered with blood, and they reminded us that this was the blood from other Jews of other ghettos, and this was what awaited us – the Jews of the Ghetto of Zborow.

Outside the Ghetto of Zborow a forced labor camp was created. In the early spring of 1943 my father was taken into the camp. My mother and I remained inside the Ghetto. I kept on working at the S.S. Headquarters.

Food was getting scarce. Some Gentile people, with heart, used to smuggle some food into the Ghetto. Between those bringing in food there was a young man from my hometown by the name of Kola Leskiv. His father was a good friend of my father, and during one of his trips, mother asked Kola if he could hide us. Without giving it a thought Kola agreed. It was hard to believe that without one word said or thought, this young man should sacrifice himself to hide two Jewish women, but we had nothing to lose; by staying in the Ghetto we knew what was coming, and by leaving we had a chance to survive.

At the end of April of 1943, with the help of a Gentile family from Zborow, we escaped. We were quite lucky, for we made it to Jezierna to the house of the Leskiv family. As Kola had promised, they accepted us and made shelter for us in the attic. For a Gentile family to keep Jews the punishment was death. The Leskiv family shared with us every piece of bread they had.

In May of 1943, the Zborow Ghetto was "liquidated" and in July of 1943 the camp of Zborow, where my father was kept, met the same fate. The day my father and his brother died, Kola came to the attic to see us. His grief was profound and I remember , as if it were yesterday, his telling Mother, "Even if I have to give my life, I shall protect you and shelter you". I shall never forget Kola and his smiling face, for he too met his maker a year later.

We stayed at the Leskiv home throughout the winter, until March of 1944. At that time the Russians were advancing and the battlefields were at the outskirts of Jezierna. The Leskiv's house was burned by the Germans, for the simple reason that it obstructed the view of the battlefield. We had nowhere to go but into the woods. We wandered from place to place and it seemed that G-d was guiding us out of trouble.

In July of 1944 we were liberated by the Russians. After a short time in Jezierna we moved to Tarnopol, where we lived with a few Jewish families.

In 1945, after the worst was over, we were allowed to leave the Ukraine and go to Poland. We settled in Byton and waited for a pass to leave for America, where my mother has brothers and a sister. Unfortunately, my mother's health was deteriorating and as soon as she was confined to bed in 1946, her brother Moris Lechowitz came from Russia and joined us in Byton, for he was alone, as his wife Netka and three children lost their lives in a concentration camp in Poland. Together with Mother, in a stretcher, we left to go to Paris. After a few months in Paris, Mother died.   On January of 1947 my uncle Moris and I left France for the United States. Behind I left only graves and bad memories, but I had to forget all this, for was going ahead to an unknown country in search of happiness and a better tomorrow.

Editor's note: The Leskiv family – Mickhail, Yekatrina, and their son Nikolai, were recognized by Yad v'Shem as Righteous Among the Nations, for risking their own lives by feeding and hiding members of the Blaustein family. Documents from Yad v'Shem can be viewed in the Introductory Pages of the book.

Appendix

Documents from Yad V'Shem
Added to the book by Editors of the English version.

🌐 Language ▾

The Righteous Among the Nations Database

70

Leskiv Mikhail & Yekaterina ; Son: Nikolai

Leskiv Mikhail (1886 - ?)   Leskiv Yekaterina (1889 - 1978)   Leskiv Nikolai (1920 - ?)

Family Name	Leskiv
First Name	Mikhail
Date of Birth	01/01/1886
Fate	survived
Nationality	UKRAINE
Gender	Male
Date of Recognition	15/02/1999
Ceremony Place	Kiev, Ukraine
Commemorate	Wall of Honor
Ceremony in Yad Vashem	No
File number	M.31.2/8380

Mykhailo and Katerina Leskiv lived with their four children in the small town of Jezierna, Tarnopol District (today Ozerna, Ternopil' District). Among their neighbors was the Jewish Blaustein family, consisting of parents, Ben-Zion and Rosa, and two children, Munio (Moshe) and Dozia. On July 2, 1941, the Germans occupied Jezierna, and during the following two days, carried out the first Aktion, which the Blausteins luckily survived. For the following months they remained in their own house, going daily to forced labor and being subject to humiliation from the Germans and many locals. When a labor camp was formed in Jezierna, Munio Blaustein was interned there; he perished in July 1943, with the liquidation of the camp. The rest of the family was marched, together with other Jezierna Jews, to the ghetto in Zborow (Zboriv). The living conditions in the ghetto worsened from day to day: hunger increased, and sanitary conditions deteriorated until there was an outbreak of typhus. In Zborow, they received a small supply of food, smuggled into the ghetto by 20-year-old Mykola Leskiv, the eldest son of their former neighbors. In March 1943, Ben-Zion Blaustein was taken to a labor camp in Zborow, and soon after, rumors spread that the days of the ghetto were numbered. It was then that Rosa Blaustein asked Mykola to hide her and her daughter, and, without hesitation, Mykola agreed. His family kept the promise: after their successful escape and return to Jezierna, Rosa and Dozia were accepted by the Leskivs and sheltered in their attic.

Throughout the following year, the rescuers shared their meager fare with their two Jewish guests. Mykola was the one who brought them, with great sorrow, the news about the liquidation of the camps in Jezierna and in Zborow, and the deaths of Rosa's son and husband. In March 1944, as the front drew close to Jezierna, the Leskivs' house was burned down by the Germans because it obstructedthe view of the battlefield. The Leskivs were taken in by their relatives, while Rosa and Dozia, having no other choice, hid in the forests and, miraculously, survived to witness the liberation, in July 1944. Shortly after the end of the war, Rosa and Dozia left for Poland, hoping to reach the USA where they had relatives. Unfortunately, Rosa's health declined and she died in Paris, in 1946. Dosia Blaustein reached the United States a year later. She and her rescuers never met again. On February 15, 1999, Yad Vashem recognized Mykhailo and Katerina Leskiv and their son, Mykola, as Righteous Among the Nations.

Show Less ▲

SUPPORTED BY

[photo from Rivka Ben Israel]

From the Gottfried *family album circa 1930.*

NAME INDEX